SJRhoads 1980

The Careers of
Professional Women
COMMITMENT AND CONFLICT

This study centers on the extent to which women with graduate
and professional degrees have been able to utilize their skills in the
labor market and on how levels of achievement are affected by sex-
based job discrimination and conflicts between career motivation
and female role expectations. The book is based on data from a
1963 survey of 226 women and a 1975 follow-up questionnaire.

OTHER VOLUMES IN THE
Conservation of Human Resources Series

The Careers of Professional Women

COMMITMENT AND CONFLICT

by ALICE M. YOHALEM
Foreword by Eli Ginzberg

LandMark Studies
ALLANHELD OSMUN Montclair **UNIVERSE BOOKS** New York

To Stephen B. Yohalem
For his affirmative actions

ALLANHELD OSMUN AND CO. PUBLISHERS, INC.
19 Brunswick Road, Montclair, N.J. 07042

Published in the United States of America in 1979
by Allanheld, Osmun and Co. and by Universe Books
381 Park Avenue South, New York, N.Y. 10016
Distribution: Universe Books

LIBRARY OF CONGRESS CATALOGING IN PUBLICATION DATA

Yohalem, Alice M
  The careers of professional women.

  "Landmark studies."
  1. Women college graduates—Employment—United States.
I. Title.
HD6053.6.U5Y63   331.4'0973   77-10187
ISBN 0-87663-821-3

Printed in the United States of America

The material in this publication was prepared under contracts 21-26-73-51,
21-36-75-20, 21-36-76-18, from the Employment and Training Administration,
U.S. Department of Labor, under the authority of Title III, Part B of the
Comprehensive Employment and Training Act of 1973. Researchers undertaking such projects under government sponsorship are encouraged to express
freely their professional judgment. Therefore, points of view and opinions
stated in this document do not necessarily represent the official position or
policy of the Department of Labor.
  Reproduction by the U.S. government in whole or in part is permitted
for any purpose.

FOREWORD

In this book, Alice Yohalem carries forward the analysis of the career and life experiences of a group of professional women who were the subjects of a prior study in the early 1960s, approximately 15 years after most of them had been graduate students at Columbia University. It therefore provides a basis for assessing the course of the careers of a group of highly educated women throughout much of their adult lives.

In the quarter-century since most of these women ended their advanced training, there have been radical changes in both the receptivity of the economy to the employment and promotion of women workers and the ways in which career-oriented women have sought to balance their multiple responsibilities in and out of the labor force. A major focus of this work is on the period 1963 through 1974 which coincides with the onset of what has come to be known as the "women's liberation movement." By tying recent experiences to earlier patterns of homemaking and work, the author enables the reader to understand the impact of this movement on a group of women who should have been in a good position to benefit from the changes it inspired.

These women represent a select component of a transitional generation insofar as their education and work experience placed them at a distinct advantage to profit from the diminution of sex discrimination in the late 1960s and early 1970s. By becoming intimately acquainted with this group, the reader will be better able to consider the spectrum of changes in American society resulting from the continuing revolution in the roles of women.

As the title of this book suggests, the analysis centers upon the career commitment of these professional women. The preceding study had revealed that some of them were closely attached to work even while rearing their children. This follow-up inquiry indicates that mothers' ties to work were strengthened in subsequent years as their children matured. Many women who had been out of the labor force in 1963 had reentered; others who had been working part-time at the earlier date had shifted to full-time jobs; a considerable number had risen in the occupational hierarchy. In light of recent legislation raising the age of compulsory retirement from 65 to 70, it is interesting to note that some of the older respondents continued to work past their sixty-fifth birthday and that many of the younger women expressed a preference for extending their working life beyond the age of 65.

Realization of the career commitment of professional women depends in considerable measure on the shape and direction of the economy. In the last decade and a half there has been both a fairly strong demand for professional personnel and accelerated efforts by private and public sector employers to increase the proportion of their women employees in response to political and legal pressures and revised social attitudes. What remains moot is the extent to which the economy will continue to expand opportunities for the highly educated population and to seek more female applicants for good jobs, especially in view of heightened competition among all persons aged 25 to 44 years resulting from the aging of the "baby boom" cohort.

There is no question that future labor market trends will have an influence upon the rate of progress of professional women in the years ahead. For instance, a number of respondents were able to maintain their ties to their careers through part-time employment while otherwise occupied with raising their children. If there should be a successful effort to reduce the average weekly hours of full-time work, the number of desirable part-time jobs might decline. It may therefore prove more difficult in the future than in the past for professional women to withdraw from full-time work without severing their connections to the labor force.

One must also consider what will happen if, as appears likely, the next generation of professional women will be more reluctant than their predecessors to remove themselves from the full-time career track for long periods. How will they be able to cope with their childrearing and homemaking responsibilities, even if they decide to limit the size of their families? Some clues are provided by our group. Whether a woman can successfully combine a career and family depends in no small measure on the attitudes and behavior of her husband. But it will require much more cooperation on the part of husbands than is yet the pattern if professional women are to avoid paying a price, often a high price, in terms of unfulfilled career goals.

The data that Ms. Yohalem presents about the earnings of these professional women demonstrate the importance of their contribution to their families' standards of living. Without giving the whole story away it suffices to say that working wives contributed a median of about 40 percent to total family income. It is apparent that dual careers generate substantial benefits, especially when both spouses are high earners.

If the economic factors that will affect the future career prospects of professional women are difficult to delineate and assess, that much more difficult are the family and social consequences of the trend towards a greater career-orientation. There are clues in the life histories of these women that suggest that a range of conflicts is inherent in deeper female career commitment.

A focus on career goals to the exclusion of marriage or children can be frustrating if a woman fails to achieve her aims. And not everyone, even among those with superior educational attainment, is able to achieve his or her career goal in a competitive environment. Moreover, these cases reveal more than an isolated instance of tension between spouses as to whose career is to take precedence, and the number of such conflicts is likely to increase as more wives seek long-lasting careers. If these women are trustworthy guides, the odds are strong that, even when spouses are mutually supportive, the career wife will continue to carry the greater share of family burdens, often with negative consequences for her peace of mind.

Ms. Yohalem has written an interesting book, an important book, a book rich in policy implications. The story that she has to tell about the experiences of this well-educated group of American women warrants close reading and reflection. She makes no specific claim that this group will prove prototypical of all women workers during the next quarter-century. But this possibility cannot be ruled out. Thoughtful readers will be able to reach their own conclusions about the extent to which the career commitments and conflicts of highly qualified women have served as the framework for a women's revolution that is still in an early stage.

Eli Ginzberg

ACKNOWLEDGMENTS

During the years following my participation in the initial survey of this group of women in the early 1960s *(Life Styles of Educated Women* and *Educated American Women: Self-Portraits)*, I maintained a proprietary interest in the respondents which was heightened by occasional published references to the accomplishments of a number of them. The evidence of achievement postdating the original inquiry coincident with intensified attention to the cause of women's rights led me to believe that an updated examination of these women's lives would be a worthwhile research endeavor. This belief was shared by Eli Ginzberg, director of the Conservation of Human Resources Project and a senior author of the original report, and it was due to his interest and encouragement that I was able to undertake the investigation I had envisioned. I am deeply indebted to him for his valuable advice and consistent support.

Major assistance was provided by Michael Freeman who was responsible for the data processing, and by Anne Wattenberg who capably performed a host of duties in connection with the survey. Other research or editorial assistance was provided by Rachel Ostow, Louise Dutka, Joanne Koeller, George Winslow and Roger Furman. Final typing of the manuscript was primarily the work of Shoshana Vasheetz and Karen Honeycutt under the supervision of Sylvia Leef. Gertrude McGrath and Ramon Lopez of the Columbia University Office of University Publications advised about the questionnaire format and handled its printing.

I wish to express my profound gratitude to the respondents for their repeated cooperation. They were the essential collaborators and their incisive observations animate the report.

Alice M. Yohalem

New York, N.Y.
March, 1978

CONTENTS

List of Tables

List of Abbreviations

Ph.D.	Doctor of Philosophy
Ed.D.	Doctor of Education
Doctorate	Ph.D. or Ed.D. except where otherwise noted
ABD	"All but dissertation" (completed course work for doctorate but not dissertation
M.D.	Doctor of Medicine
LL.B.	Bachelor of Law
J.D.	Juris Doctor (usual current equivalent of LL.B.)
M.A.	Master of Arts
M.I.A.	Master of International Affairs
M.S.	Master of Science
M.S.W.	Master of Social Work
M.P.H.	Master of Public Health
M.A.T.	Master of Arts in Teaching
ABT	"All but thesis" (completed course work for a master's degree but not thesis)
B.A.	Bachelor of Arts

The Careers of
Professional Women

1] FRAMES OF REFERENCE

Background of Study

In the early 1960s, the Conservation of Human Resources Project conducted a survey of 311 women of high scholarship who had attended graduate or professional school at Columbia University between 1945 and 1951.[1] Most of these women had prepared for professional careers and the study centered on both the influences that had shaped their aspirations and on their experiences between graduate school and 1963. Although representative of only a small minority of the total female population, the group was described as "a vanguard of the growing ranks of highly educated women who will characterize our society in the future."[2]

During the ensuing years, this prediction was verified as increasing proportions of female college graduates entered advanced courses of study. The downward trend in the annual production of female Ph.D.'s which had reached a 40-year low of 9.5 percent of the total in 1950 was reversed in the following decade; the 1950 rate had more than doubled by 1975. The proportion of women earning master's degrees rose from 29 percent in 1950 to 41 percent in 1972; and there was a twofold increase in the proportion of females awarded first professional degrees between 1960 and 1970 alone.[3]

Increasing female participation in programs of advanced study coincided with the development of a revived feminism that heightened women's self-consciousness and encouraged the community at large to support their demands for equity. At the time of the initial study (1963), however, the women's movement had not yet become a major social

3

force. In fact, a 1971 reissue of the report suggested that: "The reader of this book might find it interesting to note where and to what extent Women's Lib has made an earlier finding anachronistic and a new interpretation necessary."[4] But why leave it to the reader? Supplementation of the earlier findings with new data was bound to provide more accurate intelligence than personal impressions, and the possibility of examining these women's subsequent experiences in light of social changes that had occurred in the interim held promise of providing a body of knowledge about a distinctive group of individuals. Hence, the Conservation of Human Resources Project, under a contract with the Office of Research and Development, Employment and Training Administration, United States Department of Labor, undertook a resurvey of the original sample of women.

Although a follow-up study was not contemplated at the time of the original investigation, some of the participants had suggested that consideration be given to a future effort of this type: "I should be most curious to learn whether what is foreshadowed in each of the cases comes to pass," wrote one. As time went on, the investigators themselves became curious. They were particularly intrigued with the possibility of expanding the limited number of longitudinal studies of women. Such plaints as Papanek's that "data about the life of women are generally insufficient, especially if compared with what is known in the same society about the life of men," and pleas like Kahne's "for greater specificity in longitudinal studies of women's work histories in different occupations and in different socioeconomic groups," had not gone unnoticed.[5]

Many lacunae have been filled by research based on the National Longitudinal Surveys of Labor Market Experience of young and mature females by the Center for Human Resources Research, The Ohio State University, but these treat women who have graduate or professional education in tandem with recipients of bachelor's degrees rather than as a distinct sub-group. There have been retrospective and cross sectional surveys of women with advanced training that have explored trends over time, but these investigations either have centered upon specific academic or professional disciplines or credentials, or have dealt with current rather than former students.[6] Since the respondents to our initial inquiry were women who had studied in a large number of subject areas and who had earned various academic degrees, this diversity provided an opportunity to explore their experiences in light of the nature and extent of their graduate education.

When the initial investigation was conducted, most of the subjects were in their late thirties or early forties. Some of the women were in the labor force, either full- or part-time; the others were planning to return to paid employment when family circumstances were favorable. In a sense, the original survey left the participants stranded in midstream. An inquiry about how they had fared as they proceeded on their way was especially desirable because highly qualified women should have been in preferred positions to exploit new developments aimed at improving the occupational opportunities and status of females. Changes in the perceptions and treatment of women workers should be expected to apply not only to young newcomers to the labor force but also to women with lengthy work experience and to middle-aged reentrants; any realistic assessment of the results to date of efforts to remove sex barriers to employment and advancement cannot neglect their experiences.

In addition, a description of the responses of these women to the problems confronting females with strong career drives can serve to inform the decisions of current and prospective female graduate and professional students. Although forces that have traditionally acted to keep women in their "place" have diminished in intensity, the persistence of these barriers should not be underestimated. Highly trained women still have to negotiate an obstacle course to realize their goals, and guides from the recent past can provide valuable assistance.

Framework for Research

> That a man will spend one third of his adult life in gainful work is a premise on which the plans for his life are based. But for a woman, society creates not a decision but the necessity for a choice. She must decide whether to include work in her plans and, if so, how much of her life she should devote to it. If the answer is that she will include work in a serious way, she then arrives at the point at which the career thinking of men begins.[7]

Graduate or professional education represents such a point, but women who decide "to include work in a serious way" can rarely look forward to fulfilling their career commitments with as much certainty as most men because looming in the future is the probability that marriage and motherhood will demand modification or abandonment of their work goals. The assumption of the family role may provide the highly educated woman with a broad range of options affecting the apportionment of her time, but it tends to restrict her career options because her ability to move onward and upward is usually dependent upon her husband's job or her family's needs.

Our earlier study found that some respondents chose not to marry rather than to chance a career interruption. For the same reason, others who married decided to remain childless. Both of these decisions are essentially sex-linked, since men know that regardless of their marital or paternal status, they usually will be able to give as much time as necessary to their careers.

The woman who is seriously interested in preparing for a professional career is disadvantaged from the start. She may have the option of not getting married or of not having children, but this is not really socially acceptable (although it may be becoming more so), even if it proves to be personally satisfying, which is not always the case. She does have the option of marriage and motherhood, which *is* acceptable, even expected, but in that event she is likely to have to accommodate her career to her family. To assume that such accommodations are always satisfying is to deprecate the seriousness of purpose with which many women enter career training. To anticipate that women will make such accommodations leads to sex discrimination.

> There appears to be a general tendency on the part of employers to underestimate the career commitment of highly qualified women. . . . This leads . . . to using well-qualified women in jobs below their ability, to low morale and high turnover and to their exclusion from many opportunities and job rotations usually forming part of a career pattern at the top.[8]

In such a manner, employers' expectations that women will lower their sights becomes self-fulfilling when denial of the opportunity to progress insures abandonment of a career after a woman has had a child.

Society offers women the opportunity to prepare for careers in the professions and other high ranking occupations, but it has discouraged them from pursuing their work role in the same manner as men. Some women do combine continuous full-time careers with marriage and a family, but this type of behavior has been relatively infrequent and always controversial. Unpublished data from the 1963 survey show that continuous workers with children comprised a mere 14 percent of the total sample and represented only 24 percent of the mothers.

Since the original study encompassed a wide view of the women's lives, work was but one aspect, although a major one. In contrast, this follow-up places work in the fore. It was designed primarily to examine these women's lives from a perspective that views graduate and professional education as an implicit career commitment and seeks to determine the extent to which these women were able to realize this commitment. This assumption finds support in the proposition of Bowen and Finegan that "years of school completed may serve as a proxy for underlying taste for market work and for natural aptitudes for employment."[9]

The fact that some women attend graduate school either to mark time until marriage or to prepare for a contingency necessitating employment does not vitiate the presumption of career motivation. Graduate education is designed to provide professional and related skills. Although it does not obligate students to pursue specific careers, it is assumed that this is their intention. The initial research demonstrated that two-thirds of the respondents had clear career objectives during the course of their undergraduate and graduate studies and that only a small number never developed career goals during that period.[10]

To argue that there are unquantifiable social and family benefits to be derived as a result of women's advanced education, regardless of eventualities, not only overlooks the fundamental purpose of such schooling but also ignores the fact that most males in the pool of aspirants for the limited student places in these programs will pursue continuous careers in their fields of study. To argue in favor of giving priority to males, on the other hand, is not only morally and legally indefensible but socially pernicious. "Assuming a normal distribution of ability, society may be losing the potential skills of women superior to some percentage of the men now given preferential treatment."[11] Since nobody knows the precise use to which any student will put his or her higher studies, the arbitrary restriction of educational opportunities on the basis of sex is invidious discrimination.

It is in women's interest, however, to identify factors that have influenced the utilization of skills acquired in graduate and professional school by members of their sex. The kind of environment female graduate students are entering today may lead them to believe that it will be easier to realize their goals than it was for their predecessors. Aside from problems associated with the availability of job opportunities for highly qualified workers in the current and prospective labor market, there is reason to doubt whether the going will be as smooth as many anticipate since there is considerable resistance to pressures for equal opportunity and equal treatment among both men and women of all ages and circumstances. One need only note the bitter controversy surrounding attempts to ratify the Equal Rights Amendment to confirm the strength of the opposition.

Nevertheless, there is considerable evidence that social expectations are changing. The younger generation of highly educated females may regard some of the options that were available to their older counterparts as unacceptable. A prediction in the report of the 1963 survey that "physiological and social realities will continue to keep young women anchored in the two worlds of home and work" needs revision in light of many changes in the interim.[12]

Today, women are able to delay or forego motherhood more readily than they were in the past because the increased effectiveness and acceptance of contraceptive methods and the availability of legalized abortion enables those who wish to focus upon their careers to be less hampered by physiological realities. This is vividly demonstrated by the decline in the fertility rate. Between 1963 and 1974, the rate dropped 38 percent, representing a continuing but accelerated trend that began in 1958, a year after the rate had reached its highest peak since 1916.[13] It has been suggested that much of the decrease has been due to postponed births but even if this prediction is correct, the fertility rate is unlikely to reach previous levels because postponement should lead to smaller families.

The changes in social realities since 1963 include a liberalization of attitudes toward women who deliberately choose to forego marriage and/or motherhood—and even toward those who choose motherhood without marriage. There is also some evidence of a trend toward the convergence of male and female patterns whereby each sex gives equal attention to work and home. While it is too soon to judge whether this is indicative of pervasive change or is a deviation from a persisting norm, it is clear that any move by men towards fulfilling some measure of women's traditional responsibilities would enhance women's opportunities to fulfill their work aspirations.

Another significant change has been the legal prohibition of many of the discriminatory practices that often prevented women from fully realizing their career objectives.[14] Although many of these proscriptions have been honored more in the breach than in the observance, the very fact of their existence signifies changed societal attitudes towards women.

These changed realities have been accompanied by an increase in the female labor force participation rate. Among women educated beyond college, age 25 to 34 years, the participation rate rose from 60.4 percent in 1962 to 77.8 percent in 1974. During the same period, the proportion of 55 to 64-year-old women with similar school attainment who were in the labor force dropped from 81.4 percent to 64.9 percent, while the participation rates of women in the intervening age groups remained stable at 75 and 81 percent.[15] The increased participation of the younger women signifies greater reluctance to abandon work for family responsibilities than in the past. This, in turn, possibly has had an effect upon the availability of job opportunities for older women whose decrease in labor force participation also may have been influenced by the retirement of their husbands since the participation rate of males with graduate training aged 65 years and over dropped from 54.1 percent in 1962 to 48 percent in 1974.[16]

Despite such changes, the evidence of a weakening of the forces that have customarily served to differentiate the occupational goals of men and women is equivocal. Although more women are enrolling in graduate and professional schools, they still represent the minority of students. Moreover, women graduate students remain concentrated in a few fields, many of which serve as sources of supply for predominantly female occupations. In 1970–71, for example, women received the majority of the master's degrees in only nine out of 33 selected fields and represented a minority of the recipients of doctorates in all fields.[17] Blitz, noting that female higher degrees had peaked in the '30s, cautions that "while women are regaining their proportions of degrees at all levels of college and university education, this is taking place more slowly on the higher levels compared to the lower. This, in turn, implies that women's ability to compete for positions requiring the highest professional training will be more limited than is the case for positions requiring less rigorous qualifications."[18]

Although the inroads of women into male dominated precincts may signify the onset of a growing move to break out of traditional female occupations, most women's professional career choices still appear to be influenced by sex role expectations. The forces that have affected the life patterns of highly qualified women in the past continue to operate, albeit in slightly attenuated strength.

Yet more women are choosing non-traditional alternatives, and care must be taken to avoid generalizations to characterize female career choices. This study provides information about highly educated women who prepared for either traditional or non-traditional careers and who subsequently followed either traditional or non-traditional paths. Our earlier inquiry demonstrated that the conventional female role was merely one of a variety of life patterns and that there was no inherent relationship between choice and satisfaction. Although relatively few of these women were able or willing to fashion non-traditional life styles, changed realities may result in reformulations by succeeding generations that incorporate hitherto deviant patterns into a larger model permitting more attention to the realization of individual potential than to acquiescence to social expectations.

While a follow-up could have been confined to replication of the original analyses using updated information, certain considerations led to the decision to broaden the range of the research. The time span covered by the data available from both surveys includes the major portion of these women's adult lives so that attention to their lifetime work and non-work experiences, in addition to their experiences after the previous study, was indicated. Also, because of the changes in the larger environment it seemed advisable to examine dimensions of the women's lives that either were not covered in the earlier research or that were not covered in the detail warranted by the turn of events.

Procedure and Participants

Following pretesting and consultation, a questionnaire was prepared which was designed to update the information supplied in 1963 as well as to provide additional data that would illuminate the period between the surveys.[19] Unlike its predecessor, which had included questions exploring the women's early background, influences and attitudes in depth, the follow-up questionnaire placed its principal focus on labor market decisions and behavior. In consideration of the women's earlier cooperation and of the possibility that brevity would produce greater response, most of the questions required short answers. A small number of open-ended questions were included, however, both because they covered topics that did not lend themselves to brief answers and because anecdotal accounts had contributed a heightened dimension to the earlier study. The final question asked for additional comments and many of the women took advantage of this opportunity to illuminate some of their answers or to provide information they deemed relevant to the research.

Respondents were assured that their answers would be held in strict confidence by the investigators and, where deemed necessary, depictions of individual respondents have been altered in order to preserve anonymity.

In June 1974 the questionnaires accompanied by a cover letter explaining the general objectives of the follow-up survey were sent to those participants in the initial study whose addresses could be obtained.[20] Seven of the 311 members of the original cohort could not be located and 16 had died. Another communication was sent to women who had not responded by the following September and a second questionnaire was mailed when requested. Telephone calls were also used to encourage responses.

Of the 288 questionnaires that were presumed to have been received, 227 or 78.8 percent were returned; one of these supplied insufficient information to be included in the study. A comparison between demographic, educational, and employment data supplied by respondents and non-respondents in their 1963 questionnaires revealed no significant differences between the two groups to that date.

The data supplied by the 226 usable questionnaires were coded for computer analysis. Special codes were devised to handle replies to open-ended questions using classifications based upon detailed examination of subject matter. Data from the previous questionnaire were usually utilized as they had been coded at that time, although occasional recoding was undertaken to facilitate comparison.

Tabular analyses are used exclusively. Most of the statistical exploration centers upon determinants of labor force participation and occupational achievement. Intra-group differences permitted comparisons which utilize a number of independent variables, including highest academic degree, subject of graduate study, marital status, family size, occupation, and occupational sex ratios. Other information supplied by the respondents is also handled by using cross-tabulations to clarify relationships or to explore differences. The 12 years between January, 1963 and December, 1974 define the follow-up period; the span

Table 1.1 Age of Respondents, 1974

Age	Percent
40-44 years	2
45-49	27
50-54	41
55-59	16
60-64	8
65 years or older	6
Total percent	100
Total number	(226)

used to examine worklives encompasses the year of college graduation through December, 1974, less years of full-time study.

The tables indicate percentage responses but numerical bases are shown, as are excluded cases. Occasionally percentages were rounded to total 100 percent.

Selected Characteristics of the Respondents

The following data are presented with only brief comment since they are discussed in more detail in subsequent chapters when utilized as explanatory variables. This information is supplied at this point because age is an essential mark of identity, and education was the criterion for sample selection.

The 226 respondents represent every graduate faculty and professional school at Columbia University in 1963, dentistry and engineering excepted. Each participant had completed at least one year of graduate study and most had earned at least one graduate degree by 1963.

Year of birth did not enter into the sample selection process and the women's ages covered a wide range, spanning about a generation. The two oldest women were born in 1906; the four youngest in 1930. In 1974, their median age was slightly under 52 years. Table 1.1 gives the distribution of their ages in that year.

The respondents earned various graduate and professional credentials, including academic doctorates, first professional degrees (M.D. and LL. B.) and master's degrees. Only four of the women had not completed requirements for a higher degree by 1963. Twenty women either entered new degree programs or concluded previous courses of graduate study between 1963 and 1974.

Table 1.2 presents an overview of the group by highest degree earned by 1963 and by 1974.

More than seven out of ten of the women who received a graduate degree prior to 1963 earned the degree before 1950. By 1974, 222 of the 226

Table 1.2   Highest Earned Degree, 1963 and 1974

Degree	1963 (percent)	1974 (percent)
Ph.D. or Ed. D.	28[a]	32
ABD[b]	6	5
First Professional Degree	12	13[a]
Masters	51	48
ABM[c]	3	2
Total percent	100	100
Total number	(226)	(226)

[a] Includes one Ph.D. who subsequently earned a *J.D.*

[b] Completed all work toward doctorate except dissertation.

[c] Completed all work toward masters except thesis.

women had acquired one or more higher degrees, and at least 21 years had passed since the majority had received their last academic credential.

A detailed breakdown of degrees by subject is presented in Table 1.3. In the body of the report, academic disciplines that had relatively few students are sometimes tabulated in combination with a related study area, except where distortions would result.

Several of the women had earned more than one graduate degree, and in some cases a higher degree preceded a master's. The most frequent example of the latter circumstance was the award of a Master's of Public Health degree to respondents with M.D.'s. Another instance was an M.A.T. in Russian earned by a woman with a doctorate in chemistry. Multiple master's degrees were not uncommon. Usually the first of these was in a liberal arts discipline and the second in a pre-professional area such as teaching or library science. Women who earned a master's degree and an academic doctorate usually obtained both in the same discipline but occasionally in different areas of concentration. A description of degrees awarded between 1963 and 1974 is contained in Chapter 6.

Outline of Report

Chapter 2 sets the stage for much of the subsequent discussion by considering the extent, duration, and patterns of the women's total worklives and of their labor force participation since the initial investigation.

Chapter 3 examines the impact of marital and maternal circumstances upon the respondents' career commitment by showing how these were associated with labor force participation. Also presented are the women's retrospective feelings about the way they apportioned their

Table 1.3   Highest Earned Degree by Academic Discipline, 1974
(percentage distribution)

Graduate Discipline	Ph.D or Ed.D	ABD	First Professional	Masters	ABM	Total Percent	Total Number
Humanities	54	12	—	34	—	100	(35)
Social Science	59	9	—	22	10	100	(32)
Physical Science	76[a]	6	—	18	—	100	(17)
Life Science	83	17	—	—	—	100	(36)
Medicine	—	—	100	—	—	100	(16)
Law	—	—	100[a]	—	—	100	(12)
Education	58	13	—	29	—	100	(24)
Social Work	4	—	—	96	—	100	(28)
Library Science	4	—	—	96	—	100	(23)
Public Health	14	—	—	86	—	100	(7)
International Affairs	—	—	—	75	25	100	(4)
Business	—	—	—	100	—	100	(8)
Journalism	—	—	—	100	—	100	(14)

[a]One Ph.D in chemistry who subsequently earned a law degree is included in the latter group.

time between family and paid work. Their advice in this regard to the younger generation concludes the chapter.

The principal theme of Chapter 4 is the nature of the careers of the women who were employed in 1974 in terms of such elements as field, function, setting, and employer and career patterns. The next chapter provides information on two other important aspects of their employment: hours and earnings. Reentry to the labor force is the focus of Chapter 6 which also is concerned with volunteer activities, further education, and the identity of non-workers in 1974.

The chapter that follows appraises the women's occupational achievement in terms of their attainments in their current careers and compares it with their achievement in 1963. The respondents' perceptions about their treatment in the labor market and their reports of types of discrimination they had encountered are the major concern of Chapter 8, which also includes reports of changes in various aspects of the women's employment as a result of pressures for equal opportunity.

The penultimate chapter was largely written by the respondents themselves; it contains a sampling of their advice to able young women about both the value of graduate school and the wisdom of advanced training in their own fields of study. Additional quotations illustrate their opinions about the women's movement and its effect upon various aspects of their lives.

The final chapter summarizes the principal findings of the study, discusses their implications, offers policy recommendations, and provides a brief glimpse into a possible future.

Notes

1. Eli Ginzberg, I. E. Berg, C. A. Brown, J. L. Herma, A. M. Yohalem, and S. Gorelick, *Life Styles of Educated Women*, (New York: Columbia University Press, 1966); and Eli Ginzberg and Alice M. Yohalem, *Educated American Women: Self-Portraits* (New York: Columbia University Press, 1966).

2. Ginzberg, *et al., op. cit.,* p. 166.

3. National Center for Education Statistics, *Digest of Educational Statistics* (Washington, D.C.: U.S. Government Printing Office, 1975), p. 84; Betty M. Vetter and Eleanor M. Babco, *Professional Women and Minorities* (Washington, D.C.: Scientific Manpower Commission, 1975), p. 52; *Enterprising Women*, II, 8 (April 1977), p. 2.

4. Ginzberg *et al., op. cit.,* (paperback edition, 1971), p. vi.

5. Hanna Papanek, "Men, Women, and Work: Reflections on the Two-Person Career" in Joan Huber (ed.), *Changing Women in a Changing Society* (Chicago: University of Chicago Press, 1973), p. 91; and Hilda Kahne, "Economic Perspectives on the Roles of Women in the American Economy," *Journal of Economic Literature*, XIII, 4 (December 1975), p. 1276.

6. For example, see Helen S. Astin, *The Woman Doctorate in America* (New York: Russell Sage Foundation, 1969); John A. Centra, *Women, Men and the Doctorate* (Princeton, N.J.: Educational Testing Service, 1974); Myra Strober, "Women Economists: Career Aspirations, Education and Training," *American Economic Review*, LXV, 2 (May 1975), p. 92; Saul D. Feldman, *Escape from the Doll's House*, Carnegie Commission on Higher Education (New York: McGraw-Hill, 1974).

7. Lotte Bailyn, "Notes on the Role of Choice in the Psychology of Professional Women," in *Daedalus*, III, 2 (Spring 1964), p. 238.

8. Michael Fogarty, A. J. Allen, I. Allen, and P. Walters, *Women in Top Jobs* (London: Allen and Unwin, 1971), p. 18.

9. W. G. Bowen and T. A. Finegan, *The Economics of Labor Force Participation* (Princeton, N.J.: Princeton University Press, 1969), p. 115.

10. Ginzberg *et al., op. cit.,* pp. 40–41.

11. Marjorie Galenson, *Women and Work*, ILR Paperback No. 13 (Ithaca, N.Y.: New York State School of Industrial and Labor Relations, Cornell University, 1973), p. 7.

12. Ginzberg *et al., op. cit,* p. 178.

13. Executive Office of the President: Office of Management and Budget, *Social Indicators, 1973* (Washington, D.C.: U.S. Government Printing Office, 1973), p. 252. National Center for Health Statistics, *Monthly Vital Statistics Reports*, XXIV, 10 (Washington, D.C.: Public Health Service, 12/29/75), p. 1.

14. Among the most important of the relevant laws and regulations are Executive Order 11246 as amended by 11375 (the Affirmative Action Program); Title VII of the Civil Rights Act of 1964 as amended by the Equal Opportunity Act of 1972; the Equal Pay Act of 1963 as amended by the Higher Education Act; Title IX of the Education Amendments of 1972 (Higher Education Act); and Title VII of the Public Health Service Act as amended by the Comprehensive Health Manpower Act and the Nurse Training Amendments Act of 1971.

15. *Educational Attainment of Workers,* March 1962 and March 1974. Special Labor Force Reports Nos. 30 and 175 (Washington, D.C.: U.S. Department of Labor, Bureau of Labor Statistics, 1963 and 1975), Table E.

16. *Ibid.*

17. Feldman, *op. cit.,* pp. 7–8.

18. Rudolph C. Blitz, "Women in the Professions, 1870–1920," *Monthly Labor Review,* XCVII, 5 (May 1974), pp. 37–38.

19. See Appendix.

20. See Appendix.

2] WORKLIVES

Introduction

In most fields of work in which graduate or professional training is required or preferred, continuity of labor force participation usually is considered to be a sine qua non for advancement to the higher rungs of the occupational hierarchy. One of the most popular rationalizations for the disparity between the achievement of well qualified men and women has been that women devote less time to their careers than men and therefore must forfeit some measure of occupational success. The argument holds that although persistent dedication to work does not necessarily lead to the top, discontinuous employment almost surely retards or prevents normal career progression.

One example of the case for differential treatment of male and female professionals has been put as follows:

> Two factors help to explain a significant divergence in women's capacity or 'productivity' as teacher-scholars. . . . One is the individual's expectations that she will have a curtailment of time and effort that she can devote to professional development. . . . Two, less time and effort are actually devoted to research and scholarship, which keep one intellectually alive and on top of one's subject because so much time and attention during a vital period for progress in one's profession are taken up with family and household duties.[1]

This kind of rationalization of discriminatory treatment presumes that all female professionals assume wifely and maternal responsibilities. Yet not all women marry or have children, and not all working

16

mothers relax their hold on their careers. Nor do all professional occupations require uninterrupted employment as a condition for advancement.

The evidence provided by the respondents indicates considerable variation in both the extent of time they devoted to work and their patterns of labor force participation. This chapter lays the groundwork for determining the degree to which continuity and stability of employment was related to occupational achievement. It focuses on the proportion and timing of years spent in the work force.

Data provided in both questionnaires are used to describe the extent and duration of women's worklives to the end of 1974, and to compare employment experience before and after January 1963 in order to examine changes in work behavior in mid-life. This discussion is followed by a delineation of the respondents' patterns of work.

Years of Work

The year in which respondents earned the bachelor's degree was used as the base for computing total years spent in the labor force to the end of 1974, because it was a credential they had in common and because several women had a body of work experience between college and graduate school. Time spent in full-time graduate study was excluded, on the assumption that full-time schedules generally precluded the possibility of regular employment.

Respondents had been employed for a median of 22 years. Variations in the numbers of years of gainful employment were not only due to differences in labor force participation but also to differences in the year of college graduation. One respondent had received her baccalaureate as early as 1927 and, at the other extreme, one had earned her B.A. in 1951. Four out of five women, however, had completed their undergraduate education between 1940 and 1950, and 85 percent had devoted fewer than five years to full-time graduate study. There was a median of 31 years between the B.A. and the end of 1974; and potential worklives of most respondents, from the baccalaureate to the end of 1974, ranged from approximately 20 to 35 years: A 1950 B.A. plus four years of full-time graduate study was at the lower limit of the modal range and a 1940 graduate with no full-time advanced schooling was at the highest point.

Almost three out of five of the respondents had been employed for more than 20 years following college graduation and over a third of them had accumulated work experience totaling more than 25 years by the end of 1974. Two percent had spent more than 40 years in the labor force.

The relationship between actual and potential years of employment is presented in Table 2.1. Overall, more than one-third of the respondents were employed during every one of their non-student post-college years

Table 2.1   **Proportion of Years Worked, B.A. Through 1974[a]**
by Number of Years with Work Experience
(percentage distribution)

Percent Years Worked	Number of Years Worked					Total Percent Years Worked
	More than 30	26-30	21-25	16-20	Less than 16	
100	59	64	52	2	—	34
76-99	41	31	36	39	2	28
51-75	—	5	12	59	24	20
50 or less	—	—	—	—	74	18
Total Percent	100	100	100	100	100	100
Number =	(37)	(42)	(50)	(41)	(55)	(225)
NA = 1						

[a]Proportion derived by dividing the number of years with any work experience by the number of years between college graduation and December 1974, less years of fulltime graduate study.

and about half were employed in a minimum of 90 percent of those years (not shown). More than three out of five had been employed in at least 76 percent of the years after college graduation. (The inclusion of ten retirees prior to 1974 slightly understates the proportion of women employed annually.)

The table demonstrates a sharp dichotomy between women with more than 20 years of employment and those with shorter work histories. Among the former nearly three out of five had worked in every year after college and 94 percent had worked in more than three-quarters of those years. In contrast, only one of the 96 respondents with 20 or fewer years of work experience had been employed in each year after college and fewer than one in five had been employed in more than three-quarters of the years since college.

Because of the relationship between the number and proportion of work years, it is possible to present analyses concerned with employment duration in terms of the proportion of work time without the danger of distortion. Utilization of proportions of time devoted to work rather than total years of employment is of greater relevance to the question of career commitment and allows for differences in potential work time.

Women who were in their late fifties in 1974 were more than twice as likely to have worked during each year after college than those born a decade later (Table 2.2).

It is conceivable that differences in continuity can be attributed to external factors such as the Depression which was under way when the

Table 2.2 Proportion of Years with Work Experience, B.A. Through 1974[a]
by Age in 1974
(percentage distribution)

Proportion Years Worked	Age, 1974 (percent)				
B.A.—1974[a] (percent)	65-68	60-64	55-59	50-54	44-49
100	23	44	56	31	26
76-99	54	39	30	27	20
less than 75	23	17	14	42	54
Total	100	100	100	100	100
Number =	(13)	(18)	(36)	(92)	(66)
NA = 1					

[a]Excluding years of full-time study.

women in the older group were undergraduates, or the postwar baby boom which reverberated during the younger women's early twenties. However, one need look no further than to differences among the respondents to find a probable explanation for the greater proportion of years of employment among the older women. Those aged 55 and over were much more likely to have never married (47 percent) than the younger women (14 percent) and over two-thirds of the never married women had worked every year compared with fewer than a quarter of the women who had been married at least once. A more detailed discussion of the influence of marital status on employment is in Chapter 3.

The drop in the proportions of women with 100 percent participation after the age of 59 is an artifact of the computations which penalized retirees. When date of retirement rather than December 1974 is used to compute years at work, these proportions resemble those of the women in their late 50's.

Aside from the women with 100 percent work participation, what is of particular note are changes among women under the age of 60. Much of the progressive rise in the degree of work experience with increased age can be ascribed to reentry to the work force and subsequent continuity of labor force participation.

Although duration of work experience, in terms of proportion of years with any amount of employment, is one indication of the strength of attachment to the labor market, a more precise measure of employment continuity is the proportion of working years devoted to full-time employment (Table 2.3).

Only 19 percent of the respondents had been employed full-time throughout every non-student year after college, and there was a strong association between the percentage of years with work experience and

Table 2.3   Proportion Work Experience Full-Time, Full-Year by Proportion Years with Work Experience, Year of B.A. Through 1974[a]
(percentage distribution)

Proportion Work Experience, Full-Time, Full Year (percent)	Proportion Years Worked (percent)				Total Percent Years with Full-Time Employment B.A.–1974
	100	76-99	51-75	1-50	
100	57	31	5	22	19
76-99	35	31	36	10	28
51-75	5	22	25	27	16
1-50	3	16	34	31	36
None	–	–	–	10	1
Total percent	100	100	100	100	100
Number =	(76)	(63)	(44)	(41)	(224)
NA = 2					

[a]Excluding years of full-time study.

the percentage of work experience that was full-time. Almost three out of five of the respondents with work experience in each year after college had always worked full-time, full-year. In contrast, less than a third of the women who had discontinuous work histories had been employed full-time throughout all the years in which they had worked. When allowance is made for limited breaks in full-time employment, and for retirement prior to 1974, the percentage of women with work experience each year who had been employed full-time throughout over three-quarters of their worklives was twice the proportion of all women with discontinuous work histories and a similar extent of full-time experience.

As may be inferred from the table, a considerable proportion of work time was devoted to part-time and/or part-year employment, and any judgment about the women's career commitment cannot ignore the implications of less than full-time work. More than two out of five of the respondents who had been employed every year, and seven out of ten of those who had worked in more than three-quarters of the years after college, had spent some of those years on part-time and/or part-year work schedules. However, only four respondents had never engaged in full-time, full-year employment.

Part-time employment was rarely an indication of inability to obtain full-time work. Rather, it usually represented an accommodation which enabled mothers of young children to divide their attention between family and career. In addition, part-time employment was often the first step taken by reentrants to the work force, presumably serving as a means of self-testing after long absences.

For many of these women, part-time employment played an important role in maintaining career ties, although its utility and availability largely depended upon one's occupation. The fact that the male model of work attachment is epitomized by continuous full-time labor force participation does not necessarily mean that a period of part-time employment was ipso facto a sign of weakened career commitment. It may also be viewed as an indication of career dedication by women who refused to let go of their careers despite added responsibilities.

Many respondents did abandon their careers for lengthy periods, however, almost always in order to fulfill family responsibilities. Yet not every mother abandoned her career, temporarily or permanently, which suggests that the decision to exit from the work force may have depended as much upon personal predilection as upon perceived necessity. As Bailyn observes:

> All serious work entails drudgery and unrewarding effort, and there are times when anyone—regardless of sex—would welcome a legitimate excuse to stop. Such excuses are near at hand for the professional woman. . . . And, as a matter of fact, a decision to desist would surely have strong social support.[2]

Considering the fact that most married respondents were raising their children during the 1950's when women who withdrew from work had strong social support and those who did not faced severe community criticism, mothers who persisted in working were not only numerically exceptional but had attributes and attitudes that were out of the ordinary.

One attribute that influenced continuity of employment was educational attainment. Respondents with medical or law degrees had the highest rate of full-time work experience. Thirty-seven percent of the doctors and lawyers always worked full-time, compared with one-quarter of the doctorates and 13 percent of the women with master's degrees. No holder of a first professional degree and only one out of 13 doctorates had spent half or fewer of the years after college out of the labor force, in contrast to 28 percent of the recipients of master's degrees.

Recent Work Experience

The years between college graduation and January 1963, and the years of the follow-up, 1963-74, represent distinct segments of the lives of the respondents. For most, the earlier period covered the years of family formation and/or early career development. The nature of the latter period largely depended upon age and prior behavior. For some women, it marked the resumption of employment after a hiatus; for others it was characterized by continued career progression; and for a few it led to retirement. Only 20 respondents spent all of the years from 1963 through

Table 2.4   Proportion of Years Employed, 1963 Through 1974, by Proportion of Years
Employed from B.A. Through 1962
(percentage distribution)

Percent Years Worked 1963-1974	Percent Years Worked B.A. through 1962			Total Percent 1963-1964
	100	70-99	Less than 70	
100	86	57	33	59
70-99	8	16	20	14
1-69	6	20	28	18
No work	—	7	19	9
Total percent	100	100	100	100
Number =	(86)	(56)	(83)	(225)
NA = 1				
Total percent B.A.—1963	36	25	37	100

1974 entirely out of the labor force. Table 2.4 reveals that prior work experience was predictive of subsequent participation in the labor force.

Women who had been employed every year before 1963 were 50 percent more likely to have worked each year thereafter than those who had work experience during 70–99 percent of the earlier years and two-and-a-half times more likely to have been employed annually after 1962 than those who had worked in less than 70 percent of the previous years. No respondent who worked in every year during the earlier period did not work at all subsequently, although a few retired after 1962.

Yet despite the influence of past labor market behavior upon later work activity, there was an overall rise in employment over time. Thus, the percentage of women with work experience each year between 1962 and 1974 was more than 50 percent higher than the percentage who had worked annually in the prior period.

Similar findings obtained when full-time, full-year employment was examined. More than four out of five of the women who had worked full-time throughout every year to 1963 did so thereafter. This was the case for over three-fifths of those whose full-time, full-year employment had encompassed 70 to 99 percent of the earlier years, and of more than a quarter of the respondents with less prior full-time work experience. In toto, only a quarter of the respondents had spent the whole of each year in full-time employment before 1963; thereafter, almost half were consistent full-time workers.

A major difference between the earlier and later periods was found to be the extent of part-time employment. Prior to 1963, only seven respondents or three percent had never worked full-time, full-year. In the subsequent period, however, 29 or 14 percent of those who were in the labor force for any time, had engaged solely in part-time and/or part-year employment, most commonly part-time. The smaller the percentage of full-time employment prior to 1963, the greater the likelihood of a history of exclusive part-time employment in subsequent years. For many other women, these years consisted of a mixture of full- and part-time work.

Women of all ages under 65 years increased their involvement in work between 1963 and 1974, but the greatest rise was among those who had been between 38 and 42 years old in 1963. The proportion of these women who had worked steadily after 1962 doubled (from 32 to 63 percent), presumably because they had been relieved of major child care responsibilities during this period.

Patterns of Labor Force Participation

The preceding discussion has focused upon the length and duration of the respondents' worklives but, with the exception of the minority of continuous full-time workers, it did not touch upon the timing of their employment. Yet, as Mallan has noted, "a short worklife is by no means synonymous with an unstable one. Whether a worklife of 20 years or less is a significant commitment to the labor force depends on whether it is spread out over many years or concentrated on one period of intensive work."[3] Discontinuity is less likely to have a disabling impact upon a career if it is of the latter type, and the women's lives were examined in terms of the staging of work and non-work.

The initial report had described six patterns of labor force participation that had emerged from an analysis of the women's work histories to 1963; their patterns of work participation during the follow-up period assumed similar conformations. One pattern was continuous employment. The remaining patterns ranged from a few brief interludes of part-time or non-work in an otherwise continuous employment history to a pattern representing a total of less than four years of work experience. In between these extremes were patterns characterized by intermittent short periods in and out of the labor force, periodic withdrawal from the work force for three or more years at a stretch, and termination of employment after a substantial amount of experience. The women with discontinuous work histories prior to 1963 were fairly equally divided among these five patterns as Table 2.5 demonstrates.

Almost two-thirds of the respondents had a broken pattern of work prior to 1963, although only a quarter had been out of the labor force for any appreciable amount of time, and only 12 percent had withdrawn after less than a total of four years of work experience. From 1963 on, the majority of respondents had continuous work patterns.

The "terminated" pattern usually had a different connotation in the

Table 2.5   Labor Force Participation Patterns, B.A. to 1974

Pattern	Percent B.A. to 1963	Percent 1963 through 1974
Continuous	36	53
Minor breaks	13	11
Intermittent	13	12
Periodic	13	8
Terminated	13	1
Minimal or no work	12	15
Total percent	100	100
(Number = 226)		

latter period than the earlier one. Prior to 1963, it almost always signified withdrawal from the labor force in order to fulfill family responsibilities. Afterwards, it often indicated retirement for age or disability.

Between 1963 and 1974, nearly two out of five of all of the women who formerly had a pattern of discontinuous labor force participation worked every year, and another 18 percent had only minor breaks in employment. Of those whose earlier pattern of work had been marked by an exit from the labor force after lengthy employment, more than half had returned to the labor market by 1974, as had half of the women who had only minimal work experience before 1963. Almost three out of five of the women with patterns of intermittent or periodic work participation before 1963 worked continuously or with only minor breaks thereafter.

Eight of the ten women who had retired by 1974 had worked continuously from college graduation until their final exit from the labor force and the other two had taken only short intermissions from work. Finally, 93 percent of non-retired women with continuous work patterns prior to 1963 followed the same course throughout the subsequent period.

When patterns of work participation are examined in conjunction with duration of work experience the earlier caution about the importance of considering the timing of work is confirmed. For example, one-third of the women who had minimal work experience prior to 1963 were employed during at least 9 out of the 12 subsequent years as were a quarter of women who had previously withdrawn from the labor force after more extensive work experience.

While employment instability was characteristic of the earlier period, stability was the hallmark of the later years. Broken patterns of work participation were largely smoothed out and earlier withdrawal from

Table 2.6   Changes in Employment Status, January 1963, June 1969, and December 1974[a]

Employment Status 1963-1969	Percent
Working 1963	71
Exited 1963-1969[b]	6
Not working 1963	29
Entered 1963-1969[b]	42
Total	100
Employment Status 1969-1974	
Working 1969	79
Exited 1969-1974[b]	11
Not Working 1969	21
Entered 1969-1974[c]	32
Total	100
Working 1974	77
Number = (220)	
NA 1969 = 6	

[a]Excludes more than one change in work status in the periods between these dates. Although only 20 women, or 9 percent, were not employed at all during the entire period, about 12 percent were not working at any of the three dates in the analysis.
[b]Shows percent of those working who exited.
[c]Shows percent of those not working who entered.

work proved, in most instances, to have been temporary. These changed patterns suggest that many women who had spent relatively short periods of time in the labor force in the years preceding 1963 will eventually have an extensive body of work experience concentrated in the middle and later years of their lives.

A view of the dynamics of employment during the follow-up period is shown in Table 2.6 which indicates changes in the rates of labor force participation at the beginning, middle and end of the follow-up period.

The table demonstrates that lack of continuity of labor force participation after 1962 was primarily caused by delayed reentry to employment. Women returned to work throughout the period and usually remained at work thereafter so that, in most cases, reentrants had continuous patterns from the date of return but not necessarily from 1963. Ten of the exiters during this period were retirees.

Employment status in these years by age of respondent demonstrates a massive pull toward work as women reached middle age.

The cycle that this table describes is one of steadily increasing involvement in gainful employment among respondents during their forties and early fifties followed by a decrease in work attachment,

Table 2.7 Employment Status, January 1963, June 1969 and December 1974 by Age in 1963

Age in 1963	Percent Employed		
	1963	1969	1974
33-38 years	59	67	77
39-43	67	81	83
44-48	86	97	83
49-53	90	78	63
54-58	85	75	31
Total employment rate	71	79	77
Number employed =	(160)	(173)	(173)
Number unknown = 6 (1969)			

especially after the age of 65 (ages 54–58 in 1963). Until that age, however, the percentage of wage earners never became as low as that of women who were still in their thirties in 1963. Since peak participation occurred when the women were in their early fifties, it seems reasonable to predict increasing involvement by women in the youngest group, most of whom had not yet reached the age of 50 by 1974.

Summary

Relatively few of these highly qualified women had the continuous work history that is characteristic of their male counterparts. Only one-third of them had been employed during all of the years of their adult lives that were not devoted to full-time schooling, and merely one-fifth had been employed full-time throughout every year. There was a strong association between the percentage of years employed and of years employed full-time: the more persistent the overall work attachment, the greater the proportion of the worklife devoted to year-long full-time employment.

Continuity of employment was related to age and educational credentials. Women aged 55 and older in 1974 were more likely than the younger respondents to have been continuously employed, largely because a far higher percentage of the older group had never married. In addition, respondents with first professional degrees demonstrated the greatest propensity toward full-time, full-year work; those with master's degrees, the least.

Part-time employment experience was common and appeared to be the means these professional women used to maintain their career ties during periods of heavy home responsibilities. It also served as the first step in the reentry process for many of the women who had withdrawn from the labor force.

Although the extent of earlier work participation was predictive of subsequent labor market behavior, as many women approached and entered their forties there was a substantial increase in overall labor force participation. The follow-up period was also marked by an increase in employment stability as women who earlier had broken patterns of labor force participation resumed employment and settled down to a continuous work attachment.

Notes

1. Richard A. Lester, *Antibias Regulation of Universities,* Carnegie Commission on Higher Education (New York: McGraw-Hill, 1974), p. 58.

2. Lotte Bailyn, "Notes on the Role of Choice in the Psychology of Professional Women," in *Daedalus,* III, 2 (Spring 1964), p. 39.

3. Lucy B. Mallan, "Women Born in the Early 1900's: Employment, Earnings and Benefit Levels," *Social Security Bulletin,* XXXVII, 3 (March 1974), p. 7.

3] HUSBANDS, CHILDREN, AND CAREERS

The careers of professional women can be obstructed by forces within and without the labor market. Employer presumptions that a woman's family will have a negative influence upon her work decisions can lead to differential treatment of the sexes, and strong social pressures beyond the labor market often persuade women to modify or abandon their career goals after marriage or childbirth.

The respondents' histories provide illustrations of the danger of inferences derived from traditional female behavior. Many of them never married and consequently remained continuously attached to the labor force. Also, marriage, per se, rarely impeded wives' employment, although conformity to the view that a husband's career interests are overriding sometimes imposed a penalty. Children represented the primary barrier to the continuous pursuit of a career, but some of the mothers defied convention by working consistently after their children were born.

This chapter describes changes in the women's marital and maternal status over time and then examines how these characteristics were associated with their labor force participation. Also discussed is the time spent on homemaking and paid work and the wives' contributions to family income. The reflections of mothers about the way they had apportioned their time between family and career are presented as a measure of their satisfaction with the outcomes of earlier work decisions. The chapter concludes with a discussion of the respondents' advice to younger women about the desirability of combining family and career.

Table 3.1   Marital Status, 1974, by Marital Status, 1963
            (percentage distribution)

1974 Marital Status	1963 Marital Status					Percent Marital Status 1974
	First Marriage	Remarriage	Separated or Divorced	Widowed	Never Married	
First marriage	87	—	—	—	3	55
Remarriage	2	85	100	58	—	11
Separated or Divorced	6	—	—	25	—	5
Widowed	5	15	—	17	2[a]	5
Never married	—	—	—	—	95	24
Total percent	100	100	100	100	100	100
Percent Marital Status 1963	63	6	1	5	25	100
Number = 226						

[a]Married and widowed between 1963 and 1974.

Marital Status

Three-quarters of the respondents had been married prior to 1963 and 84 percent of the women who had ever married were living with their first husbands at the beginning of that year. Thereafter, as a result of divorce and widowhood, there was a decrease of 11 percent between 1963 and 1974 in the number of ever married women living with their first husbands. Table 3.1 details the changes.

The proportion of never married women (24 percent) is in striking contrast to national rates of four percent of women aged 45 to 54 years in 1974 and of less than six percent in the 55 to 64 year age group.[1] The desire for extended education often takes precedence over matrimony during graduate training, and it is possible that the pool of "eligible" males was being depleted while many respondents were engaged in prolonged study. This inference is supported by the disproportion of never married women in the group that had spent the longest time in earning advanced degrees—the academic doctorates. Unmarried respondents with Ph.D.'s and Ed.D.'s represented 39 percent of all doctorates in 1974 (41 percent in 1963). This was about twice the proportion of unmarried women with first professional or master's degrees, whose rates were also above the norm. Most of the husbands of respondents with doctorates either had doctorates themselves (54 percent) or had first professional degrees (17 percent).

Traditionally, a wife's school attainment is less than, or, at most, equal to her husband's. At the highest academic level where the number of men with equivalent education is relatively small, adherence to this convention affords limited marital opportunities for women, especially for those who have postponed marriage.

Centra found a similar proportion of single women among doctorates who had received their degrees in 1950 and 1960—about the same time as most of the respondents.[2] Noting that the rate of never married women fell to 30 percent among 1968 Ph.D.'s, he predicted a trend toward more marriages, but even if his forecast is correct, female doctorates would have far to go to match the national marriage rate.

An additional explanation for the high percentage of never married women among the respondents is provided by comparing the marital status of women who attended graduate school shortly after college with those who enrolled after a fair amount of work experience. Half of those with work experience remained single in contrast to only 15 percent of the women who had no substantial break between undergraduate and graduate studies. Perhaps the belated pursuit of credentials that would improve occupational opportunities was in itself a reaction to fading marital prospects.

It may be that, as Havens asserts, "the higher the economic achievement of females, the less their desire to accept the confining traditional familial sex-role of wife-mother-homemaker."[3] Since economic achievement rarely precedes marital decisions, this assertion is open to question. It is possible, however, that women who are strongly motivated toward careers may refrain from marrying in order to concentrate upon their occupational goals, thereby *eventually* achieving greater economic success than those who do marry. Nevertheless, spinsterhood was not necessarily the result of a voluntary decision: "I like my job. I like being a woman. I am sorry I never married and had children," said a 59-year-old professor who was among the respondents.

Inquiries into the female condition too often neglect those who never marry. Yet they represent a significant component among women with superior academic qualifications, in particular. Comparisons between single and married women are useful measures of the impact of marital responsibilities on the shape of women's careers and such analyses appear at various points in this report.

The proportion of ever married respondents who were still living with their first husbands (75 percent) was higher than the national percentage among ever married women aged 46 to 55 in 1975 (70 percent).[4] This difference appears to be due primarily to differences in the divorce rate. Among the 171 ever married respondents, 28 or 16.4 percent of the first marriages had been broken by divorce by 1974. The national rate in 1975 for women of comparable ages was 18.5 percent.[5]

The rate of remarriage among respondents who were divorced after their first marriage (73 percent) was similar to the national rate for their female contemporaries.[6] The rate of remarriage among those whose first marriages left them widowed (31 percent) was considerably below that of divorcees, possibly because divorce occurred at younger ages. Although divorce was more common among women whose first marriages had occurred when they were below the age of 25, early marriage did not lead to quick divorce. In most cases, at least ten years elapsed between marriage and divorce and in 40 percent of these instances marriages were not dissolved until the passage of 20 years or more.

Most respondents had first married at relatively late ages, more than half after the age of 24 and one-quarter after the age of 28. In contrast, only 20 percent of the first marriages of all ever married women of similar ages took place after the age of 24.[7] The lower divorce rate of respondents relative to their female contemporaries may be related to the large proportion of late marriages among the highly educated group since, in general, the older the wife's age at first marriage, the lower the divorce rate.[8]

There was no evidence that extended extramarital commitments had a place in the lives of many respondents as they appear to be having in the lives of large numbers of their younger counterparts. A few women did volunteer information about relationships with men that played important parts in their lives, however, and some others appended general comments about changing sexual mores.

Husbands

As already noted, women tend to marry men of equal or higher school attainment and the respondents were not exceptions to this rule. The proportions of husbands whose academic degrees were comparable to or higher than those of their wives ranged from nearly two-thirds of the men married to women with master's degrees to almost three-quarters of those whose wives had doctorates or first professional degrees. Only 12 percent of all husbands had not graduated from college and four out of five of the non-graduates were married to women with bachelor's or master's degrees. The median age of the husbands was 54 years.

With the exception of 12 retired men and one student, all husbands were employed in 1974. About two-thirds of them, both working and retired, were professionals, almost half of whom were academics. A quarter of the husbands had positions as officials, managers or administrators in business, non-profit or government organizations or were self-employed businessmen. All but one of the remaining seven were in white-collar staff jobs. The exception was a skilled blue-collar worker who had married after retirement.

Stiehm has pointed out that, despite the tendency of the best educated

Table 3.2   Number of Children[a], Ever Married Women, 1963 and 1974[b]

Number of Children	1963	1974
	(percent)	(percent)
0	14	13
1	16	15
2	36	33
3	24	25
4 or more	10	14
Total percent	100	100
Total number	(168)	(171)
Never married	(58)	(55)

[a]By birth or adoption.
[b]Excludes one unmarried mother.

women to marry men with the same or superior education, very few of these women "enjoy the position of *most* college educated men—that of not only having attained a high educational level but also that of outranking their spouse." She goes on to say

> this makes it possible to understand why even well-educated women defer to their husband's interests when family decisions are made. . . . [E]ven if their education is equal, he will be able to profit more from his training; even if she aspires to ultimate equality, because he is older he is more likely to be ready to use opportunities which may arise.[9]

Children

Relatively few of the women who had ever married remained childless: about 87 percent had at least one child by 1974, most having completed their families by 1963. Only 15 percent of the mothers bore or adopted children between 1963 and 1974, including one unmarried woman who adopted two children. Table 3.2 presents the distribution of family size in 1974.

After 1962 there was a rise of 15 percent in the proportion of families with three or more children and an increase in average family size from 2.0 to 2.16 children. Nationally, the mean family size among all females of similar ages in 1975 was between 2.8 and 3.0 children.[10] This difference may be, in part, a reflection of relatively late marriage among the respondents.

Family size was associated with the highest academic degree mothers had earned prior to 1963. Table 3.3 sets forth this relationship.

The family size of mothers with academic doctorates and of those with first professional degrees was similar; but the proportion of childless wives among the former (28 percent) was more than six times greater than among the M.D.'s or LL.B.'s. Only one of the 22 ever married women with a first professional degree had no children in contrast to eleven of the 39 ever married doctorates. The rate of childless married women among the 1950 and 1960 doctorates surveyed by Centra was even higher than that of doctorates among the respondents—33 percent— indicating that our finding is no anomaly.[11]

The decision to have children, not how many children to have, distinguished respondents with doctorates from those with other graduate degrees. To quote a childless Ph.D. anthropologist: "I cannot imagine having accomplished what I have if I had children." Since wives with doctorates had married later than those with other degrees, they may have had stronger grasps upon their careers at the time they wed than many who had married at younger ages, and may have been reluctant to risk relaxing their hold by having children.

Most women of high educational attainment probably made deliberate decisions about family size so that the smaller than average number of children reported may reflect the desire to avoid or minimize career disruptions. Although the majority of married respondents opted to have children, the ability to control the number and spacing of their offspring provided some of them with the opportunity of combining continuous work and motherhood and others with the chance of resuming their careers without too long an intermission. Most of the mothers left the labor force for some period of time and their date of

Table 3.3   Number of Children 1974 by Highest Degree
as of 1963, Ever Married Women
(percentage distribution)

| Number of Children, 1974 | Highest Degree[a] (percent) | |
	Doctorate or First Professional	Masters[b]
None	11	10
1	19	14
2	36	31
3	10	31
4 or more	14	14
Total percent	100	100
Total number	(61)	(105)
Not applicable = 61		

[a]Excluding B.A.
[b]Includes ABD.

reentry usually was governed by their perception of their children's need for their presence in the home.

In general, it is during the preschool years that a mother is most likely to believe that her continuous presence is required in the home. Reentry to the labor force by mothers starts when the youngest child enters elementary school and gathers momentum as children proceed through school. Among the respondents, more than half of the mothers had children of kindergarten age or below in 1963 and the youngest child of another 40 percent was below the normal high school entrance age. By 1974 fewer than a quarter of the mothers had children below high school age.

There was a direct relationship between size of family and the age of the youngest child in both years; in 1963 about two-fifths of the mothers of one or two children had at least one child under six years of age but there were children of this age in most of the larger families. In 1974, the youngest child in the majority of families of every size was at least 14 years old and only two mothers had children under the age of six.

Among the children of respondents, there were 223 who had graduated from high school, 94 percent of whom had entered college. Nine out of ten of this group were current undergraduates or had already earned the baccalaureate. The remainder had left college prior to graduation. Nine children had terminated their education at the end of high school and four were high school dropouts.

The percentage of offspring who had enrolled in college was considerably higher than that of all youth aged 20 to 24 years in 1974, only 41 percent of whom had entered college by that year.[12] Moreover, almost three out of five (58 percent) of the college graduate children of respondents went on to graduate or professional school compared with less than two out of five (39 percent) of all graduates aged 20 to 29 years.[13]

Of the children who were in the labor force, two-thirds were in either professional, technical, or managerial occupations, mostly in jobs in the first of these categories. The remaining workers included laborers, farmers, craftsmen, and operatives, as well as clerical, sales, or service workers. Many of the workers in blue collar and agricultural occupations appeared to have adopted alternate life styles—some mothers mentioned common-law marriages, for instance—which was par for the course among many members of their generation from middle-class families. Nevertheless, most of the children appeared to be following in their parents' footsteps, although the majority were still at low rungs of the career ladder. Many daughters had opted for teaching and other predominantly female pursuits, full-time homemaking excepted.

One respondent, a recent Ph.D. and presently a professor of economics wrote:

My children [a self-employed farmer-toymaker son and a daughter described as a writer-farmer-mother] are free in a way we weren't, but even they are dogged by some of the same difficulties and conflicts over role-definitions and conflicting expectations. But at the least they recognize the possibilities. I'm not sure we always did.

Marital Status and Work Experience

The labor market behavior of the respondents was closely dependent upon their family composition. The presence or absence of a husband or of children, the number and ages of offspring, and a husband's attitudes toward his wife's career were strongly associated with a woman's work decisions.

Respondents who never married had more extensive work histories than those who had been married for any length of time. By 1974, 92 percent of the non-retired single women—but only 36 percent of other women—had been employed during at least nine-tenths of the years since college. Furthermore, marital stability also influenced the extent of work experience (Table 3.4).

Women who never had husbands were more than three times as likely to have worked consistently as those who had ever been married and more than twice as likely to have been employed in a minimum of 90 percent or more of the years since college. Women with broken marriages stepped up their labor participation, especially the divorcees, presumably because divorce (usually having occurred earlier in life than widowhood) propelled them back into the labor force that much

Table 3.4   Proportion of Years Worked, B.A. to 1974[a] by Marital Experience
(percentage distribution)

		Marital Experience (percent)			
Percentage Years Worked to 1974	Never Married	Married Once, Still Married	Divorced After First Marriage	Widowed After First Marriage	Total Percent Years Worked
100	67	21	29	23	34
90-99	18	11	25	15	15
70-89	13	18	25	23	18
less than 70	2	50	21	39	33
Total percent	100	100	100	100	100
Total number	(55)	(129)	(28)	(13)	(225)
NA = 1					

[a]Retirees included.

sooner. Young divorcees possibly had greater financial incentives to work than older widows.

Marital status was also associated with the extent of a woman's full-time employment. The proportion of never married respondents who had been employed full-time throughout a minimum of 90 percent of the years after college (75 percent) was more than three times higher than the proportion of continuous full-time workers among women who had ever married (23 percent). Moreover, the percentage of women who had spent less than half their adult years working full-time was 12 times higher among the ever married (47 percent) than among the never married (four percent).

The influence of marital status on work participation was also revealed by examining 1974 labor force participation rates. In December 1974, the rate of divorced or separated respondents who had not retired was 100 percent, eight points higher than the never married rate. In contrast, 82 percent of the widows and less than three-quarters of wives with husbands present were in the labor force. Nationally, the labor force participation rate of divorcees with five years or more of college was 88 percent in March 1975; that of women with husbands present was 68 percent.[14] Divorced mothers of children of school age had a much higher participation rate than divorcees with preschoolers, however, and none of the divorced respondents had children under 12 years of age in 1974.[15]

Some respondents commented upon the influence of divorce or widowhood upon their work decisions. A sociologist recalled that "divorce prior to 1963 left me unhappy as I would then have preferred a homemaker role. Subsequent career was fascinating, enjoyable. . . . Recent marriage is very sensible—comfortable, blends well with career which is now at its best." A divorced public administrator said: "If I had had a happy marriage, I would have preferred to spend more time on family concerns when the children were younger and a job or extensive volunteer activity later."

A widow with intermittent teaching experience reported: "The death of my husband has put me in the position of having to find paid employment of some kind; hence at the moment, I am forced to wish that I had spent more time developing an independent career." Another respondent remarked: "Being a widow with three children to support, one through medical school . . . and one through law school . . . and a daughter who will at least get a Bachelors degree. . . . I am very grateful for my degrees and CPA certificate. Without them I probably wouldn't have been offered the opportunities that I have been able to accept which now enable me to raise my family in a comfortable fashion. . . ."

Many husbands encouraged and supported their wives' careers aims and sometimes they adjusted aspects of their own work in order to enable

their wives to fulfill their job commitments. For example, a college professor and department chairman married to a dean at another institution said: "My husband and I have always worked out the problem of dual careers, home, family, etc. He moved three times for my position; the last time I moved for him. I owed him one!" And a librarian with a librarian husband remarked: "I think too little credit is given to the positive contribution a good marriage makes towards the family and career combination. At a number of points in my professional life, it has been at my husband's insistence that I have taken on responsibilities for which I would otherwise have lacked the confidence. The converse is equally true: I am sure my marriage is the stronger for my having a life of my own and satisfactions independent from it." The psychologist wife of a journalist wrote: "I have an egalitarian husband which makes everything much easier. He has always encouraged me in my career."
One teacher warned:

> One should choose a husband—if one marries—with great care. My husband, a psychiatrist, has often been urging me to expand my horizons, and has consciously been assuming an ever-increasing share of household burdens. We have tried to rear all five children to assume their own responsibilities. . . . Anyone who assumes that, since she is born female, she is automatically foreordained to clean up after everyone else, is *asking* to be looked down upon! And anyone who marries a man who feels women were created to look after him and other men had better believe she's in for a lifetime of trouble! A double, triple, quadruple pox on those men who welcome their wives' working and then expect them to carry all responsibilities for household, children, etc. as well! *Ugh!!*

Some husbands were hindrances to their wives' careers. There were those who forbade their wives' employment at any time or at specific times. Others gave precedence to their own career concerns so that their wives were forced to suit their own employment to the requirements of their husband's jobs. Of course, compliance on the part of wives was required in support of these positions, and many highly qualified women who had firm intentions to pursue careers came to view their own work goals as subordinate to those of their husbands.

Nevertheless, relatively few wives explicitly assigned responsibility for thwarted careers to their husbands. One who did, a non-working social scientist married to a business administrator, said: "A continuing problem for me has been the 'workaholic' aspects of my husband's work life. He has always worked long hours—granted, enjoying those hours!—traveled quite a bit when the children were younger, etc. Therefore, given my own personality, being a 'worrier,' a perfectionist about my own paid work, I soon found that the children were being short-changed when I got too involved in my own work problems."

There were other comments that referred to ways in which a husband affected his wife's work. For example, a woman who had recently achieved success as a free-lance writer said: "My husband [a corporation executive], who is ten years older than I, is approaching retirement age; I feel that my life is just beginning. There may be conflicts ahead. But I hope that as I was supportive of his efforts when he was climbing to the top he will be helpful to me. It's my turn now." A professor married to a physicist noted: "My husband is very successful and almost 20 years older than I am—I feel that this helped. He could afford to be magnanimous toward me."

A part-time adjunct professor made the following plea:

> I wish you would utilize your influence to alter the language of the "anti-nepotism" debate. Nepotism implies the hiring of unqualified persons solely because of a familial relationship. Every women hired by an institution which also employs her husband is thus more or less guilty of something by virtue of her marital status. In point of fact, the married women I know have had one hell of a time getting themselves hired, and many have credentials superior to those of persons not caught in the "nepotism" bag. Now that it is no longer immoral for a woman to work outside the home, cannot we drop this semantic relic of the past?

While anti-nepotism regulations were rarely cited as a reason for lack of employment or for under-employment, there were additional instances in which wives were employed at the same institution as their husbands but as temporary, adjunct, or subsidiary appointees with no assurance of regularity of employment or of placement on a tenure track. The experiences of these women echo the findings of a study of faculty wives that concluded:

> Faculty women were sought out for their positions, while for the faculty wife it was far more often the case that her husband was sought by the University and that she found her job through her own efforts.[16]

Another problem often encountered by wives is the need (or desire) to accompany their husbands to new job locations. With some notable exceptions, the respondents adhered to the general view that the husband's career interests are overriding. Therefore, if husbands were able to advance their careers by relocating to a different community, their wives were forced to seek new employment opportunities.

Examination of the women's reasons for leaving jobs revealed that more than two out of five wives had left employment at least once prior to 1963 to accompany their husbands to new job locations and that 12 percent had done so between 1963 and 1974. The decrease during the latter period may reflect not merely a smaller number of years but also the fact that most husbands were likely to have reached stable career niches at this point in their lives.

Overall, about half of the ever married women had left at least one job because of their husbands' relocation. In the case of 55 percent of these wives, however, or 28 percent of the total, this type of job change occurred only once, and for a quarter, or 12 percent of the total, just twice. Thus, less than 10 percent of all ever married respondents left more than two jobs due to the transfer or voluntary move of a spouse. One wife left eight jobs for this reason!

Job loss caused by husbands' moves had some impact upon wives' employment continuity. A smaller proportion of wives who left jobs to accompany their husbands to new employment locations had worked each year (16 percent) than of those who did not have to make this decision (29 percent). However, among wives who were in the labor force during nine-tenths of their adult years the resemblance between these two groups was closer—31 percent and 39 percent, respectively. Many women apparently were able to obtain new positions without much difficulty, possibly because their high qualifications facilitated placement.

About half of the wives with doctoral, law, or master's degrees had to leave jobs at least once in response to their husbands' plans. Wives with medical degrees were half as likely to give up jobs for this reason as other women, possibly because their husbands, usually physicians themselves, were less likely to be involved in locational changes than men in certain other fields. It is also possible that women physicians may have especially high stakes in their jobs so that their husbands paid special deference to any desire to stay put.

In general, a third of the wives of professionals, other than academics, had left jobs to accompany their husbands to new posts, as had two out of five wives of non-professional husbands who were in public, private, or self-employment in 1974. It was the wives of men who held academic positions who demonstrated the greatest frequency of job loss due to their husbands' moves. Almost three-quarters of them had quit at least one job and 36 percent had left two or more positions for this reason. While the corporate wife has been the stereotype who is buffeted hither and yon by the exigencies of her husband's career, among the respondents this peripatetic pattern was typically within academe.

In 1963, about three out of ten of the married women had indicated that their husbands were either strongly opposed or had certain objections to a work role for their wives. The attitudes of the remaining husbands ranged from neutrality to outright enthusiasm. Only six percent of the wives of disapproving husbands defied their spouses by working at least 90 percent of the years between college and 1974. In contrast, more than half of the wives of men with more positive attitudes toward their wives' careers had worked this amount of time.

Of the 19 married women who were not in the labor force at any time between 1963 and 1974, five noted their husband's preference that they not work for pay as a reason for not working. Considering that there were 171 respondents who were married and living with husbands in 1974, and that nearly a third of the husbands had previously been described as having some reservations about having a working wife, the small number of wives who had consistently refrained from working in response to their husbands' preferences provides a perspective upon the wives' determination to continue or resume their careers. However, in many cases a husband's opposition was based upon his feelings about a work role for a wife who was a mother as well. Most of these men were not against their wives working at *any* time but rather against their working at specific times, namely at points in their children's lives at which fathers judged a mother's presence was required.

Children and Work Participation

Most respondents may have defied the conventions of the postwar period by preparing for professions at a time when their contemporaries were increasingly dedicating themselves to *Kinder* and *Kuche,* but relatively few of those who married went so far as to pursue their careers with the same ardor that led them to train for careers. This was certainly the case among women who had children.

Although employment experiences during World War II convinced many married women that paid work was a highly attractive alternative to housework, those who remained in the labor force after the war were more likely to be women who had already fulfilled their family obligations or who had not yet assumed them. The labor force participation rate of all women in the prime childbearing years dropped after the war and did not regain (and surpass) its wartime level for more than 20 years. In contrast, participation rates of younger and older women rose steadily.[17] The postwar period was inhospitable to women who wanted to have children and also to engage in a full-time career and, when respondents became mothers, most chose to modify their career goals in order to accommodate them to their families' needs.

The decision to continue working without a break after childbirth was exceptional. It was especially rare among mothers who gave birth to their first child in the early 1950's. They were not only three times less likely to have worked continuously than wives who first became mothers in the prior and subsequent decades, but they also had the largest families. Their behavior implies that many women of high educational status were moved by the postwar exaltation of hearth and home to abandon or to defer their careers.

Nevertheless, most mothers left the labor force for periods of varying lengths regardless of their first child's year of birth. Only three out of ten

Table 3.5   Percent Ever Married Women with Work Experience[a] in 90-100% of Years to December 1974, and between January 1963 and December 1974, by Number of Children, 1974

Number of Children 1974	Worked 90-100% of Years (percent)	
	B.A.-1974	1963-1974
None	78	77
1	65	69
2	38	61
3 or more	9	42
Total percent wives	36	57
Number wives = 171		
Never married = 55		

[a]Excluding full-time study.

had been employed during a minimum of 90 percent of the years since college graduation (Table 3.5).

While the proportion of childless wives who spent nine-tenths of all available years in the labor force was somewhat smaller than that of never married women (85 percent) it was greater than that of mothers with families of all sizes. Marriage, alone, may have influenced some women to refrain from paid employment, but it hardly matched the influence of motherhood upon withdrawal from the work force.

Size of family had a determinant effect upon the extent of a mother's work experience. Only 18 percent of all mothers, but 46 percent of the mothers of one child did not miss as much as a year of employment (not shown). The birth of each additional child exerted increasing pressure upon a mother to leave the labor force. Mothers of one child were only slightly less likely than childless wives to have worked during nine-tenths of their adult years. However, they were 42 percent more likely to have done so than mothers of two, and over seven times as likely as mothers of three or more children. Restricting family size to one child, therefore, did not seriously limit married women's ability to engage in gainful employment, but the birth of a second child was much more of a constraint upon labor force participation, and the presence of more than two children was a strong disincentive to work.

Since most of the children were born before 1963, increasing numbers of their mothers had returned to the labor force by 1974, after having been home for nine to ten years, on the average. The percentages of mothers who worked almost every year after 1962 shown in Table 3.5 do not indicate the true dimensions of this change, because reentry occurred throughout the period. In January 1963, 56 percent of all mothers were in the labor force; in June 1969, their participation rate had risen to 71 percent; and by December 1974, it was 77 percent. More than two out of five of mothers who were not employed in January 1963 were in the work force in 1969, and an additional 16 percent were working in 1974. Since about 14 percent of the mothers who had returned to work after 1963 were not employed in 1974, the net maternal reentry rate as of 1974 was 86 percent.

Size of family also influenced the extent of the mothers' full-time, full-year employment. Only a small minority of mothers had worked full-time, year round for at least 90 percent of their adult lives and the proportion who did so decreased with increases in family size.

A substantial number of the mothers with the lengthiest work histories spent a considerable portion of their working years in other than full-time, full-year employment. In fact, differences between the work participation of wives with and without children were much greater with respect to full-time employment than total employment. For example, the proportion of mothers of one child who spent a minimum of nine-tenths of their lives at work was only 17 percent lower than that of childless wives, but the proportion of the former who had as much full-time work experience was 40 percent lower.

Only little more than half of the mothers who had worked continuously or nearly so in the years after college always had been employed full-time, full-year. In most cases, the alternative was part-time full-year work; in the others, some time was spent in part- or full-time work for less than a full year. However, only four mothers had no full-time, full-year work experience.

Also an indicator of a mother's propensity to work was the age of her

Table 3.6   Labor Force Participation Rates of Mothers in January 1963, June 1969, and December 1974 by Age of Youngest Child in January 1963

Age of Youngest Child, January 1963	Participation Rate (percent)			
	1963	1969	1974	N
Under 6 Years	47.3	64.9	75.7	(74)
6 to 13 Years	63.8	77.6	75.9	(58)
Total rate, mothers	56.4	70.7[a]	75.7	(132[a])
Total rate, all respondents	70.9	78.6[b]	78.2	(220[b])

[a]Excludes four mothers with unknown work status.

[b]Excludes six respondents with unknown work status, 1969.

youngest child. Practically all mothers had completed their families by 1963 and Table 3.6 indicates how the increase in the work participation of mothers from then on was linked to the maturation of their last born.

The trend in the participation rates indicates that, over time, the age of the youngest child was a major determinant of a mother's labor force status. Thus, by 1969, when a youngest child who had been below the age of six in January 1963 was between 6 and 13 years, a mother had about the same participation rate as one whose youngest child had been aged 6 to 13 in the earlier year.

As their youngest child reached high school age, mothers' participation rates closely resembled the rate for all respondents. If retirees are excluded, the difference is slightly larger because no retired women had any children. Of the 43 non-retired respondents who were out of the labor force in 1974, about four out of five were mothers, more than half of whom had children under 18 years of age. Only half of these mothers had not worked at all after 1962. Thus, the table understates the recent work experience of the mothers because almost nine out of ten (88 percent) of those whose youngest child had been under six years of age in 1963 had been in the labor force for some period of time during the subsequent years.

Consideration of children's ages, alone, conceals the combined effect of age of youngest child and family size upon a mother's work decision. A substantial number of the mothers had children below the age of six in 1963. Yet, their labor force participation rates differed according to the number of children they had. In families with three or more children, the presence of a child under six years was far more of a deterrent to a mother's employment than in families with fewer offspring, and this difference persisted thereafter. More than half of the mothers with one or two children, at least one of whom was under six years in 1963, worked in every subsequent year compared with 28 percent of those with larger families and at least one child under six.

Educational attainment also exerted an influence upon a mother's work decision. In January 1963, more than four out of five doctorates or FPG's with two or more children were in the labor force, compared to slightly more than half of mothers who had master's degrees and families of similar size. In fact, the proportion of working mothers of three or more children among doctorates or FPG's (64 percent) was about the same as the proportion of working mothers with one child among those with a master's degree (63 percent).

Moreover, almost twice the proportion of mothers with the higher credentials and children under the age of six were working in 1963 (70 percent) as that of mothers with children of similar age and master's degrees (37 percent). The 1963 participation rate of doctorates and FPGs who had children below the age of six (70 percent) was higher than the rate of women with master's degrees and children aged six years or older (66 percent).

Homemaking

The definition of homemaking was addressed by a physician who estimated that it consumed three to four hours of her time each week.

> This question sparked a dinner table debate. What is homemaking? I include making my own (half of the) bed and my own breakfast, and my husband and son protest, especially my husband, who says this questionnaire will not assume that *he* makes his own half of the bed and his own breakfast. My standard is that homemaking includes any work that would be considered "homemaking" if anyone else did it. Thus, brushing my teeth and going out to eat in a restaurant are not, but grocery shopping and picking up and the above chores are. I did *not* include "child care" time on telephones with teenagers re their worries, etc.

Despite the strength of a woman's original career commitment, if she opted for a husband and children, or even a husband, alone, she was bound to face the problem of integrating her work and family roles, and it was not an easy problem to solve, primarily because of the unavailability of substitute providers of child care.

> Because of decreased domestic help, the difficulties confronting a highly educated mother today may resemble those of a manual worker's wife more closely than those of professional women two or three generations ago.[18]

An examination of the time the respondents reported that they normally spent on homemaking in 1974 can be instructive in demonstrating the dual burdens that women with strong career motivations have to shoulder if they are to fulfill the domestic responsibilities that traditionally devolve upon a wife and mother, and simultaneously remain seriously committed to work.

Most of the women, regardless of family composition, spent a considerable amount of time attending to household affairs. Almost nine out of ten devoted some amount of time to domestic duties, about half spending 20 weekly hours or more, and one quarter, 30 or more hours. While it may not seem remarkable to find women doing what is normally deemed women's work, it is worthy of note if they are women with professional training, most of whom are working.

Homemaking time was closely associated with both marital and maternal status. Women living with husbands were almost twice as likely to be spending 30 or more hours on homemaking as divorcees or widows, and four times as likely as the never married. Furthermore, the proportion of mothers with at least one child under the age of 18 who devoted this much time to household duties in 1974 was twice that of mothers with no young children. Yet, although the presence of a husband or children made heavy demands upon the free time of wives and mothers, more than half of the never married women reported that they spent at least ten hours a week keeping house and two out of five of them spent a minimum of 20 hours on this activity. One may conclude that regardless of a woman's marital status she usually had to act like a wife, either her husband's or her own!

Irrespective of marital or maternal status, the response to home-making demands was influenced by a woman's academic qualifications. Married women and mothers of young children devoted considerably less time to homemaking activities if they had doctoral or first professional degrees than if they had other scholastic credentials.

There was a high correlation between hours of work and hours of homemaking. The proportion of women who spent 30 or more hours attending to homemaking responsibilities was three times higher among non-workers and part-time workers than among full-time employees. In addition, homemaking time decreased as working hours increased. Thus, the percentage of non-workers who were engaged in homemaking for 30 or more hours weekly was more than four times that of the workers who devoted 49 or more hours a week to employment.

Nevertheless, only slightly more than one in ten of the full-time workers spent no time on household duties; three out of four spent a minimum of ten hours; and two out of five at least 20 hours in such activities. In other words, the combination of gainful employment and homemaking consumed a substantial portion of the weekly waking hours of many of the respondents.

A professor of psychology commented that divisions of weekly hours into time spent in separate activities "don't really work. I combine activities. For example, a mother spends a great deal of time waiting for car pools. For years I graded papers and prepared lectures while waiting in the car."

There were striking differences between the homemaking hours of working and non-working mothers and between mothers who worked part-time and full-time which are set forth in Table 3.7.

The more their involvement in work, the less time mothers with children living at home devoted to household activities. Although working mothers did spend more time attending to household concerns than full-time workers without young children, only eight percent of whom devoted as much as 30 hours a week to homemaking (not shown), it is apparent that combining work with a family largely resulted in reduced participation in home-related tasks. While the substitution of paid domestics may have helped to replace the unpaid services normally

Table 3.7   Weekly Hours of Homemaking by Work Status of Mothers, 1974[a]
(percentage distribution)

Mothers' Homemaking Hours	Work Status of Mothers (percent)		
	Full-time Work	Part-time Work	No Work
0	2	5	6
1-9	12	—	—
10-19	25	21	23
20-29	34	26	6
30-39	12	32	18
40 or more	15	16	47
Total percent	100	100	100

Total number = 77
Not applicable = 149

[a] Mothers of children under the age of 18 living at home.

supplied by housewives, it is also possible that judgments about homemaking requirements are variable and depend on subjective determinations of need rather than upon any universal standard. Such a determination is likely to be influenced by the strength of a wife's career commitment as well as by her husband's willingness to support her goals.

Despite the substantial amount of time that many of the respondents gave to the care of home and family, only about 13 percent mentioned a preference for fewer hours of homemaking. The desire for more time for work, leisure, study, or volunteer work which was expressed by several women sometimes may have implied less homemaking as a corollary, but their explicit remarks gave the impression that most respondents accepted their current housekeeping schedules with resignation if not delight.

It cannot be inferred that women who devoted no time to homemaking were necessarily completely carefree. An assistant professor commented:

> My biggest problem is housework. I like a well-ordered house but I cannot have it without becoming a nervous wreck, so I let housework go. My husband [also a professor] is happy to share chores—but we both put professional and personal matters before the housework. Some system for making more household help easily available on a part-time basis is one of the most pressing needs for people like us. Cooking I like; the problem is cleaning.

The infrequency with which minimal homemaking time was noted by wives suggests that even with the most cooperative husband or most efficient domestic assistance, a wife usually has at the least ultimate responsibility for planning and supervision and is the party of first resort in an emergency.

Single women also had home responsibilities as the following remarks of a professor of physics demonstrate:

> As a widow living alone I tend a garden, wash clothes and dishes, cook for myself and occasional guests, clean the house and do some repairs. Is this "homemaking"? I think I spend 10 hours a week at it and so stated. WOULD A WIDOWER WHO DOES THESE THINGS FOR HIMSELF ANSWER THE SAME WAY?

A widower might not describe these activities as "homemaking" because of its sex role implications. He might be less likely to do them himself, however.

Recent attention to two career marriages which feature equal division of labor between spouses may lead to the conclusion that the respondents' behavior is passé, but notoriety may have been given to exceptional cases. As Komarovsky has noted: "The ideological support for the belief in sharp sex role differentiation in marriage has weakened but the belief itself has not been relinquished."[19]

Family Income

The respondents were requested to specify the dollar range of their total 1974 incomes—either their own or their family's, if married with husbands present. Considering the high educational attainment of both the respondents and their husbands and its correlative occupational status, and in view of the substantial number of two-earner families, it was not surprising to find that the proportion of families and individuals who had incomes at very high levels was greatly in excess of that of the total population. Table 3.8 shows the distribution of family income according to the respondents' marital status in 1974.

The presence of a husband, currently or in the past, largely accounted for income differences among the three groups of women. The median income of husband-wife families was $44,083. Wives living with husbands tended to be the most affluent; former wives were less so; and the never married were concentrated at the lowest end of the income distribution. Thus, 36 percent of wives with husbands had total 1974 incomes of $50,000 or more, compared with 5 percent of the formerly married and only 2 percent of the never married.

Yet, regardless of marital status, these were relatively prosperous households. In 1974, only about one percent of all families in the United States had total money income of $50,000 or greater, and under 12 percent had incomes of $25,000 or more.[20] Among the respondents, almost one third of the families headed by ever married persons had

Table 3.8   Family Income by Marital Status, 1974
            (percentage distribution)

| | Marital Status (percent) | | |
Family Income	Married Husband Present	Formerly Married	Never Married
Less than $15,000	2	5	22
$15,000-19,999	4	10	24
$20,000-29,999	14	35	39
$30,000-39,999	23	20	6
$40,000-49,999	21	25	7
$50,000-74,999	21	5	2
$75,000 or more	15	—	—
Total percent	100	100	100
Number =	(141)	(20)	(46)
NA = 19			

incomes of at least $50,000, and more than three-quarters had incomes of at least $25,000.

Never married respondents were also better off than individuals of similar status. Whereas two-tenths of one percent of all never married women had incomes of $50,000 or more in 1974, and the incomes of one percent were $25,000 or more, two percent of the single respondents were in the $50,000 and over income category and 15 percent had incomes of at least $25,000.[21]

In addition, husband-wife families among the respondents tended to be more prosperous than those headed by individuals of similar age and educational attainment. The 1974 median total money income was $29,539 for all families having heads aged 45 to 54 years with education beyond college and full-time year round employment.[22] About two percent of all families headed by males aged 45 to 54 had incomes of $50,000 and over in 1974, compared with one-third of husband-wife respondent families,[23] and less than 9 percent of all such families whose male heads had completed five or more years of college had 1974 incomes of $50,000 and more compared with 30 percent of the comparable families among the respondents.[24]

These differences probably are partially attributable to differences in the labor force participation rates of women. About 75 percent of the married respondents were in the labor force in 1974 compared to 49 percent of wives in all families headed by males between the ages of 45 and 54 years.[25] It is also likely that income comparisons between families of respondents and all those headed by men with five or more years of college are imprecise because of the large proportion of husbands of respondents who had earned doctorates and first professional degrees and who consequently were in relatively high paying occupations.

Satisfaction with Work Decisions

Respondents with children were asked how they felt, in retrospect, about the amounts of time they had allocated to family concerns and to career pursuits. Their responses follow:

Satisfied with the apportionment of their time: 66%
Wish more time had been spent on family concerns: 8%
Wish more time had been spent on career development: 26%

Most of the mothers had no regrets about the way they had handled their time, and mothers with the most work experience showed the highest degree of satisfaction with their decisions in this regard (Table 3.9).

Most dissatisfaction not only centered on inadequate attention to careers but such regrets were closely related to the extent of employment. In fact, the proportion of mothers with the least work experience who wished they had given more time to their careers was about double the rate of mothers with the longest employment histories who wished they had spent more time with their families.

Half of the mothers of one child were dissatisfied with the way they had used their time compared to about one-third of those with two or three children and to only 22 percent of the mothers of four or more children. The dissatisfaction of the mothers of one child largely related to insufficient family time; that of other mothers principally concerned lack of career involvement.

Some of the women added comments to their answers to this question.

A newspaper reporter with two children who had continuously held a

Table 3.9   Mothers' Satisfaction with Allocation of Time by Percent Years Worked between College and December 1974

Attitude towards	Years Worked Since College (percent)			
Time Allocation (percent)	100	80-99	50-79	1-49
Satisfied	79	61	69	57
Wish had more time for family	21	13	2	—
Wish had more time for career	—	26	29	43
Total percent	100	100	100	100
Total number	(24)	(31)	(49)	(35)

Other or NA = 7
Not applicable = 80

part-time job said, "In my case, working worked better for husband and kids than reluctant confinement at home."

Another mother described how she had satisfactorily combined family and career:

> I changed my career from journalist to teacher-counselor in order to have the time . . . . I began when the children were 4-6-8 years old. They are now successful well-adjusted adults . . . . I feel my working while the children were young contributed to their growing up with a sense of responsibility and necessity for contributing to the family in terms of helping with the work, etc. I feel that the fact that my schedule pretty much coincided with theirs accounts for everyone's success.

An art historian and mother of two remarked:

> I did not realize that I was a "pioneer" in a sense, 30 years ago when I opted to have a Ph.D., be a professor *and* raise a family *and* be a good wife and housewife. In many ways, I know that I did the right thing for me, anyway.

A former librarian and mother of three wrote:

> I have found full-time parenthood immensely gratifying—well worth sacrificing the comforts a second income would have provided.

A physician with three children and a continuous work history said:

> Let me say, it gets easier as you get older! I had much more conflict when my children were very young. I hated being home full-time [she never was] but felt I should be. As they—and I—grew older we were all gratified that I had a rich and rewarding life of my own!

A part-time public relations worker who returned to work after a long hiatus went into considerable detail about why she was satisfied with the way she had allocated her time. Here are some of her comments:

> I think that question 22 was really the key question—How do you feel about what you did, now that you've done it? And I found it remarkably easy to say I wouldn't have done it any other way. This despite all the times when I've rapped and griped and had my consciousness raised (without benefit of formal groups, I might add) and played all the "what if" games about my own life had I married in a less sexist society. Sure I would have been more intensely career-oriented. . . . But . . . a very big BUT . . . *given the era* in which I made various decisions or slipped into various ruts as to life style and role, I would do it the same all over again!

A professor of psychology who had also expressed satisfaction with her decision to stay at home while her children were young added:

> The curious thing about one's *children's* responses is that they are opposing wishes: to have mommy home *lots* while they grow and to have mommy doing interesting *work* and feeling non-dependent on them for

emotional support when they grow up! Society needs to research ways to let kids and mommies have their cake and eat it too!

Among women who wished they had spent more time with their families was a professor of home economics who said:

I've published, had a top level job, am president of my state professional group and my children are off to college. I feel I've done all I want except be with them. I'm a little old to start with babies again.

A mother who was rueful about lost career time was a writer who suggested:

A useful additional question: Do you feel that the time and effort spent on your children has been worth the sacrifices you have made? My answer—and the answer of most middle-aged professional women of my acquaintance—would be a sad and sorry no. However, we are the mothers of the drop-out generation (2 out of 3 in my case). We gave up. the additional education and work opportunities we yearned for to raise children who do not care for education or learning. What a waste!

The dissatisfaction of a professor of education at a small college took a different tack:

Having children before finishing Ph.D. made the pursuit of the highest degree impractical for me. Not getting a Ph.D. has made the salary range I can command smaller. I regret not having had the opportunity to finish that work as a younger woman. The competing demands of family and career can make a woman's choice very difficult, especially if she marries after 30 as I did.

A working mother of three with an M.A. said:

I wish I had kept up in my field (math). I audited some courses in a rather casual way but I should have made more effort to study, although in retrospect it was very difficult when the children were small, mainly because I preferred to be with them myself—competent help not available.

A chemist (M.A.) remarked:

I wish I had returned to work and/or grad study in my field the instant my youngest went to college. I did work from '63–'65 but wish I had had better help at home so I could have continued.

At the time she responded to the questionnaire she was a student of library science and chemistry.

There were also women who modified their answer for various reasons, such as a sociologist with three children who thought that the way one felt about this subject "depends on stage of family and of career." She wished she had spent more time developing her career "in early stages of family life" when she had worked part-time but regretted not having spent time on family concerns in the past eight years when she was working from 50 to 70 hours weekly.

A non-working mother answered the question by noting that she was satisfied "up until children were 16 or so," but that she regretted lack of career "starting after children were no longer a responsibility (but by then lethargy had set in!)."

Advice to Younger Women

In addition to the mother's reflections upon the way they had utilized their time, all respondents were given the opportunity to advise a hypothetical able woman undergraduate about whether to combine family and career.

More than one-quarter of the women favored the combination without reservation. For example a professor of anatomy with one child remarked:

> It can be done—do it. There are many satisfactions. It is considerably more acceptable to pursue such a plan now than it was 30 years ago. For me and for those women who think and feel as I do, it is the only way to remain a human person.

A non-working M.A. in English and mother of three said: "I counsel my daughter to have a family and a career. It's expected now and therefore easier to arrange." Another mother of three, a newspaper editor, also offered encouragement: "Yes, do combine a family and a career for self-fulfillment that will reflect in richer family relationships." A widowed business executive with three children reflected:

> The young career-minded married women I know seem not to want children. While I could never have been happy being "just" a mother, I think I would have felt equally unfulfilled without children. They are my deepest joy. I hope that educated women who choose to remain childless do not later feel that they've blown it.

The advice of one respondent in ten was noncommittal on the grounds that such a decision had to be tailored to the individual. "Consult yourself and do what feel's right—there is no rule of thumb— both can be done if you are willing to give up *some* satisfactions in each," from a school psychologist with one child. A social worker and mother of two stated that "until one has family and children [it is] difficult to know how one will react to the change in status and responsibilities—therefore 'stay loose' and do not prejudice situation— you may decide you like to stay home—or conversely can't stand it."

There were a few responses (5 percent) that opposed combining career and family. "Do not marry or have children," warned a physician and mother of three who had been widowed, remarried and later divorced. A childless statistician advised: "Decide on one or the other. Doing both is too stressful and makes woman into a drone."

The largest group of responses—about half—gave qualified approval to the family-career combination. In many of these instances, the qualification concerned the effort, stamina, and energy that were required to handle career and family needs simultaneously. "It's hard— but do it. The worst is to be left in middle age, widowed or divorced, without an identity or passionate interest of your own," said an executive with three children, who had been widowed since 1972.

An unmarried retired professor ruminated: "A full-time professional job demands much time and energy if she wishes to make it a career. Some women of my acquaintance, bringing up a family, seem to have two full-time jobs." A college dean with three children said that "the physical strength of a horse" was necessary to do both, and a professor of chemistry who had never married claimed that combining is "risky, if real contribution in chosen profession is the goal. It takes a very unusual individual to do this well and most of us have neither the ability nor the stamina to make a success of both."

Another type of qualification concerned relationships with husbands. "Important thing is to have an understanding husband with a healthy ego who loves you enough to want you happy and fulfilled," commented a self-employed attorney, mother of two, who had remarried after widowhood.

A zoologist with four children said: "If she wants to have both a family and career, she should marry a man who would agree with these goals and be willing to devote time to their attainment." The advice of a childless lawyer was "Don't try it without a strongly supportive husband (come to think of it, an able woman should only marry a strongly supportive husband!)."

Some women thought a career and family could be compatible but advised that family should come first. Others suggested modifying career goals when children were young.

"If one has children a mother should be involved in upbringing, in establishing emotional security, structure and sense of values. In early stages, this 'career' is more important than advancement in job market. One possible exception: creative arts," noted a teacher with two children.

"OK if job is enjoyable, but children and home must come first. Being too busy away from home during their years at home is a mistake for most mothers," remarked a college instructor with four children.

"Take time off when children are young if needed, but carry on part-time if you can, and get back full-time as soon as you can comfortably do so, or even if it causes a little discomfort," advised a teacher and mother of five.

Caution was sometimes expressed about the possibility of being forced to make compromises in one or the other sphere. A lawyer and mother of three citing her own experience said:

> Excellent if you are willing to compromise on goals of perfection. If you are a perfectionist stick to one or the other—I think my life style of 10 years of career followed by full time family responsibilities and volunteer work and perhaps return to career is a good one.

Another piece of advice based on experience from a professor of chemistry and mother of three was:

> I would tell her that it might mean falling short of aspirations in one or both but is probably better than denying yourself family or career. I would tell her that I am now sorry that I took part-time work and in other ways acted more like a housewife than like a career woman.

Then there were the women who advised adjusting work schedules, career timing or occupations to fit family needs, such as a teacher and mother of three who advised: "Try to avoid a long period of years in which she is concerned *only* with young family, followed by re-entry into a career. Try to combine part-time career and part-time domestic help, part-time family care."

Another teacher and mother said: "Teaching is an ideal career for a woman who wants to have a family too. I was able to leave the field for 13 years and return with no penalties."

One point raised had to do with the need for mother substitutes and other domestic assistance. A childless retired professor wrote:

> In my experience a career demands full attention—to build and to progress. Otherwise it is not a career but a job. Providing you can find an excellent house-mother for your children and on condition that your husband (or their father) shares equal responsibility, then combine. If there is no husband, and you have a good house-mother, in some ways it may be easier.

A psychiatrist and mother of three urged: "Do it! If you can be as lucky as I was and have a dear mother-in-law who will look after many of the routine household chores it is easy. Otherwise there is more conflict—but do it anyway."

Some respondents felt that the timing of marriage and/or family was important. "Marry latish, have children at once, keep going at all costs, part-time if necessary," said a professor of English with two children.

A caseworker mother of two children advised:

> I would recommend that she get as much of her training completed prior to marriage and motherhood. Then work in field until career aspirations are somewhat fulfilled—when she and the children's father feel ready to have a family, plan to care for children as a priority responsibility during

their preschool years working part-time as desired to keep her career alive . . . Return to work to whatever amount meets her and family's needs.

Some women's comments were quite inclusive, and give a good idea of the tenor of many separate pieces of advice. A childless social scientist said:

Do so only if you have strong physical stamina, a strong desire for professional self-expression, a husband who is tolerant of your ambitions and cooperative about the family problems that arise and if you have few or no young children.

A writer-editor with two children claimed:

It's possible with a husband who supports you; it's desirable if you have a specific job goal and don't feel uptight or guilty and if you can arrange home life simply and not try to be too organized—otherwise one slight problem or change could throw you off kilter. Above all, stay calm and don't feel you always have to prove yourself.

Another respondent, a divorced professor and mother of two remarked:

It can be done and it is worth doing. You need a liberated husband, to bring up self-reliant children and to be strong and energetic, have a sense of humor—not a sense of self-importance. Some careers are easier to mesh with family—teaching is a good one—others you have to compromise in one way or another—but it is worth it.

The support of her husband for a woman's decision to combine family and career was the qualification that was cited most frequently. Next in order of importance, although far behind, was the necessity for stamina and career dedication. As a group, the respondents might best be described as cautiously encouraging, several predicting that the career-family combination will become easier to manage because of a changing social climate.

Summary

While husbands and children can be sources of great personal satisfaction, marriage and motherhood were not conducive to the maintenance of enduring career commitments. The amount of time devoted to career development by the abnormally large minority of respondents who had never married was considerably in excess of that of ever married women, and childless wives tended to have had greater employment continuity than mothers. Nevertheless, some mothers did demonstrate strong attachment to the labor force, primarily those who had limited the size of their families, since each additional child resulted in a substantial progressive decrease in total working time.

The divorce rate among the respondents was somewhat lower than that of all contemporaries, possibly because they married late. Most broken marriages were eventually succeeded by remarriage, but had the immediate effect of inducing homemakers to reenter the work force.

The period between 1963 and 1974 was characterized by a marked movement into the labor market by mothers whose youngest children had reached school age. Most of the women who had been out of the work force in 1963 were working in 1974, by which date another, smaller group had retired.

Husbands' job mobility did not appear to have resulted in major interruptions in the employment of working wives, presumably because the women's high qualifications facilitated placement in new locations. In general educational credentials were found to be closely associated with the women's employment behavior. Women who had spent prolonged periods in graduate or professional study appeared to have been considerably more reluctant to abandon their careers, even temporarily, than those whose investment in graduate education had been less costly of time, money or effort. Thus, where family size and the age range of their youngest children were the same, it was mothers with doctorates and first professional degrees who were more likely to be working than those with master's degrees.

The women devoted a considerable amount of time to homemaking, regardless of marital or maternal status, indicating that the pursuit of a career rarely exempted a woman from performing the chores that have been conventionally assigned to them.

The family incomes of the respondents were far above the national average and those of husband-wife families were higher than the incomes of households headed by men of similar age and school attainment. This was probably due to the superior occupational status of respondents' husbands and to the relatively high labor force participation rate of the wives.

Most of the mothers were satisfied with the way they had apportioned their time between work and home. Of those who had reservations, the great majority wished they had spent more time in career development.

Asked to give advice to the younger generation about combining family and career, respondents most commonly recommended this course of action but with certain reservations. It was clear that they generally supported the combination in theory but reality intervened to cast doubts upon its feasibility under all circumstances.

Notes

1. U.S. Bureau of the Census, *Current Population Reports*, Series P-20, No. 271, "Marital Status and Living Arrangements: March 1974" (U.S. Government Printing Office, Washington, D.C., 1974), p. 13.

2. John A. Centra, *Women, Men and the Doctorate* (Princeton: Educational Testing Service, 1974), p. 101.

3. Elizabeth M. Havens, "Women, Work and Wedlock: A Note on Female Marital Patterns in the United States," in *Changing Women in a Changing Society*, Joan Huber, ed. (Chicago: University of Chicago Press, 1973), p. 218.

4. U.S. Bureau of the Census, *Current Population Reports*, Series P-20, No. 297, "Number, Timing, and Duration of Marriages or Divorces in the United States: June 1975" (U.S. Government Printing Office, Washington, D.C., 1976), p. 20.

5. *Ibid*.

6. *Ibid.*, p. 3.

7. *Ibid.*, p. 23.

8. *Ibid.*, p. 7.

9. Judith Stiehm, "Invidious Intimacy," *Social Policy*, Vol. 6, No. 5 (March/April 1976), pp. 13–14.

10. U.S. Bureau of the Census, *Current Population Reports*, Series P-20, No. 301, "Fertility of American Women: June 1975" (U.S. Government Printing Office, Washington, D.C., 1976), p. 61.

11. John A. Centra, *op. cit.*, pp. 109–10.

12. U.S. Bureau of the Census, *Current Population Reports*, Series P-20, No. 274, "Educational Attainment in the United States: March 1973 and 1974" (U.S. Government Printing Office, Washington, D.C., 1974), Table 1.

13. *Ibid.*

14. Allyson S. Grossman, "The Labor Force Patterns of Divorced and Separated Women," *Monthly Labor Review* (January 1977), p. 52.

15. *Ibid.*, p. 49.

16. Myrna Weissman, Katherine Nelson *et al.*, "The Faculty Wife," *AAUP Bulletin* (Autumn 1972), p. 289.

17. U.S. Women's Bureau, 1975 *Handbook on Women Workers*. Bulletin 297 (Washington, D.C.: U.S. Department of Labor, 1975), pp. 11–12.

18. Barbara Thompson and Angela Finlayson, quoted in Angrist and Almquist, *Careers and Contingencies* (New York: Dunellen, 1975), p. 24.

19. Mirra Komarovsky, "Cultural Contradictions and Sex Roles: The Masculine Case," in *Changing Women in a Changing Society*, Joan Huber, ed. (Chicago: University of Chicago Press, 1973), p. 117.

20. U.S. Bureau of the Census, *Current Population Reports*, Series P-60, No. 101, "Money Income in 1974 of Families and Persons in the United States" (Washington, D.C.: U.S. Government Printing Office, 1976), p. 1.

21. *Ibid.*

22. *Ibid.*, Table 36.

23. *Ibid.*, Table 25.

24. *Ibid.*, Table 36.

25. *Ibid.*

4] CAREER DESTINATIONS

A career, as customarily defined, signifies consistent attachment to an occupation usually resulting in increasing responsibilities and rewards. Although occasionally applied to a wide range of fields of work, in everyday usage a career is associated with professional and other prestigious white-collar employment. The respondents' graduate training was almost always the prelude to entrance into conventionally designated career fields, and the principal purpose of this chapter is to describe the career destinations they had reached by 1974.

This chapter commences by describing the women's 1974 employment in terms of field, function, setting, class of employer, and occupational sex ratios. Career patterns and recent occupational changes are then delineated, and the respondents' views on future job change are presented. The concluding section is devoted to the women's choice of options for the years after the age of 65.

Field of Work

The salient feature of the respondents' current employment was that it was almost exclusively professional. Only nine out of the 173 women who were working in December, 1974 were employed in non-professional occupations, primarily as public and business administrators. The ratio of professionals to non-professionals was the same in 1963 and 1974.

Table 4.1 presents a breakdown of the occupational fields of the respondents' 1974 employment. The categories correspond to the subject areas of graduate and professional study that encompass the relevant occupational classification.

For classification purposes, academics were assigned to their broad subject areas, but women teaching below the college level were placed in the category of education, which included a wide range of occupations from college dean to fifth grade teacher; professor of education to program specialist for the U.S. Office of Education; assistant superintendent of schools to substitute high school teacher of languages.

Another category which encompassed a variety of occupations was journalism and communications. Included were such workers as newspaper reporters, free-lance writers, book editors, an advertising executive, a public relations director, and an editor-translator.

The most recent fields of work of the women who were not employed in 1974 closely resembled the occupational distribution of the 1974 workers, and the distribution of the occupations of the women who were employed in 1963 also approximated the 1974 distribution. In the earlier year, however, the percentages of social scientists and librarians exceeded those of physical scientists and journalists, and business occupations were at the bottom—only one percent of the total. These changes in the occupational distribution primarily reflected retirement, on the one hand, and reentry to the labor force, on the other.

All of the women whose highest earned degrees were in the physical or life sciences, medicine, law, library science or business were employed in these fields in 1974.* This was also the case for more than seven out of ten women with degrees in all other fields, except the social sciences where only 46 percent of degree holders were working in either the field of their graduate study or in a related social science; few of the remaining social scientists were employed in areas completely unrelated to their graduate majors, however; most were in such fields as social work, business, or education below the college level, in which they were frequently able to utilize their training. Training in the social sciences apparently produced a considerable capacity for transference of skills.

Employment Setting

Employment settings largely reflected the pattern of opportunities available to women with particular types of training (Table 4.2). In fields in which substantial proportions of the respondents had doctorates—liberal arts and education—the majority of women were employed in colleges or universities. Differences in setting within these

---

*Physicians who were in public health jobs, and lawyers who were officials of national membership organizations were classified according to their professional status.

Table 4.1   Occupational Field, December 1974

Field	Percent
Arts and Humanities	18
Education	13
Social Work	13
Medicine	9
Physical Science	8
Social Science	8
Journalism, Communications	7
Library Science	7
Law	6
Business	3
Public Health	3
Life Science	3
International Affairs	2
Total	100

Number = 173
Not working 1974 = 53

particular fields resulted not only from dissimilar proportions of doctorates, but also from variations in the availability of alternative employment settings. In the humanities, where such alternatives are relatively rare, the proportion of women in higher education was greater than in fields with more sources of employment. For instance, some doctorates in education were school administrators; certain scientists worked in independent research institutions; and several social scientists were employed in federal agencies.

The patterns of employment of physicians and lawyers were not typical of these fields. Only one doctor and three attorneys were in private practice. With the exception of a part-time employee of an insurance company, all other physicians worked in medical schools or hospitals or were employed in the public health sector. The remaining lawyers served in the administrative or judicial branches of the government or in voluntary membership organizations. In other fields, the respondents were concentrated in customary settings.

The distribution of 1974 employment settings was similar to that in 1963; the greatest stability was shown by women in higher education, 87 percent of whom had worked in colleges or universities in both years. In addition, most change between 1963 and 1974 involved movement into higher education.

Class of Employer

The employer of respondents in public administration, non-profit membership organizations, business, and of the self-employed is

Table 4.2 Field of Work[a] by Employment Setting, 1974
(percentage distribution)

Field of Work

Employment Setting	Human-ities	Soc. Sci. or Int. Aff.	Phys. or Bio. Sci.	Educa-tion	Med-icine	Law	Business or Communications	Library Science	Soc. Wk. or Pub. Health	Total Setting
Higher educ.	78	53	63	64	26	–	6	33	11	41
Other educ.; Library	16	12	–	32	–	–	6	67	–	13
Hospital; Research org.	–	12	26	–	40	–	–	–	11	9
Welfare; Membership org.	–	–	–	–	–	18	16	–	57	12
Publ. Admin.; Judiciary	–	23	11	4	20	55	–	–	14	12
Business; Prof. firm	3	–	–	–	7	9	50	–	–	7
Self-employed	3	–	–	–	7	18	22	–	7	6
Total percent	100	100	100	100	100	100	100	100	100	100
Total number	31	17	19	22	15	11	18	12	28	173
Not working 1974: 53										

[a]Combinations of fields reflect similar distributions among settings.

evident. Table 4.3 shows how the other job settings were distributed in terms of class of employer.

A predominance of jobs in educational institutions explains the high rate of government employment. If educators are excluded, total government employment drops to 45 percent, still a substantial proportion, although no longer a majority.

A high rate of government and non-profit employment was predictable considering that, with few exceptions, respondents had prepared for careers in fields in which there are relatively few job opportunities in the profit sector. The only occupational area in which employment in the profit making sector predominated was communications (journalism, advertising, publishing, public relations, and so on). Even employment in business per se was evenly divided between the profit and non-profit sectors since some employees were faculty members or business administrators in the latter class of institution. In medicine and law, as in business, class of employer deviated from normal patterns. Epstein has pointed out that women professionals enter government service in far greater proportions than men because of "the prejudicial structure of the professions rather than the attraction of unique qualities of government work."[1] While such considerations may have motivated many of the physicians and lawyers to shun private practice, the majority of the respondents trained to enter fields in which government and non-profit employment is characteristic, regardless of sex.

Table 4.3　Employment Setting[a] by Class of Employer, 1974
(percentage distribution)

| | Setting[b] (percent) | | | | Percent Employer |
Class of Employer	Higher Education	Other Education	Hospital or Social Agency	Library or Rsch. Org.	Class, All Employed Respondents
Government	56	82	38	62	53
Non-profit	44	18	62	23	33
Profit	—	—	—	15	8
Self-employed	—	—	—	—	6
Total percent	100	100	100	100	100
Total number	(71)	(17)	(26)	(13)	(173)

Not applicable = 46
Not working
  1974 = 53

[a]Excluding public administration, business, non-profit membership organizations and self-employment.

[b]Combinations of settings reflect similar distributions.

Table 4.4   Major Job Activity, 1963 and 1974

Activity	Percent 1963	Percent 1974
Teaching	38	36
Research	14	5
Writing, editing	5	5
Administration, mgt.	26	34
Professional service	14	16
Other professional	2	4
Other white collar	1	—
Total percent	100	100
Total number	160	173
Not working	66	53

The distribution of respondents by type of employer closely resembled that of all female professional, technical and kindred workers in 1970 when government employees comprised 51 percent of the total, private workers, 44 percent, and the self-employed, 5 percent.[2]

Among women who were working in both 1963 and 1974, there had been substantial movement into government employment which resulted in an increase of 22 percent in the number of public employees by the latter year. The outcome was a net loss in the non-profit sector largely due to job changes in higher education—from private to public colleges and universities. This change may have been due to more attractive earnings opportunities for women in the public sector.

Job Function

The major job activity of women employed in 1963 and 1974 is shown in Table 4.4. Teaching and administration were the most common of the respondents' principal occupational responsibilities in both years.

The table describes the workers' *primary* function. Many women were also engaged in one or more additional job activities to which they often devoted a considerable amount of time. Large numbers of college teachers, for example, also were involved in research and writing, and numerous administrators had teaching, research, or service responsibilities.

The principal change since 1963 was an increase of more than 30 percent in the proportion of women engaged in administration, representing substantial upward career mobility. This change appears largely to have come about at the expense of the research function, although promotion of researchers to administrative positions usually signified an added supervisory function rather than a subtracted research involvement. Examples of changes in principal job functions between 1963 and 1974 include a part-time consulting psychologist for several school districts who became full-time director of special services and psychologist for one district; a school librarian who was later employed at a public library as a senior librarian with supervision over personnel in the technical services department; a social scientist with a research appointment in 1963 who was a full professor at a university in 1974; and a senior caseworker in a private agency who eventually advanced to principal clinical supervisor of a children's unit at a state mental hospital.

Both field of work and employment setting were associated with job functions. Table 4.5 presents a view of the relationship between field and function.

The relative infrequency of administrative status among women in the humanities, sciences, and social sciences reflects their concentration in higher education where few women were in executive positions. On the other hand, social workers and librarians were second only to physicians in the extent to which they functioned in administrative capacities. This seems to be counter to the general impression that women in predominantly female fields rarely advance to the supervisory level. These were women with master's degrees, in the main, in contrast to most respondents in higher education who had doctorates. In colleges and universities, the plum is full professor and the job of department chairman is often on a rotating basis and is not necessarily a coveted position. While many other professional workers also prefer to avoid assuming managerial duties, there is no hierarchy comparable to that in the academic world, so that they usually can advance only by promotion to supervisory positions.

In some occupations where the provision of personal service is a primary function—social work, library science, law, medicine—the proportion of workers principally concerned with client contact was relatively low. In the case of the first two of these fields, this was due to advancement to administrative positions; in law, it was largely judicial status subsumed under "other professional" that reduced the proportion providing service. And in medicine, the assumption of administrative duties overshadowed any personal services provided, although there is no evidence that it necessarily resulted in the complete abandonment of patient services.

Teaching predominated in higher education, but administration almost matched teaching in education below the college level where professional service (guidance, psychology, etc.) was also quite common. In all other settings, except business and research organizations, at least half of the workers were administrators. The self-employed were principally engaged in the provision of professional services. Part-time workers primarily functioned as writers (56 percent).

Table 4.5 Field of Work by Principal Function, 1974
(percentage distribution)

Job Activity	Human-ities	Soc. Sci., Int. Aff.	Phys. or Biol. Sci.	Educ.-Pub. Hlth.	Medi-cine	Law	Bus. or Comm'ns	Library Science	Social Work
Teaching	77	53	58	54	7	–	11	–	–
Research	–	12	26	4	–	–	–	–	6
Writing, Editing	–	–	5	–	–	–	44	–	–
Administration	13	23	11	36	73	18	39	50	61
Professional Service	7	12	–	3	20	46	–	50	33
Other Professional	3	–	–	3	–	36	6	–	–
Total Percent	100	100	100	100	100	100	100	100	100
Number	(31)	(17)	(19)	(28)	(15)	(11)	(18)	(12)	(22)

Not Working 1974 = 53

Women whose principal activity was teaching at the college level had the longest workweeks. At the opposite extreme were full-time workers engaged in teaching below the college level or in providing library or social services. Academics regularly spent a substantial amount of time in research or writing and in other job-related activities which are integral to their employment and to progress in academic careers, and which rarely can be performed within stipulated time schedules. School-teachers, librarians and social workers generally are not faced with similar expectations and, in their case, additional work time beyond a prescribed schedule is more likely to be a voluntary decision rather than an explicit or implicit job requirement.

Academic Employment

Teaching at the college or university level lent itself to closer examination than other types of occupations both because it embraced the largest single group of respondents and because the faculty hierarchy permits detailed analysis of career progression.

Most employees of institutions of higher education were members of teaching faculties. The remainder primarily had administrative, research, or library positions. The proportion of full professors had more than doubled by the end of the 12-year period when this rank was held by 65 percent of academics. In contrast to 1963 when about half of the academics were assistant professors or instructors, more than four out of five were at the level of associate or full professor in 1974. As a rule, a principal distinction between the lower and upper ranks is that tenure is granted at the level of associate professor.

Non-workers in 1963 who later entered college or university employment had not had time to make as much progress as those who had been there already or who had changed from non-academic to academic employment.

Illustrations of changes related to the academic arena are provided by the following women:

A 58-year-old social worker had been employed as director of social service in a university department of psychiatry from 1958 to 1967 when she became an associate professor and director of a local branch of a state university school of social work as the result of a job offer from the dean of the school. Her reason for accepting this offer was her "desire for full time academic teaching." She held this position until 1974 when she retired due to a disability.

A respondent who earned her Ph.D. in a social science in 1963 while she was employed as a consultant for a large research organization continued this association until 1969. She spent a semester in 1963–64 as a visiting lecturer at a four-year private college, and in the latter year became a part-time lecturer and executive secretary of a program of special studies at a state university. By 1966 she was a full-time faculty member at the university, starting as an associate professor. She was a full professor and director of the special program in 1974.

An ABD in English who had had a series of jobs in miscellaneous fields up to 1960, left the labor force in that year due to illness and to care for her two children. During this time she devoted about ten hours a week to writing poetry and fiction. In 1966, through a friend who was the vice-president of a community college, she was hired by the institution as an English instructor and by 1974 she had become an associate professor and director of a program in English as a second language.

Among women who were faculty members in both 1963 and 1974, at the rank of professor in the latter year were all those who were professors in 1963; nine-tenths of those who had been associate professors; almost three-fourths of the 1963 assistant professors; but less than three-tenths of the former instructors. In fact, the majority of 1963 instructors who were working in 1974 had not yet reached the rank of associate professor.

Differences in faculty rank correlated with age differences. Fifty-five percent of the assistant professors and instructors in 1974 were under the age of 50 but only 17 percent of the women of higher rank were that young. Moreover, 55 percent of the women in the lower ranks had neither an academic doctorate nor a first professional degree. In the higher ranks, fewer than 12 percent of the incumbents had not yet earned either of these degrees.

Continuity of work experience was also related to faculty level. Forty-one percent of the full professors and 26 percent of the associates had worked full-time every adult year, but no one at lower ranks had worked as consistently. Four out of five of the full professors had worked full-time for a minimum of three-quarters of the years since college, as had seven out of ten of the associates; this was the case for only 14 percent of the assistant professors and none of the instructors.

While differences in rank resulting from differences in attachment to work were predictable, what is worthy of special note is that four women who had worked full-time for no more than half their lives were full professors! All academics who had never married or who were childless wives had attained full professorships, as had 80 percent of those with one child; 60 percent of those with two children, and 13 percent of those with three children or more, differences which largely reflect differences in labor force attachment.

Of the 57 members of non-medical faculties in 1974, 46 percent were working in universities offering doctoral studies, 49 percent were in four-year non-doctoral institutions, and the remaining five percent were teaching in two-year colleges. There was very little difference between the distribution of faculty positions at universities and four-year colleges: More than 60 percent of the women in each type of institution had attained professorial rank and over three-quarters in each were above the rank of assistant professor. There were three department chairpersons at four-year colleges; one at a university.

Despite the rapid growth of community colleges in recent years, only three women, one each at the rank of associate professor, assistant professor, and instructor were employed in two-year institutions, possibly because most faculty women had entered the academic marketplace at the senior college level before the community college expansion. Moreover, most of the academics were doctorates (the exceptions were largely ABD's or masters in pre-professional fields such as social work or library science) who not only often have been deemed over-qualified for junior college faculties but who probably concur in this judgment. One junior college faculty member had an M.A.; one was an ABD; and the other had received a Ph.D. in chemistry as recently as 1970 and was aiming for employment at a senior institution.

According to the American Council on Education's rating of graduate programs by quality of graduate faculty, ten of the 26 graduate departments (38 percent) in which respondents were employed were rated "above the cutting score." Four of these ten departments (15 percent of the total) were ranked in the highest score category (3.0 or higher) in the country; two (8 percent) scored in the middle range and the remainder (15 percent) were given lower scores. One respondent served as chairman of a department in the last category. The remaining 16 university faculty members were either in departments with lower ACE scores; in institutions that were not evaluated; or in fields such as education, in which departmental quality was not assessed.[3]

Academic social scientists were more likely to be at universities offering doctoral studies than respondents in other subject areas. More than 60 percent were employed in this type of institution, compared to 36 percent each in academic science or humanities. In other fields— education, primarily—women in universities comprised 30 percent of the total.

Although most of the respondents with doctorates received their degrees from Columbia, only two were employed at Columbia and none was employed at any other Ivy League university. The four-year colleges and non-doctoral universities that provided a considerable amount of the academic employment were primarily publicly supported institutions, several of which had been recently promoted to liberal arts status from teachers colleges. No woman was employed on the faculty of a "Seven Sisters" college, although one respondent was a dean at one of these schools, and one woman was a member of the faculty of a highly prestigious private co-educational college. The number of faculty members at women's colleges was six in 1963 and had dropped to two by 1974.

Members of medical school faculties were considered separately because they ordinarily have service as well as teaching and research responsibilities. Thus, many physicians served on both hospital and medical school staffs. The most prestigious rank in this group was that of professor and chairman of the department of medicine at a university medical center. Other professors of medicine included chiefs of oncology, endocrinology, diabetes, and immunohematology. One physician was professor of clinical psychiatry and director of a hospital department of psychiatry. None of the physicians, academic or non-academic, were surgeons or general practitioners.

Publications and Prizes

Publications often serve as a gauge of career achievement especially in academe where they are a major criterion for advancement. The respondents were asked to note any books or other publications and to describe other forms of recognition they may have received for vocational or avocational accomplishments.

Forty-seven of the respondents (21 percent) had published at least one book as senior, sole, or co-author; 23 (10 percent) had produced at least two books. In addition, 12 had been junior authors or editors of one or more books, and 79 (35 percent) had published at least one article in a journal or magazine. Seven out of ten of the article writers had produced a minimum of ten published pieces. Fifty-six percent of the sole or senior authors of books, and 62 percent of the article writers, were academics. However, almost two-thirds of all academics employed in 1974 had published no books as sole or co-author, and 31 percent had no articles to their credit.

Many other types of achievement or recognition were noted by the respondents. These ranged from the sale of sculptures produced by a woman who became involved in art after retirement from teaching, to alumni awards and honorary degrees; from fellowships to government appointments; from membership on public or private boards and committees, to several listings in Who's Who and similar publications; from selection as an outstanding teacher or professional, to developer of college or university programs of study.

Occupational Sex Ratios

The distribution of the respondents in terms of the proportion of women employed in their occupation was atypical of female workers in general and of female professionals in particular since it did not demonstrate the

Table 4.6   Most Recent Employment of Respondents in Occupations Classified by Extent of Female Representation in 1970[a]

Occupations in which women were: (percent)	Percent of Respondents
0-25 (Underrepresented)	37
25-45 (Well represented)	31
45-100 (Overrepresented)	32
Total percent	100
Total number = 206	

[a]Excludes 20 non-workers 1963-1974.

characteristic concentration of female professional employment among a relatively small number of occupations. This was the result of survey selection which sought representation from diverse graduate and professional programs of study without reference to student sex composition. Since the respondents' fields of study, in most cases, were designed as preparation for specific professional occupations, their occupational distribution was primarily a reflection of the variety of graduate curricula in which some number of women studied and excelled. The consequent occupational heterogeneity fortuitously provides an opportunity to examine certain aspects of their employment in relation to the sex ratios in their fields of work.

The respondents' most recent occupations were classified according to the proportion of female employment in each in 1970 and placed in a threefold schema based upon the degree of female representation (Table 4.6).[4]

Table 4.7   Female Representation in Occupations by Highest Degree[a]
(percentage distribution)

Female Representation in Field of Work (percent)	Ph.D. or Ed.D.	First Pro-fessional	ABD	Masters[b]
1-25	52	85	27	16
25-45	38	4	46	32
45-99	10	11	27	52
Total percent	100	100	100	100
Total number = 68				

[a]Excludes 20 non-workers 1963-1974.
[b]Includes four women who did not complete masters degrees.

Examples of the occupations of respondents working in fields in which women were underrepresented include physicians, lawyers, economists, chemists, state, federal and college administrators, and most college and university faculty. Among workers in occupations where females were well represented were psychologists, journalists, biologists, statisticians, school administrators, and college teachers of English, German, Spanish, social work, and education. Illustrative of respondents in occupations with overrepresentations of women workers were librarians, social workers, teachers below the college level, and college instructors of French, library science, and home economics.

Directly correlated with the female occupational representation in the respondents' jobs were their scholastic credentials as Table 4.7 demonstrates.

Because all first professional degrees were either in medicine or law, the concentration of physicians and lawyers in occupations dominated by men was to be expected; the exceptions were public health administrators and a local public administrator. On the other hand, one might have anticipated more than a bare majority of doctorates with employment in male dominated occupations, since most of them were academics and males are overrepresented in college and university teaching. However, as we have already indicated, female representation in academe differs according to subject area and many of the doctorates among the respondents were in departments of English, modern language, or education, where women are well represented; a few others were in French, social work, or library science, where women are overrepresented.*

Nevertheless, the proportion of doctorates in fields where women are underrepresented was about double that of respondents with ABD's and more than triple that of those with master's degrees. This difference largely mirrors differences in fields of study. Most master's degrees qualified their holders for employment in predominantly female fields, while most doctorates were awarded to respondents in fields usually leading to either male dominated occupations or to those in which women are well represented. Although respondents were classified according to their current occupations, few career changes involved

*It is of incidental interest that academic departments in general are more heavily populated by males than corresponding non-academic occupations, even in fields where women represent a majority of total employment. Thus, the nationwide proportion of female social workers is 46 percent higher than the proportion of female social work faculty; the proportion of female librarians is a third higher than women teachers of library science, and the percentage of women elementary school teachers is more than double the percentage of women in university departments of elementary education. In fields with a larger male component such discrepancies also exist. For instance, the proportion of female academics in psychology and political science is less than half the proportion in non-academic employment.

moves to occupations with different sex ratios. Thus, in general, the interrelationship among fields of study, graduate degrees and current occupations continued over the course of time. In other words, it was not the type of graduate degree, per se, that was related to current occupational sex composition, but the fact that the degree largely reflected a respondent's earlier career choice.

The choice of a traditional feminine profession has often been viewed as having an element of contingency because breaks in labor force participation by women in these fields do not demand the payment of as heavy a toll in lost promotional opportunities and foregone earnings as they do in occupations dominated by males. "Female professions are more likely to be those in which long and set career lines are not essential and those with little tradition of professionalization."[5] While there is disagreement about whether this is the case *because* these are female occupations or whether these are female occupations *because* they do not invoke large penalties for interruptions, differences in the patterns of the respondents' worklives are associated with the character of their occupational choice. Respondents who were in occupations with an underrepresentation of women show a stronger attachment to work than those in fields with larger proportions of females (Table 4.8).

Female representation in an occupation was strongly associated with both the proportion of total adult years with work experience and of

Table 4.8   Female Occupational Representation by Proportion Time Worked to 1974[a]
(percentage distribution)

Percent Life Worked to 1974	Under- represented	Well Represented	Over- represented
100	50	32	25
80-99	26	25	31
less than 80	24	43	44
Total percent	100	100	100
Total number	77	64	64
Percent Life Worked Full-time Full-year to 1974			
100	34	16	11
80-99	27	25	25
less than 80	39	59	64
Total percent	100	100	100
Total number	77	63	64

[a]Excludes 20 non-workers 1963-1974.

time spent in full-time full-year work. The fact that the percentage of respondents in disproportionately female occupations who had continuous or nearly continuous work histories was far lower than that of the women in male dominated professions confirms the existence of a relationship between occupational sex composition and strength of career commitment. Whether this was a cause or effect of career choice is unclear. That is, whether respondents entered female fields primarily because such occupations permit flexible work patterns, or whether discontinuity was in response to a subsequent discovery that inter-mittent work participation was acceptable and even expected, cannot be determined. In the initial survey, which investigated career choice, only a small minority (18 percent) of all respondents indicated that they had originally intended to limit or abandon their careers for family concerns. However, the possibility that acceptable discontinuity was an inherent component of some career choices cannot be disregarded.

The proportion of never married women among respondents in occupations in which females were under- or well represented was about 45 percent higher than the percent in fields dominated by females; but the proportion of mothers of three or more children in fields with male majorities was about a quarter lower than in occupations with larger representations of women. Since family decisions tend to follow career choice, the fact that there was some association between family characteristics and occupational sex composition suggests that women in male occupations were less willing to encumber themselves with responsibilities that would prevent them from competing on equal terms with their male peers.

While most respondents in occupations that had minority female representations spent greater portions of their lives at work than most of those in female fields, two out of five respondents in occupations with underrepresentations of females, and three out of five in those where women were well represented, had short worklives relative to their male counterparts who are presumed to be continuous workers. It is possible, however, that in many cases women found they were *not* the counterparts of males with similar qualifications, but instead were concentrated among the lower echelons of their profession. While women in female fields may leave the work force because they know they can readily return to their exit status, women in occupations dominated by men may leave because they perceive limited opportunities for advancement relative to their male peers. Nevertheless, those in traditionally male fields did demonstrate substantial continuity of employment, presumably because of their reluctance to relinquish a high status acquired at great cost.

While we have postulated that the respondents' advanced education and superior scholastic performance were indicative of strong career motivation, the extent of work attachment has been found to depend upon various personal and vocational characteristics, one of which is the extent of sex segregation in their chosen profession. Yet, insofar as discontinuity is an acceptable feature of disproportionately female professions, comparisons between women in these fields and those in fields with smaller female components may be unjust. Career commitment may have different implications in different occupations and workers may have simply done what was normal for women employed in their fields. The fact that ultimate status and rewards were dissimilar for women in fields with different representations of the sexes, as shall subsequently be demonstrated, may not have been so much the result of career *commitment* as of career *choice*.

Career Patterns

The 1974 occupations of the majority of women were in the same general area as their highest academic degree. Some women had shifted to occupations within the same broad area of their degree or were in different but related fields. Relatively few of the respondents were in occupations that radically differed from the field in which they had received their most recent academic credential.

Among women who had shifted within their field of training was a one-time professor of geology with a Ph.D. in paleontology who was working as an editorial consultant and writer for a center engaged in research in the physical sciences; a former newspaper reporter with a degree in journalism who was engaged in public relations and related activities for a non-profit educational facility; and a lawyer serving as village clerk, treasurer, and assessor.

Examples of shifts to occupations in other fields that are related to the field of their graduate studies include a woman with an accounting degree employed as a high school commercial teacher; the holder of an M.A. in public administration serving as a college dean of students; and the recipient of a library degree whose last position before retirement was associate professor of English.

Women who were employed in occupations unrelated to their most recent graduate studies included a sales representative for a pharmaceutical company with an M.A. in Chinese language and history; and an antiques dealer with a master's degree in history, although a case could no doubt be made that the last two are related fields.

More common than shifts and changes in field were shifts and changes in function. For example, a lawyer with four years of prior work experience received a research fellowship in the early 1960's and then engaged in legal research for a government commission for two years.

Thereupon she became associated with a law firm in which she later became a partner.

Another illustration is that of a woman who had spent nine hours a week as a church organist in 1963 and about eight hours as a self-employed piano teacher. In 1967, she was hired as a staff accompanist by a college music department where, by 1974, she was teaching music.

An instructor of freshman English in 1963 was a freelance writer in 1974, and a physician who had been engaged in part-time cancer research in 1963 was working as a company physician, also part-time, in 1974.

In the 1963 report, women with more than three years of work experience were classified according to four career patterns: straight, broad, changed and variant. The women were similarly classified according to the shape of their careers between 1963 and 1974.

Prior to 1963, the broad career pattern, characterized by horizontal movement within the original area of work, was most characteristic of the respondents' work experience. Between 1963 and 1974, however, the straight pattern, consistent progression within the same field, was typical of the majority of careers. It may be concluded that by the end of the earlier period, most of the women had found acceptable occupational loci and had settled into them. If this interpretation is correct, then it is not surprising that women who had made radical changes in their careers prior to 1963 or who had variant patterns which found them floundering in indecision in 1963, or who had a minimal amount of work experience prior to that year, were less likely to have had straight career patterns in the 1963–1974 period than those whose careers showed greater stability. The respondents were at different stages of career development when first studied, and many of them turned out to be late bloomers who ultimately reached a satisfactory occupational resolution.

In terms of their entire work lives, the most common career pattern was the broad configuration which characterized two out of five careers. The primacy of the broad career pattern indicates a tendency to embark upon new liaisons while remaining essentially faithful to original career choices. An additional 50 percent of the women were equally divided among the straight and changed patterns. About 10 percent could not be categorized because of insufficient work experience; a few had abandoned careers before 1963 and had not been employed again. Only one woman had a variant pattern after 1963—a series of unrelated jobs with no sign of consistency or advancement. All those who had variant patterns prior to 1963 were eventually able to find an occupation to which they became attached.

Among the women who had a straight career pattern throughout their work lives is a biostatistician who had worked for a state health department from 1947 through 1955 with time out for graduate school, had then retired to raise her family, and returned to work in 1969 as a health statistician for a federal bureau, changing to another federal agency in 1971, where she was employed in 1974.

Another example of the straight pattern is a woman with a Ph.D. in biology who worked periodically between 1952 and 1961 as a postdoctoral fellow and instructor and was continuously employed thereafter as a research biologist, first by a college and then by a research institute.

A straight career that was marked by broadening after 1962 was that of an attorney who had worked continuously in a variety of local and state agencies, following a three year stint with a private law firm after law school. During the 1960's and early seventies she served as counsel to city officials and as assistant administrator of a municipal agency. In 1974 she was a judge, having been elected to that position two years earlier.

A broadened career both before and after 1962 was that of a woman who received an Ed.D. in Religious Education after several years of work in the field of social welfare. After being employed from 1953 to 1966 as the educational director of a state council of churches and for seven years thereafter as an urban consultant with a national organization in the same field, she joined a college faculty as an associate professor of education in 1973.

Broadening after 1962 is exemplified by a social worker who returned to the labor force in 1961 after an absence of 12 years, resuming a career as a part-time psychiatric caseworker for a voluntary agency. She held this position until 1967, supplementing it with editorial work for a psychoanalytic journal. Then she became a staff assistant in the department of public affairs of another voluntary social agency until 1970, when she joined a municipal mental health department as a senior consultant. The following year she became a clinical coordinator for an institute devoted to psychotherapy, leaving in 1973 because of retrenchment. In 1974, she had two work roles: one as a part-time public affairs associate for a voluntary health organization, and the other as a part-time self-employed psychotherapist.

Another broadened career pattern between 1963 and 1974 was that of a former freelance writer with a journalism degree who joined a newspaper as copyeditor and occasional reporter in 1964. Upon relocation to another city in 1966, she was employed by a large advertising agency in a public relations job that she described as being "created for me." By 1974 she had become vice-president and director of public relations.

In 1967 a respondent with a M.S. in hospital administration, who had been associate director of a membership organization in the health field, took the first step toward expanding her career interests by joining a university faculty as a part-time assistant professor, following her remarriage and relocation. Two years later she left this position in order to begin doctoral studies in health organization research, acquiring a Ph.D. in 1973 at the age of 55. In 1974 she was a professor at another university. About her belated pursuit of the doctorate, she said,

> Like Mallory said about Mount Everest, "it was there." I had married and no longer had to support myself. I worked part time, heard about the Ph.D. program and decided to try it. My husband paid "cash on the line" every semester.

Prior to 1963, one respondent had a fairly checkered work history after receiving two master's degrees in the mid-1940's, in history and in education. Initially, she spent about five years working for a testing service in a psychology department and as a test writer for a publisher. The remainder of her experience in the fifties and early sixties centered on music. Over a period of two years, she spent ten hours weekly as a church organist and choir director, and later served as an occasional substitute music teacher in local public schools and as a self-employed piano teacher. She changed course in 1965, becoming a lecturer in history at a four-year college. Two years later, she started working as an assistant professor of history at a state college where both she and her husband, who wished to teach after a career as a clergyman, had been offered positions by the dean. She was still employed in that position in 1974. She commenced doctoral studies in 1971 and anticipated earning her degree in 1976 at the age of 53.

Career change is also illustrated by a respondent with an ABD in business who had a variety of white collar jobs prior to and during business studies and had served in the Navy during World War II. After a seven-year interlude, she returned to the labor force in 1957 as a teacher and director of a suburban private primary school, later becoming local Head Start director and a supervisor in the local public schools as supplements to her other position. She moved to another part of the country in 1972 when her husband, a professor of sociology, was offered a post-retirement position on the faculty of a small liberal arts college which also hired her as professor of education.

One of the more extreme career changes was that of a Ph.D. in chemistry who was employed part-time at a university as an assistant research specialist in chemistry in 1963. She had become a research associate by 1967 when she left her job in order to enter law school. After receiving her law degree in 1972, at the age of 48, she was employed as a legal analyst by a city council. Her sole comment about her new career direction was that it stemmed from a change of interests.

Another radical career change also involved a Ph.D. in chemistry who undertook Russian studies in 1958 to translate chemical articles at home while caring for her children. This led to an interest in Russian literature, so she decided to earn a teaching degree, and she obtained an M.A.T. in 1966 at the age of 39. By 1974 she had been employed for eight years as a Russian teacher at a university high school and was also engaged in writing computerized Russian lessons for the university.

Career change was not always preceded by further training. The decision to pursue additional education depended not only upon the requirements of one's new vocational goal but also, where formal preparation was not a prerequisite, upon the nature of skills developed during earlier training and employment—and sometimes during periods of volunteer activity. Some women who decided to test themselves in new work roles before coming to a decision about the desirability of additional education were able to change careers without a period of formal retooling when they discovered they could function adequately without it.

The respondents were asked to note the considerations that prompted any shift in emphasis within the same general area of work or any change in their line of work after 1963. Two reasons predominated: a change of interests, which comprised 78 percent of all reasons for such decisions, and the offer of a good job opportunity in another area or field, totaling 59 percent.

Following are some comments by women who had made recent shifts of emphasis or career changes. One respondent with a master's in international affairs changed her field of college teaching from political science to history after her husband accepted a faculty position elsewhere. She commented:

> There is only one teaching institution in A .... : Latin American studies happened to be taught in history rather than political science. I then became more interested in history and moved into that area for my Ph.D. [expected in 1975 at age 47].

A caseworker who had not been employed since 1957 returned to the labor force in 1964 and spent many of the succeeding years as a self-employed, part-time therapist. She said:

> I could be said to have shifted emphasis to "private therapy" and individual and family therapy as no part-time psychiatric and medical social work jobs [were] available in this rather troglodytic community.

Between 1949 and 1967 a Ph.D. in education had been employed by a state board of education, ultimately as supervisor of the division of instruction and in other related capacities. She then became a professor of education at a state college because of her "desire to work with students and not be tied to administrative tasks which were increasing under Federal programs."

Table 4.9   Circumstances That Would Motivate Future Changes of Employers

Circumstance	Percent[a]
Chance to make better use of skills	39
Offer of more responsible position	38
Dissatisfaction with future employment conditions	34
Higher salary offer	32
Husband's relocation	32
No foreseeable circumstances	20
Husband's retirement	17
Job opportunity nearer home	13

Number = 155
NA = 18
R = 375

[a]Based on number of respondents (155).

Future Change

In order to obtain some idea about the way workers viewed their current employment situation, we asked them to use a checklist to note the circumstances under which they would probably change their employer (Table 4.9).

Answers to this question averaged more than two per respondent, and circumstances intrinsic to work—skill-utilization and responsibility—were cited most often as reasons for a job change.

Only one-third of the workers noted dissatisfaction with future conditions of employment as a reason for changing jobs. Taken at face value, this suggests that the great majority would stay put even if they were discontented. It could also mean that some women could not visualize being dissatisfied or felt that they were in no position to make a change regardless of future dissatisfaction. Many respondents may have found this choice to be so ambiguous—as indeed it was—that they simply ignored it.

There were no common denominators among those who explicitly envisioned no foreseeable circumstances that would prompt a job change, and it is possible that this sentiment was more closely related to the nature of particular jobs than to the nature of particular job holders.

When responses of wives alone were examined, the proportions who predicted a job change in the event of a husband's job relocation or retirement were 45 percent and 25 percent, respectively. While these rates may seem high, especially in cases in which wives appeared willing to permit the requirements of their husband's jobs to take precedence over their own, the reverse side of the coin is of even greater interest—55 percent of working wives did not say they would leave their jobs if their husbands relocated, and 75 percent did not intend to do so when their husbands retired, although most of both groups cited other circumstances that would lead them to change employers. Examination of their careers does not shed light on these views, and these differences possibly had more to do with personal relationships than career characteristics.

Among those who thought that they would probably leave their employers in the event of a change in their husbands' places of work were a university social science research associate married to a professor of psychiatry; a pediatrician with the Public Health Service wed to a government psychologist and program planner; a professor of economics whose husband was similarly employed; and a professor of chemistry married to an attorney.

On the other hand, there were women at similar occupational levels who did not note that job changes would be dictated by their husbands' moves to new locations. These included a physician in public health whose husband was a professor of medicine; a partner in a law firm married to a government physician; the social worker wife of a supervising social worker; a college dean wed to a university research physicist; and a college professor whose husband was a banker.

Where a husband's retirement was mentioned as a reason for leaving a job, it was always noted in conjunction with the expectation of leaving if he made a job transfer, although as the figures indicate, many women who cited the latter cause for a job change did not express the intention of doing so if and when their husbands retired.

Among those who commented about reasons for changing jobs was a part-time adjunct professor.

> I would attempt to re-locate if I were offered a full-time position in teaching or related field. But it would be necessary to consider alternative employment for husband as well (not easy at his age).

Another professor:

> Since I am recently widowed and would like to remarry, I would change if such a marriage made relocation desirable and necessary. I'd rather have a husband happy at his job—I've always adapted to new job circumstances.

A social worker in a large city said she would change for a "location nearer to home or easier public transportation since I freeze up when the roads freeze up."

A divorced professor of psychology gave "marriage to someone in another city" as a probable reason for change. She also would change employers for "opportunities for again working on a research project. Ours just had its funding terminated."

A professor in a major university who noted that she would probably change if she received a higher salary offer or in case of her husband's retirement, added that a new position would have to be in "a comparable university" and to have a "low teaching load."

A part-time clinical social worker employed by a diagnostic clinic for young children wrote:

> Present job funded by Federal Government and very unstable as a result. I become anxious when my job is in jeopardy and would like it to be more stable. I need to work. We don't seem to make it on my husband's salary anymore.

Finally, a director of a master's program in student personnel administration at a private coed college, formerly a vice-president of student affairs at a women's college, indicated that she would leave her job if offered a more responsible position, adding "am seeking Presidency." She did not say which presidency but it seems reasonable to assume that it was either of her current institution or of another college.

The fact that only 20 percent of the workers responding to this question could not define any circumstances that would lead them to voluntarily terminate their current employment should not be interpreted as indicating job dissatisfaction among the remaining 80 percent. In the first place, 34 percent of the women noted *future* dissatisfaction as a reason for leaving their jobs, thus implying that they were currently satisfied. Moreover, not all of the circumstances that would result in a job change were job-related. While reasons that did have specific application to conditions of employment may indicate reservations about current positions, mention of such possibilities does not necessarily imply a high degree of dissatisfaction. It is not unusual even for contented employees to accept a better job opportunity if it comes their way, but it appears that relatively few of these workers actively sought a job change. An illustration was provided by a college dean who said she would change to a more responsible position and a chance to make better use of her skills and who also checked "a higher salary offer." She noted that this would have to be combined with the latter of the first two inducements—"this would be a joint considera-tion," she commented, and added, "it would have to be an excellent offer. I am NOT seeking a change."

Options for Later Years

The questionnaire anticipated the debate over the age of mandatory retirement by asking respondents who were employed in 1974 and were below the age of 65 to indicate what option they would choose at that point in their lives, financial considerations aside. The inclusion of this question was based upon the premise that many women with discontinuous work patterns had belatedly embarked upon professional careers which they might be reluctant to abandon at the age of 65.

Independent of employment continuity was the factor of life expectancy which, for the majority of the respondents who were aged 44 to 54 in 1974, ranged from 34.8 to 26.1 years, respectively, or to ages 79 to 80.[6] Since each added year of life extends expected longevity, retirement at age 65, or earlier, would lead to a substantial period out of the labor force for most of the current workers.

Table 4.10 indicates the respondents' choice of options for the years after age 65. Although they were requested to make *one* selection from a list of possibilities several women specified multiple choices.

The most popular preference for the years after age 65 was to continue working on the same or a similar job on reduced schedules, an option already selected by three of the respondents who had reached the age of 65. Next in popularity was independent writing and/or research. Dual responses most often noted the latter option in conjunction with part-time employment.

Several of the respondents gave fuller explanations of their choice of options for their later years. Among them were the following:

Return to college teaching, part-time, to build up eligibility for Social Security [plus] part-time writing and research. I am not ready to give up outside contacts and retreat to any kind of living in isolation. [Program specialist, U.S. government agency, age 56]

I might like to go back to school and study something quite different. [Professor of sociology, age 51]

It is difficult to project how I will feel at 65. I think (if still well and vigorous) I would like to continue to practice medicine on a part-time schedule plus continue my other area of interest, poetry. (Course again possibly, study, writing; attempts to get published.) [Physician, age 48]

Table 4.10   Preferred Activity after the Age of 65

Activity	Percent[a]
Continuation in same job or field on a reduced schedule	41
Independent writing and/or research	32
Retirement	21
Continuation in same job or field full-time	17
New career	11
Number = 157	
NA = 69	
R = 192	

[a]Based on total N.

Travel, part-time work, part-time study and research in same or related fields. [Social worker, age 48]

Actually continuation on reduced schedule would suit me best—but I feel strongly that mandatory retirement age is good, because it prevents what could be exceedingly embarrassing burdens on a department chairman to decide whether or not a given individual still has all his marbles and therefore should be retained! Some people should retire at 65, and I would not care to be the chairman who must single out such individuals. [Assistant Professor of History, age 50]

Only a judicial appointment. Retirement age in my firm is 70—so otherwise I will practice until 70. [49 year old attorney]

Those who envisioned new careers after 65 included a college dean who hoped to engage in "part-time or volunteer work in a service-related organization"; a professor of English who looked forward to "field work in geology"; a librarian who had a dream of "catering cocktail parties"; a 46 year old newspaper reporter who wanted to be a travel agent "maybe before age 65"; and a professor of public health who hoped to engage in "political activity."

Choice of options was related to a large number of respondent characteristics, including age, work experience, earnings, education and marital status.

Respondents below the age of 55 were about half as likely to opt for retirement (17 percent) as those aged 55 to 64 (32 percent). The alternative which contributed to most of this difference was part-time employment in one's current occupation which was the preference of 44 percent of the younger group compared to 32 percent of the older. Age differences with respect to the other options were minimal.

The proportion of respondents with the greatest continuity of work experience (a minimum of 90 percent of adult years in the labor force full-time) who expected to retire at age 65 (32 percent) was almost three times higher than the proportion of workers with less continuity of employment (12 percent), almost half of whom hoped to work full-time in their present fields compared to fewer than a third of the continuous workers.

Among workers with doctorates 14 percent looked forward to complete retirement at age 65, compared with one-fifth of workers with first professional degrees, and slightly less than one-third with a master's. On the other hand, the FPG's were the most inclined to continue working on a full-time schedule: 29 percent of them chose this option, compared with 20 percent of the doctorates, and only 12 percent of the master's. The remaining workers largely opted for part-time or free-lance employment.

While only 15 percent of women academics at all faculty levels indicated the desire to retire at age 65, a mere 12 percent expressed a preference for staying on full-time. Their most common choice was part-time employment in their current field (47 percent), closely followed by independent research and/or writing (40 percent), options which were frequently selected in tandem.

It is possible to conclude from the foregoing findings that the extent of labor force participation was a crucial element in the decision to opt for retirement at age 65. Relatively few women chose retirement, but those who did tended to be older and to have worked more consistently than those who preferred other alternatives. It is conceivable that younger respondents, many of whom were fairly recent reentrants to the labor force, will change their plans as they grow older, although if they consolidate their positions in the labor market, they may continue to welcome an opportunity to compensate for lost work time.

Summary

Most of the respondents who were gainfully employed in 1974 were in professional occupations which were similar or related to the field of their terminal graduate study. Higher education was the dominant employment setting and government was the principal employer. Only a small minority of respondents were employed in the profit sector, reflecting the occupational concentration in the professions. Teaching and administration were the major job functions of the majority of respondents, with the proportion of administrators showing a substantial rise between 1963 and 1974.

Among academics the proportion of full professors had more than doubled after 1963 and the rate of women in ranks below associate professor had dropped by more than 60 percent. Relatively few faculty members were employed in highly rated university departments, however.

Respondents who were employed in male dominated occupations demonstrated a stronger attachment to work than those who worked in predominantly female fields, presumably because discontinuity of labor force participation is less acceptable in the former fields and consequently produces higher penalties for withdrawal. To the extent that discontinuity is an inherent feature of disproportionately female professions, continuity of labor force participation may be an unsuitable measure of career commitment.

Over their worklives, respondents' careers had broadened as a result of horizontal movement toward new functions and/or responsibilities. Most of this movement had occurred prior to 1963, however; thereafter the women tended to exhibit straightforward progression suggesting that the earlier period was marked by exploration and discovery, and the latter, by settlement and entrenchment.

The most frequently noted conditions that would prompt a job change were related to opportunities for greater skill utilization or responsibility. Although only one woman out of five could not define any circumstances that would lead to a change of employer, there was no evidence of much current job dissatisfaction. To the extent that plans for one's later years are conditioned by one's earlier experiences, the fact that only about one-fifth of the women expressed a preference for retirement after the age of 65 may be received as an affirmation of their career commitment. Part-time work was the most popular alternative to retirement, followed by independent writing and/or research, a choice which was often combined with the former option. Long-time workers were more likely to want to retire than those with less employment continuity, which suggests that the desire to continue working is at least partially engendered by the hope of compensating for lost work time.

Notes

1. Cynthia F. Epstein, *Woman's Place* (Berkeley: University of California Press, 1971), p. 171.

2. U.S. Bureau of the Census. Census of Population: *1970 Detailed Characteristics*, Final Report PC (1)-D1, U.S. Summary (Washington, D.C.: U.S. Government Printing Office, 1973), Table 225.

3. Kenneth D. Roose and Charles J. Andersen, *A Rating of Graduate Programs*, American Council on Education (Washington, D.C.: 1970), *passim*.

4. Employment data were obtained from the 1970 Census (PC 51-32) and, for specific academic disciplines, from Feldman, *Escape from the Doll's House, op. cit.* The threefold categorization was suggested by B. Bergmann and I. Adelman, "The 1973 Report of the President's Council of Economic Advisers: The Economic Role of Women," *American Economic Review* (September, 1973), p. 510.

5. Saul D. Feldman, *Escape from the Doll's House*, Carnegie Commission on Higher Education (New York: McGraw Hill, 1974), p. 38.

6. National Center for Health Statistics, *Vital Statistics of the United States 1974*, "Life Tables," Vol. II, Section 5 (Washington, D.C.: U.S. Department of Health, Education and Welfare), Table 5-3.

5] HOURS AND EARNINGS

No valid judgment of the respondents' career progress can be made without a consideration of their earnings from employment. Since hours of work are a major determinant of income from work, the chapter first focuses upon the amount of time working respondents devoted to gainful employment in 1963 and 1974. This is followed by a discussion of their earnings in these two years and of their contributions to 1974 family income.

Hours of Work

Respondents were asked in 1963 whether they anticipated any change in their employment status. Most of those who answered, both workers and non-workers, looked forward to some type of change, primarily to increased time at work. Table 5.1 compares 1963 anticipations with subsequent work activity and indicates that, except for those predicting no change in status, the women's plans were largely fulfilled.

The greatest congruence between plans and results was among women who expected to devote more time to work. Seven out of ten of the 1963 workers who anticipated additional work time and about four out of five of the non-workers who wished to return to the labor force realized their intentions, although one returnee subsequently exited.

While there was a slight decrease in the proportion of part-time* workers among employed respondents between 1963 and 1974, the

---

*"Part-time" is defined as a total of less than 35 hours a week, in either year.

Table 5.1   Changes in Work Behavior 1963 through 1974 by 1963 Anticipations
(percentage distribution)

| Actual Behavior 1963-1974 | 1963 Anticipations | | | | Total Percent Change |
	Increased Work Time	Decreased Work Time	Reentry to Work	No Change	
Increased work time	70	54	—	22	27
Decreased work time or exit from labor force	21	31	2[a]	27	20
Entry to labor force	—		77	7	25
Same work time	9	15	—	37	19
Remained out of labor force	—	—	21	7	9
Total	100	100	100	100	100
Number	23	13	39	60	135
Not applicable = 91					

[a]Entered, then exited.

principal change in the work schedules of the employed women during this period was at the other end of the hours range: a rise of 74 percent in the proportion of women working 49 or more hours a week (Table 5.2).

This table presents *total* weekly work hours, combining hours routinely spent on all types of gainful employment. If subsidiary employment is disregarded, a slightly smaller percentage spent 35 hours or more per week on their primary jobs, but such exclusion is unjustified in view of the regularity of their supplementary work.

More than 95 percent of the workers were engaged in salaried employment in 1974, but 28 percent of these employees regularly devoted additional weekly hours to self-employment and/or other paid work such as consultation, free-lance assignments, etc. For example, the clinical director of a child guidance clinic spent an average of 45 hours at that job and 11 hours in private practice as a consultant social worker. A health education officer worked 40 hours a week at a public health hospital and also spent two hours weekly as an adjunct associate professor at a community college, five hours on a special health education project and one-half hour as a consultant to a professional examination service. A staff piano accompanist and teacher employed by a college music department for 25 hours a week also gave six hours of private music lessons.

A few salaried employees spent the same number of hours or more in self-employment as they did in salaried employment. One psychiatrist, for instance, was in private practice for 20 hours a week and spent a similar number of hours working for a municipal health department. Only a minority of self-employed or free-lance workers had no other type of employment. These were primarily physicians, lawyers, editors, or writers.

In comparison with their female contemporaries and with all female professionals, the respondents had much longer weekly work schedules: the percentage working 41 or more hours a week was more than triple that of all working women age 45 to 64 (13 percent), and more than twice that of all female professional and technical workers in 1974 (20 percent). With respect to part-time employment the respondents did resemble all working women of similar age (24 percent) or occupational status (21 percent).[1]

Women with doctorates and first professional degrees were more likely to be working full-time in 1974 (87 percent) than those with master's degrees (71 percent). Moreover, the former group tended to spend considerably longer hours at work each week than women with lesser credentials.

More than half of the workers with first professional degrees regularly spent 49 or more hours at work each week in 1974 as did nearly half of the doctorates. These proportions were more than double the percentage of women with master's degrees who had work schedules of similar length.

One-third of the respondents worked 49 hours or more in 1974 compared with only 11 percent of all female professional or technical workers. Further, only 14 percent of all full-time female professionals worked at least 49 hours a week compared with two out of five full-time workers among the respondents.[2] This difference may be attributed to

Table 5.2 Weekly Hours of Work, 1963 and 1974

Hours of Work	Percent 1963	Percent 1974
1-14	6	6
15-34	19	15
35-39	14	11
40	21	22
41-48	21	13
49 or more	19	33
Total percent	100	100
Total number =	145	167
NA =	15	6
Not working =	66	53

Table 5.3   Weekly Work Schedules, 1974 by 1963 Work Schedule
(percentage distribution)

1974 Work Schedule	1963 Work Schedule		
	No Work	Part-time	Full-time
No work	45	9	20
Part-time	22	35	18
Full-time	33	56	62
Total percent	100	100	100
Total number	69	34	107
NA = 16			

the atypicality of the respondents' occupational distribution which covered a broad range of professions, some of which tend to be extremely time-consuming, whereas female professionals in general are clustered among a small number of occupations which normally have fairly circumscribed work schedules.

As Table 5.3 indicates, not only were the majority of non-workers in 1963 in the labor force in 1974, but most of the part-time workers in the earlier year were employed full-time 12 years later. Three out of five of the 1974 employees who had reentered the labor force after 1963 were full-time workers, although they tended to be on shorter schedules than women who had been working in 1963 (not shown). Almost half of the full-time workers who were on 35 to 40 hour schedules in 1963 had increased their work time by 1974, and a similar proportion of those who had been on longer work schedules in the prior year were devoting the same or more time to work currently (not shown). Generally, the respondents demonstrated a tendency toward increasing work time over the 12-year period: non-workers returned to work; part-timers became full-time workers; and full-time workers spent more hours at work.

Part-time work was largely the result of voluntary decisions; two-thirds of the part-time workers in 1974 said that they preferred having additional free time. Half of the part-time workers cited family responsibilities as a reason for part-time status. Only 17 percent gave the unavailability of acceptable full-time job opportunities as the cause of their part-time work status.

In many instances, the job responsibilities of part-time workers matched and sometimes exceeded those of full-time employees in similar occupations. Examples include a lawyer who spent an average of 28 hours a week as an administrator of a department in a voluntary social action organization; a 30-hour-per-week writer-editor who, as a joint owner of an all-female firm, engaged in providing public information services in the health field; and a federal government bureau chief who worked between 30 and 35 hours on the average.

At the other extreme were part-time workers whose weekly work time and whose work responsibilities were minimal. One woman was a part-time English instructor at a university college who spent three hours a week teaching and five in preparation. Another respondent devoted about five hours weekly to duties connected with her membership on the board of advisors of a charitable trust fund. There was also a free-lance writer of newspaper articles whose weekly time normally amounted to five hours.

Only one respondent was regularly employed on a part-year basis. (Teachers usually work part-year but are regarded as full-year employees). This was an accountant who regularly worked 40 hours a week preparing tax returns for an accounting firm between January and May 15th and was self-employed for an additional two hours a week for most of the same period.

These illustrations of the disparate work activities of women who were engaged in less than full-time employment suggest that inferences about the weaker career commitment of voluntary part-time workers may not always be applicable to persons with superior skills and qualifications. The achievements of several women who had spent substantial portions of their worklives in part-time work were on a par with professionals who had consistently worked full-time. While the part-time employment of a number of the respondents was a temporary expedient for the purpose of maintaining ties to their professions while simultaneously fulfilling child care responsibilities, others who may have originally regarded part-time work as a provisional arrangement continued on a shortened work schedule after they found that it did not prevent them from realizing their career goals. Although such women represent a small minority of the total, their experiences may have important implications for professionals of both sexes and for employers of professional workers in the future, especially if it becomes necessary to provide job opportunities for an enlarged pool of highly skilled workers.

Although family responsibilities were less frequently cited as a reason for part-time work than the desire for more free time, women with children were more likely to be part-time workers (26 percent) than single or childless women (11 percent), and the incidence of maternal part-time work was correlated with both size of family and the age of a mother's youngest child.

Only 13 percent of the mothers of one child worked part-time in 1974, compared with 29 percent of women with two or more children; and working mothers with at least one child under the age of 14 in 1974 were almost three times as likely to be in the labor force part-time (50 percent) as those with no children below this age (19 percent). Thus, the desire for additional time was often linked to the presence of family responsibilities even if the latter reason for part-time work was not made explicit. Although this finding appears to indicate that many of these part-time workers will increase their working hours when their children are older, only 18 percent of the part-time employees anticipated such a change.

About two out of five non-workers looked forward to reentry into the labor force. About one-fifth of the non-workers had retired because of age and a few others due to ill health and, if they are excluded, the actual motivation toward work among younger or healthier women becomes proportionately higher.

In general, the working women found the amount of time they were devoting to work to be satisfactory, although almost a third of those who spent an average of 50 hours or more at work each week preferred shorter workweeks.

Most of the women who wished to *increase* their hours of employment cited the availability of appropriate employment as the means of achieving this aim; next in order of frequency was fewer family responsibilities. The principal conditions mentioned as permitting a desired *decrease* in work hours were improved financial circumstances and retirement. Several women also sought changes in their current job duties which would relieve them of time-consuming chores. Others had no complaint about their working hours but deplored time spent commuting to work.

Examples of respondents who wished to increase their weekly schedule of work were the following: an associate professor of chemistry and mother of three children aged 8, 16, and 18 worked 25 hours a week and anticipated a 30 to 35-hour workweek when she had fewer family responsibilities; an adjunct professor of history at a four-year college, who regularly spent about ten hours in teaching and associated duties, hoped to complete her doctoral dissertation and prepare it for publication and then teach an additional class; and a six-hour-per-week worker wished to have a 10- to 20-hour workweek, noting that such a possibility required "more 'get up and go' on my part!"

Among respondents with hopes of spending fewer hours at work were a college professor of art history with a 35-hour workweek who preferred spending 30 hours in self-employment (research and writing) but did not foresee this occurring until retirement. "I like my job," she wrote, "though the committee work and administrative reports, etc. are too demanding in proportion to what they achieve. The teaching I love." An adjunct professor of English who taught for six hours per week and spent 12 hours weekly writing a book wished to stop working and increase her writing time to 18 hours but felt she could do so only if there were less need for her earnings which were under $2,500 in 1974 (about six percent of her total family income).

Miscellaneous remarks about working time included those of a music professor who commented: "Would prefer to spend less time commuting, otherwise the schedule is great! (Even commuting can be constructively used since I ride public transportation—therefore can study while traveling.)" She stipulated a preference for a job nearer home, preferably within walking distance. A lawyer and federal department section chief who was spending 52 hours a week at work and wanted to spend 45 hours thought that the only way this change could be made would be through "training subordinate personnel." A physician serving as department chief at a V.A. hospital and as a member of a medical school faculty had no criticism about her 55-hour workweek but indicated that she would prefer devoting 10 more hours to teaching, an alteration which would only be possible through a "change in departmental structure"; and a community college assistant professor of science who was spending more than 40 hours weekly in teaching and committee work listed a preference for 20 hours of teaching and related duties and 20-plus hours of research, instead of her current 10 research hours. She felt that this change could occur only if she obtained employment in a "senior college with graduate work rather than community college."

As a whole, these findings suggest a high level of job satisfaction insofar as time on the job can be associated with life on the job. Under a narrower interpretation which considers the amount of working hours

Table 5.4   Distribution of Annual Earnings, 1963[a] and 1974

Earnings	Percent 1963		Percent 1974	
	Total	Full-time	Total	Full-time
Less than $5,000	14	4	4	—
$5,000-7,499	5	3	2	1
$7,500-9,999	8	6	6	2
$10,000-12,499	13	14	6	5
$12,500-14,999	27	33	13	15
$15,000-19,999	18	24	22	22
$20,000-29,999	15	16	28	33
$30,000 and over	—	—	19	22
Total percent	100	100	100	100
Number =	142	101	166	126
NA or not applicable =	84	125	60	100

[a]1974 constant dollars

to be a proxy for labor force status, at a minimum the current workers may be described as content with the fact of being gainfully employed.

Earnings

There was a marked upward movement in the earnings of employed respondents over the 12-year period from January 1963 to December 1974. The changes in the distribution of earnings between these two dates are shown in Table 5.4.

The 1974 median full-time earnings of the respondents were about $24,000. The 1974 median money income of all year-round full-time female workers with five or more years of college, aged 45 to 54 years, was $12,784, about half that of the respondents.[3] The difference may be partly due to the disproportion of women with doctorates and first professional degrees among the participants in the study.

Between 1963 and 1974, there was more than a tripling in the proportion of employed respondents with salaries of at least $20,000 in 1974 dollars. In the earlier year the earnings curve peaked at the $12,500 to $15,000 range; in 1974 it peaked in the $20,000 to $30,000 bracket. No respondent earned the 1974 equivalent of $30,000 or more in 1963; women with salaries in that range represented 19 percent of the total in 1974.

Inclusion of part-time earnings had a slighly depressant effect upon the distribution of total earnings since most part-time workers were at lower salary levels than the full-time workers. Yet, ten of the women on part-time schedules in 1974 earned $15,000 or more and three earned a minimum of $30,000, which suggests that, in professional occupations, rewards from work are not necessarily a function of time at work.

Nevertheless, among full-time workers in 1974, those who reported that they devoted 49 or more hours a week to work were almost three and a half times as likely to be earning $30,000 or more (37 percent) as those on shorter full-time schedules (11 percent). Since no full-time employee was an hourly worker, it is unclear whether this finding implies cause or effect, that is, whether full-time workers who were paid more money worked longer hours or whether women who paid more attention to their work were rewarded commensurately. Many of the women with the longest work schedules were in such professions as law and medicine which commonly produce relatively high earnings.

In only about one in ten instances was a woman's 1974 earnings range the same or lower than in 1963. A picture of change over time is provided by Table 5.5 which shows the relation between the 1963 and 1974 earnings of those respondents who were employed full-time at both dates.

Table 5.5   1974 Full-time Earnings by 1963 Full-time Earnings[a]
(percentage distribution)

Earnings Range 1974	Earnings Range 1963			
	Less than $12,500	$12,500-14,999	$15,000-19,000	$20,000-29,000
Less than $12,500	10	4	—	—
$12,500-14,999	35	9	6	—
$15,000-19,999	30	33	6	—
$20,000-29,999	20	50	69	14
$30,000 and more	5	4	19	86
Total percent	100	100	100	100
Number =	20	24	16	14
Not applicable = 152				

[a]1974 constant dollars.

Among all respondents with full-time earnings in 1963 and 1974, more than three out of five were in the $20,000 or over range in the latter year and a quarter had salaries of $30,000 or more. Among those who were part-time workers in the earlier year and were employed full-time in 1974, slightly more than half earned a minimum of $20,000 in the latter year and 15 percent had earnings of $30,000 or more. Earnings of women who had not been in the labor force in 1963 and who were working full-time in 1974 were considerably lower: only about one out of five made $20,000 or more, and fewer than one out of twenty made at least $30,000.

Continuity of labor force participation was strongly correlated with size of earnings. Table 5.6 which presents 1974 full-time earnings by

Table 5.6   1974 Full-time Earnings by Percent of Adult Years Employed, Full-time, Full Year
(percentage distribution)

Full-time Earnings, 1974	Percent of Years Worked Full-time			
	Less than 50%	50-79%	80-99%	100%
Less than $15,000	52	26	17	8
$15,000-19,999	26	32	17	17
$20,000-29,999	13	27	47	36
$30,000 and over	9	15	19	39
Total percent	100	100	100	100
Number =	23	34	36	36
Not applicable = 97				

proportion of full-time full-year work experience demonstrates the relationship between attachment to work and income from work.

The table demonstrates that the stronger one's ties to the labor force, the greater likelihood of being in a top earnings bracket. A toll was paid even by workers who had only brief periods of retirement or of part-time or part-year employment.

While respondents generally paid a price for employment discontinuity in the form of lower earnings, the price was not the same in all occupations. For example, high earners were not evenly distributed among occupational fields, even when they exhibited similar work patterns. Table 5.7 shows how the chances of women with the same proportion of full-time employment experience having salaries of $20,000 or more were associated with their career field.

It is clear that the ability to recuperate from discontinuity varied widely. However, since the table is limited to minimum earnings of $20,000, it does not reflect differentials at higher salary levels. Thus, the apparent absence of penalties for discontinuity in some fields may conceal actual losses in professions with superior earnings potential.

The proportion of high earners was related to occupational sex composition: the larger the proportion of females, the smaller were the

Table 5.7 Proportion of Years with Full-time Employment, B.A.—1974, Respondents with 1974 Earnings of $20,000 or more, by Field

| Field | Years Worked Full-Time—Percent Workers Earning $20,000 or More | | |
	100%	80-99%	Less than 80%
Medicine	100	100	80
Law	100	100	75
Social Service	100	80	40
Science	100	63	33
Public Health	100	67	—
Education	75	75	17
Social Work	100	25	14
Business and Journalism	a	50	16
Humanities	33	33	13
Library Science	—	50	—

Number = 78
Not applicable = 148

[a]No workers with 100% full-time experience.

Table 5.8   Full-time Earnings 1974 by Female Employment
(percentage distribution)

| Full-Time Earnings | Female Occupational Representation | | |
	Females Underrepresented	Females Well Represented	Females Overrepresented
Less than $15,000	9	30	35
$15,000-$19,999	20	12	35
$20,000-$29,000	34	46	22
$30,000 and over	37	12	8
Total percent	100	100	100
Number =	56	39	37
Not applicable = 104			

percentages of workers at top salary levels. This finding is clarified in Table 5.8 which presents 1974 full-time earnings by female occupational representation.

The distribution of the earnings of respondents in male dominated fields was the reverse of the salary distribution in predominantly female fields. The earnings of women in occupations in which females were underrepresented tended to be skewed toward higher income levels; salaries in fields in which women were well represented tended to cluster about the mean; and earnings in female occupations were largely bunched toward the bottom.

Respondents in male dominated occupations were three times as likely to have been continuous workers as those in disproportionately female occupations, but they were four times as likely to be in the top earnings bracket. Employment continuity among respondents in the former group was twice as high as it was among those in fields where women are well represented, but the proportion of top earners was three times higher. Apparently, occupation exerts an influence on earnings independent of career attachment. Similar amounts of work experience resulted in lower monetary returns for respondents in female professions because, in general, wages in such occupations are relatively depressed. "The higher the percentage of female employment, the lower are earnings, but this is true for men as well as women."[4]

Earnings were also related to class of employer and type of workplace. Government employment was more lucrative than private (non-profit and profit). Almost two-thirds of government employees had full-time earnings of $20,000 or more, which was about 70 percent higher than the proportion of private employees at the same salary level (38 percent). Among workers with minimum salaries of $30,000, there was more than twice the proportion of public as private employees. Full time earnings under $15,000 were almost twice as frequent in the private sector (31 percent) as the public (17 percent).

Because a substantial proportion of the respondents in public employment worked in educational institutions, an analysis of full-time earnings with respect to both employer and setting was performed. Among full-time public employees, those in government administration, who primarily worked at the federal level, were the highest paid: approximately nine out of ten made $20,000 or more and almost two out of five earned a minimum of $30,000. Among employees of public institutions of higher education, the proportions in these salary ranges were 60 percent and 23 percent respectively. In contrast, 37 percent of workers in private colleges and universities earned a minimum of $20,000 and only eight percent, at least $30,000.

Other settings (social agencies, hospitals, libraries, schools, etc.) showed a close resemblance in the proportions of top earners: half of the public workers and 42 percent of the private workers had earnings of $20,000 or more; and about 17 percent of each group made at least $30,000. Public colleges and universities were principally state controlled; publicly sponsored employment settings other than administrative agencies and higher education were mainly under the aegis of local governments.

A comparison of the salaries of full professors (excluding medical faculty) revealed that one-quarter earned $30,000 or more and 44 percent received $20,000 to $29,999. There was a close similarity between the proportions of top-earning professors employed by private and public universities, but the percentage of full professors at four-year colleges who were in each of these earnings ranges was only half that of faculty at universities.

The higher a respondent's earnings, the less time she regularly devoted to homemaking duties. The percentage of women who earned $20,000 or more in 1974 and spent no time on housekeeping or related activities (15 percent) was twice as large as the percentage whose earnings ranged from $10,000 to $14,999, and triple the proportion of women at still lower earnings levels. Similarly, only five percent of the top earners allotted 30 or more hours a week to homemaking, compared with 19 percent of the middle group, and 48 percent of those who earned less than $10,000. The last group was mainly engaged in part-time work, which probably had both a cause and effect relationship to the greater attention given to household responsibilities.

For top earners, the lesser amount of time involved in homemaking may reflect the ability to pay for domestic help. It may also indicate a reverse Parkinson effect, whereby time spent in housework decreased as time ordinarily allotted to it contracted due to the substitution of full-time employment.

Table 5.9   Wife's Earnings as Percent of Family Income by Total Income of Husband-Wife Families, 1974

Percent Contributed by Wife's Earnings	Family Income					Total Percent Contribution
	Less than $30,000	$30,000-39,999	$40,000-49,999	$50,000-74,999	$75,000 or more	
No earnings	25%	28%	20%	24%	16%	22%
With earnings	75%	72%	80%	76%	84%	78%
1-9	4	9	3	3	–	7
10-19	11	6	–	14	5	7
20-29	11	6	10	3	11	8
30-39	14	9	20	14	26	16
40-49	7	16	33	24	21	20
50-74	21	25	13	18	21	19
75 or more	7	–	–	–	–	2
Total percent	100	100	100	100	100	100
Number =	28	32	30	29	19	139

Not applicable = 77
NA = 10

Most wives who work do not earn much, regardless of their husbands' earnings. But the respondents were exceptional and, although the wives' salaries rarely approached their husbands' earning level, many had earnings that were, alone, above the median income of two-earner families which was $14,750 in 1974.[5] The median income of all husband-wife families among the respondents in that year, regardless of the wife's work status, was about $44,000.

There was a strong association between the amount of money a wife earned at her job and the amount of a family's total 1974 income. Thus, close to a majority of working wives earning under $10,000 were in families with incomes of less than $30,000, while the family income of three-fifths of the wives who earned $30,000 or more was $75,000 or over.

Although many wives made substantial contributions to family income, Table 5.9 suggests that the absence of a wife's earnings would have caused few families to slip from prosperity to poverty. More than three-quarters of the married respondents contributed earnings to family income in 1974, in contrast to less than half of all wives of comparable ages.[6] Instances in which the loss of a wife's earnings would have produced objective financial hardship appear rare. Nevertheless, while the loss of a wife's contribution may not change a family's position in the national income distribution by very much, it surely can be a family misfortune, especially if her earnings had been depended upon as a regular income source.

The median proportion of family income contributed by all wives was 30.5 percent. Only about a fifth of the families received half or more of their total income from wives' earnings. Thus, in the great majority of households, husbands maintained their conventional role as the major breadwinner. (It is possible that unearned income was an important income source in some families and that, in such cases, the ratio between the earnings of husbands and wives was smaller.)

The median percent of family income accounted for by the earnings of working wives, alone, was 39.6 percent. In contrast, the 1974 median contribution of all working wives in families with incomes of $15,000 and over was 26.6 percent. The respondents' median contribution did resemble that of all working wives who were employed full-time, full-year (37.5 percent), but about one-fifth of the former were part-time workers.[7]

The earnings of more than one-quarter of the working respondents accounted for at least 50 percent of family income. The most substantial contribution made by working wives was in families with incomes below $40,000: more than one-third received half or more of total income from wives' earnings. This high a proportion of family income was provided by about one-fifth of the working wives at higher family income levels.

Women with high earnings made differential contributions to family income. For example, among wives with earnings of $20,000 or more in 1974, the contribution of 42 percent represented between half and three-fourths of total family income; that of 52 percent comprised one-quarter to one-half; and the earnings of the remaining 6 percent represented less than one-quarter of the total.

To obtain some idea about the size of the respondents' earnings in relation to the earnings of males with similar educational attainment, a comparison was made between the incomes of husband-wife families in which husbands were the sole wage earners and the earnings of respondents who had always worked full-time, full-year. This analysis revealed a smaller proportion of these respondents at upper income levels than of men with similar educational attainment. Fewer than one out of five of the female doctorates had earnings of $30,000 or more in contrast to three-quarters of doctorate husbands without working wives. Among holders of master's degrees, only 14 percent of continuously employed respondents, but half of the husbands who were sole earners, made $30,000 or more. Only among recipients of first professional degrees was the financial position of men without working wives and women with continuous work histories the same—100% of each sex had incomes of $30,000 or more. Two caveats are in order when interpreting these comparisons. The $30,000 top-earnings range conceals differences at higher levels; and not all income can be assumed to be derived from earnings. Nevertheless, this comparison may be viewed as being suggestive of sex discrimination, since despite similarity of educational attainment and duration of employment (the men are presumed to have been continuous workers) there were wide disparities in income between male and female contemporaries.

Summary

Between 1963 and 1974 the respondents showed a general tendency toward increasing their weekly hours of work: non-workers returned to work; part-time workers became full-time employees; full-time workers spent longer hours at work. Part-time work status was principally a voluntary decision influenced primarily by a personal desire for more free time and, secondarily, by the need to fulfill family responsibilities. Few women worked part-time because they were unable to secure full-time employment.

Respondents on part-time work schedules were employed in diverse capacities and many had ranks and responsibilities on a par with full-time employees. This finding suggests that hours of work may be an improper criterion for judgments of the career commitment of professional women.

Women who were employed in 1974 were generally satisfied with their work schedules; a desire for a decrease in work time was primarily expressed by those who regularly worked 50 hours or more per week. The impression given was of a group of workers who, at the least, were content with their labor force status.

Respondents' earnings showed a marked upward movement between 1963 and 1974, with full-time workers in both years showing the greatest improvement. While continuity of labor force participation was strongly associated with size of earnings, the income realized from persistent attachment to work varied by occupational field, in large part, because of occupational differences in salary scales. Women who had worked continuously in female dominated professions, which command relatively low pay, were less likely to be among the top earners than respondents in predominantly male fields.

Respondents in government employment had higher earning profiles than women in private employment, but most private employment was in the non-profit sector which is not notable for high pay scales. There were too few respondents employed by business firms to permit any conclusions about the relative earnings position of women employed in the governmental and profit sectors.

Among families with working wives, the women's median contribution to family income was 40 percent of the total; in over one-quarter of these families, wives contributed at least one-half of total income. The majority of the highest earners ($20,000 or more) among the working wives contributed less than half of their family's total income in 1974. Thus, while the qualifications of many husbands and wives were parallel, it was the rare wife who was able to match or surpass her husband's financial contribution to the family.

Notes

1. Paul O. Flaim, Thomas Bradshaw, and Curtis L. Gilroy, "Employment and Unemployment in 1974," *Special Labor Force Report 178* (U.S. Department of Labor, 1975), pp. A-22, A-24.

2. *Ibid.,* p. A-24.

3. U.S. Bureau of the Census *Current Population Reports,* Series P. 60, No. 101, "Money Income in 1974 of Families and Persons in the United States" (Washington, D.C.: U.S.G.P.O., 1976), p. 121.

4. Victor R. Fuchs, "Differences in Hourly Earnings Between Men and Women," *Monthly Labor Review,* XCIV, 5, May, 1971, p. 14.

5. *Current Population Reports,* Series P-60, No. 101, *op. cit.,* p. 3.

6. U.S. Department of Labor, Women's Bureau, *1975 Handbook on Women Workers,* Bulletin 297 (Washington, D.C., 1975), p. 19.

7. Howard Hayhge, "Marital and Family Characteristics of the Labor Force, March 1974," *Special Labor Force Report 173* (U.S. Department of Labor, Bureau of Labor Statistics, 1975), p. A-27.

6] EXIT AND RETURN

Many respondents, as we have seen, withdrew from the labor force for varying periods, usually in order to fulfill family responsibilities. This chapter discusses two supplementary activities of many respondents during their absence from the labor force, and sometimes while they were in the labor force—volunteer work and education. It then focuses upon women who were not employed in 1963 by describing those who reentered after that date and those who remained out of the labor force.

Volunteer Work

Volunteer work played a significant role in the lives of many respondents. Such activities were wide-ranging. At one extreme was the professional career in every sense of the word except monetary payment for services rendered; at the other extreme was occasional time spent by paid workers on professionally related concerns. In between was a variety of activities usually involving the provision of services to the community in both its parochial and broader sense.

Like paid work, the volunteer activities of the respondents can be classified in certain ways. They can be related to a woman's training, for example. Some volunteer time was exclusively or primarily devoted to work that was identical or closely related to a respondent's field of study; in other cases, it had only a peripheral relationship, and in still others was completely unrelated to a volunteer's graduate subject area.

Volunteer work can also be categorized in terms of class of "employer." Some women were essentially solo professionals; others served as their husbands' assistants, usually as professional or non-professional staff aides, not equal partners. Still others were "government" workers, serving as unpaid elected or appointed members of public boards, commissions, and the like. In addition, voluntary services to professional organizations can be assigned to the profit-making sphere since they usually enhance career prospects. But by and large, the most common type of volunteer work was akin to services performed in the non-profit sector, embracing civic, school, youth, health, social welfare, charity, cultural, and religious concerns. In many cases, of course, workers in the voluntary "government" or "non-profit" sectors, like independent professionals, also utilized graduate training and skills honed in the labor market. In some cases, like unpaid professionals, they too had eliminated the profit motive from their constellation of career expectations while retaining all other elements of vocational aspiration (such as prestige, honors, productivity), and they were as ambitious for these hallmarks of success as the gainfully employed. However, such women were exceptional. Most of the respondents who engaged in volunteer work viewed it either as a temporary part-time activity performed between periods of employment, and/or as a supplement to paid employment. Typically, it was a substitute for gainful work.

The proportion of respondents engaged in volunteer work dropped from 56 percent in 1963 to 45 percent in 1974, a rate of decrease corresponding to the increase in labor force participation during this period. The relatively few instances of an increased volunteer commitment between these dates principally involved retirees. Otherwise, despite a relationship between volunteer hours in 1963 and in 1974, even women who had spent the most time as volunteers in the earlier year were likely to have either curtailed or withdrawn from voluntary activities by 1974. Nevertheless, whereas in 1963, only eight women spent 20 or more hours on voluntary activities, twice that number did so in 1974. Hand in hand with the phenomenon of reentry to the work force and a consequent decrease or abandonment of volunteer involvement was a rise in the amount of unpaid employment of some women who, when relieved of child care duties, preferred intensified volunteer commitment to paid work.

While gainful employment was contraindicative of volunteer work, more than two out of five of the respondents in the labor force regularly spent some time as volunteers in 1974. Table 6.1 shows the relationship between work time and volunteer time.

The inverse relationship between the amount of time devoted to paid work and to volunteer work is clearly demonstrated in this table. Almost 7 out of 10 of the non-workers were volunteers, but only half of the part-time workers and slightly more than a third of the full-time workers also

Table 6.1   Average Weekly Hours of Volunteer Work by Hours of Paid Work, 1974
(percentage distribution)

Hours Volunteer Work	Hours Paid Work		
	No Hours	1-34 Hours	35 Hours and over
No hours	31	50	64
1-9 hours	31	44	31
10 hours or more	38	6	5
Total percent	100	100	100
Number =	(52)	(32)	(129)
NA = 13			

engaged in voluntary activities. Moreover, five of 52 non-workers spent 30 hours or more in unpaid work, compared to only one of 161 workers (not shown). Women who were not in the labor force were more likely to be volunteers than were paid workers, and also tended to give more time to volunteer work than volunteers who were also gainfully employed. This is hardly a surprising finding. Perhaps what is surprising is the high volunteer rate among the gainfully employed since, in many people's minds, volunteer work is an activity of housewives, not of working women. This belief is counter to the evidence, for large numbers of male and female members of the labor force give time to volunteer affairs, sometimes attaining positions of considerable power and prestige. In some cases respondents who commenced their volunteer work while out of the labor force continued to pursue these interests after reentry, although usually at a lower level of intensity.

Although the amount of volunteer work among the gainfully employed may be generally underestimated, the woman without gainful employment is the prototypical volunteer. If this woman is highly trained and anticipates reentering the labor force, the nature of her volunteer work may be relevant to these plans.

Among the respondents who were not in the labor force were many who had heavy volunteer commitments. For example, included among the volunteer activities of an M.A. in government who had been employed for only one year after 1962 (as a high school teacher) were Democratic county committeeman; chairman of local Democratic committee, board member of county and local Leagues of Women Voters; director, county women's political caucus. Her current volunteer concerns consumed almost 30 hours a week. She remarked that "really bright—and idealistic—women are greatly needed in government— good place to make a contribution through politics, campaigning, funding and advertising important issues."

An attorney who was not in the labor force in 1974, and had been gainfully employed for only two years after 1962, provided the following list of her volunteer positions: County Citizens Advisory Committee for Allocation of Housing and Community Development Funds; Secretary and Director of State Housing Corporation; Vice-President of State Dance Council; and Section Vice-President of the National Council of Jewish Women. She also noted that she was cited in her state *Who's Who of Women* and also in *Who's Who of American Women*.

A master of social work had taught elementary school French from 1964 to 1967, but currently she spent 30 hours a week as a member of a city welfare advisory board. She commented:

> I am lucky to be able to do volunteer work because my husband's salary is enough [$30,000–39,999]. I am sorry that so many women need to take paying jobs to satisfy their emotional needs because in our town [a university community] those jobs are needed by poor grad students and their wives. I am glad to have earned my living in the past and not to need the ego-boost of a salary, although I work as hard at my volunteer activities as most salaried women do.

Most of the women who had devoted corresponding amounts of time to similar kinds of voluntary efforts had reentered the labor force between 1963 and 1974 and various aspects of their volunteer activities prior to 1963 were described in their initial questionnaires. Subsequently, these data were utilized in an investigation of the economic determinants of voluntarism which concluded that these women were volunteers "in part for their families but also to a great extent for themselves—to build or maintain their human capital and to aid in job search."[1] In recognition of this intent, it appeared desirable to discover whether respondents had found that volunteer work had, in fact, improved their marketability in the paid labor force. Therefore, respondents who had *ever* dropped out of the labor force for a year or more to fulfill family obligations, and who had been volunteers during that period, were asked to use a checklist to indicate how their volunteer experiences contributed to their subsequent employment.

More than half of these women (116) indicated that they had dropped out for a minimum of a year to fulfill family responsibilities, and 72 percent of this group (84) reported that they had engaged in volunteer work during that time. Table 6.2 indicates the response of the volunteers regarding the influence of voluntary experiences upon their subsequent labor force activity.

More than four out of five of the respondents who had been volunteers while absent from the labor force indicated one or more ways in which their volunteer experiences had been of value upon reentry. Most of these women noted multiple benefits.

Table 6.2   Contributions of Volunteer Work to Employment

Contribution	Percent[a]
Advanced personal growth and self-confidence	68
Maintained and/or improved career skills	41
Developed new career skills	30
Inspired new career interests	25
Provided useful contacts in job search	24
No effect	17

R = 184 (including 13 "other")
Number = 84
Not applicable = 142

[a]Based on number of respondents.

The single type of assistance most commonly attributed to volunteer work was advancement of personal growth and self-confidence, which superficially may appear to have a less specific relation to employment than other types of aid. Yet, since the resumption of paid employment after a lengthy recess can provoke anxiety and discouragement, volunteer activities that provide sufficient self-assurance to cope with the transition and to handle new responsibilities surely are directly pertinent to employability.

Some respondents clarified their responses to this question. One reported: "My first career reentry job, in 1963, was writing a report on team teaching for the M_____ Board of Education. I knew the Superintendent of Schools well through my volunteer work in the League of Women Voters, PTA, and the Unitarian Church."

An attorney who had not been gainfully employed between 1964 and 1973, when she resumed the practice of labor law, had been a member of a local commission on human rights and of a county task force on women, delegate and alternate to state judicial conventions of her political party, and a Legal Aid Society director. In addition to skill maintenance, job contacts, and improved self-confidence, she declared that her volunteer work had "increased my knowledge of and experience with social problems."

Another lawyer and mother of three remarked:

I realized at one point that being chairman of a department of a law firm has much in common with being a den mother, but which helped which is another question.

A publicist reviewed her volunteer career thus:

My periods of "retirement" from the working world had begun before your 1960's survey and quite a few of the years covered in this 1963–1975 survey have constituted a gradual "coming out" stage—from volunteer work closely connected with women and children (e.g., cooperative nursery schools, PTA's, auxiliaries based on my husband's career as a psychiatrist) to volunteer work in the community and politics because I was fortunate enough to have both the time and financial resources to do such, to part-time paid work, and finally to my present job.

She went on to describe her volunteer "peer group" as women

reaping a major if unplanned benefit from their years of being off the career track: having a chance to discover new talents, new interests and new directions, and being able to pursue them. . . . We know what a family-wrenching upheaval it usually is when a male head-of-family decides to change careers in midlife. Hasn't our generation of middle and up-permiddle class women been really quite fortunate to have had the opportunity to search out their own futures at a relatively comfortable, non-pressure time of life?

A different perspective was provided by an ABD in philosophy who became a rare book dealer. While she asserted that volunteer activities had "made me enough dissatisfied with committee meetings and endless talk to drop most of them and go into business," she was still devoting 15 to 20 hours a week to them. But she had become more discriminating in her choice of activity as the following quotation indicates:

I abruptly cut out and off those involvements which seemed to be socially unproductive (though certainly sustaining for me in a narrow, self-preening way, like state PTA, church junior and senior choirs, money-raising, etc., etc.). I began to view my involvement in them as critically as I would view the present or future of a paying job. And I decided I was playing tricks, indulging in cannibalism with other women on committees . . . and altering nothing. I quit and looked for direct action. I found it first in the assistance-to-migrants programs which take many forms, all of them undernourished; then closer to home . . . the county narcotics guidance council and a program for bussed mental patients. . . . So—a purposeful switch was made from volunteer activities that were self-serving only, to some that also carry a measure of relief directly.

Her volunteer work was not economically motivated but was essentially altruistic, and she devoted almost the same amount of time to it as to her gainful self-employment. Of course, altruism does not preclude collateral economic causes or effects but, in this instance as in others, the desire to serve the community was the guiding motive. This respondent mused that "an educational background gives additional clout in the midst of community searchings and wranglings. But whether the educated person is better equipped to carry out the human imperative of stirring things up to good purpose is debatable. (I expect that education enters into one's definition of purpose)."

These educated respondents' "definition of purpose" was composed of various elements—humanitarian, ego gratifying, vocational, among others. In general, Mueller's conclusion that human capital enhancement was a principal determinant of volunteer work is buttressed by the finding that it was also a principal consequence. While volunteer work could not compensate for lack of market work, most volunteers gave it credit for making a positive contribution to their later careers.

Additional Education

Twenty of the 226 respondents had either received academic degrees between 1963 and 1974 or were currently candidates for degrees. An additional 15 had received teaching or other certification during this period. Another 35 women had taken work-related courses, and 14 more had pursued miscellaneous educational programs. This listing includes women who combined studies and paid employment and those who did not work while attending school.

Ten women received Ph.D.'s between 1963 and 1974, and four others were doctoral candidates in 1974. One respondent earned a J.D. during this period; four completed master's programs; and one woman was a current master's degree candidate. Course requirements for the majority of the doctorates had been fulfilled prior to 1963, and most candidates were employed while they completed their dissertations. The three exceptions left the labor force in order to undertake full-time doctoral studies—in history, in quantum chemistry, and in public health, as did the student of law. Three of the four women who earned master's degrees, as well as all of the ABD's, were gainfully employed during their studies.

The ten doctorates required an average of 9.2 years to complete, although one 1966 Ph.D., noted that while her latest course of study lasted four years, her original graduate work, in the same field but in a different area of specialization, had begun in 1948.

It took one respondent 21 years to earn her doctorate and another needed 18 years. The former received an M.A. in history in 1945 and then pursued doctoral studies in anthropology until 1947. She married in that year and became a college instructor, continuing in this field until 1955, except for two short intervals—the first devoted to homemaking (she had children in 1950 and 1952), and the second to courses leading to certification in elementary school teaching (which was the only job she could get in the rural area to which the family had moved). She taught school for ten years during which time she decided to write her thesis on a subject related to her teaching experience. She finally received her Ph.D. in 1966. By 1974, she was a full professor at a public university.

The respondent who embarked upon doctoral studies 18 years before obtaining her degree was born abroad and received her B.A. in her native

country. She then spent a year at a Canadian university, followed by
marriage and four years at Columbia studying political science.
Children were born in 1951, 1956, and 1960, and she stayed home for two
separate periods totaling five years between 1954 and 1962. In the
interim, she had worked as a research assistant and later as a college
instructor. In 1963, she resumed her graduate studies but continued to
teach part-time at a state university. She earned her doctorate in 1966 and
was a full professor at the same institution in 1974.

A physician and mother of four earned a master's degree in public
health in 1973. In the same year she was appointed assistant state
commissioner of public health after four years of experience in various
capacities in the same general area of work. She had commenced her
studies 17 years earlier, in 1959. She reported that she "Took course work
1956–59. Wrote final papers 1970–73."

Respondents who had undertaken any courses of study after 1962 were
asked to use a checklist to specify their reasons. Their responses are
presented in Table 6.3.

Most of the women who had pursued studies in recent years were
employed at the same time and, in large measure, they provided various
work-related reasons for their additional education. Some added
comments such as the following:

> Undertook personal studies in electronic film-computer music; took course
> (industrial arts) in electricity and electronics in order to update myself in this
> important field. [Professor of music]

> I don't know whether I can ever be employed full-time if we remain in B____.
> My motives are a compound of personal fulfillment, desire to be prepared *in*

Table 6.3   Reasons for Studies after 1962

Reasons	Percent[a]
Updating of knowledge in original field	50
For personal fulfillment rather than vocational aims	46
Improvement of chances for job promotion	30
In compliance with employer's requirements	25
Change of interests	20
Wish to enter field with better job opportunities	14
Completion of course of study begun earlier	13

Total R = 167
Total Number = 84
NA = 142

[a]Based on total number of respondents answering question (84).

case—and lack of anything else to do in this burg. [Adjunct assistant professor of history, Ph.D. candidate, wife of faculty member]

Teachers are supposed to take 6 units of work every three years. I decided to channel mine toward a supervision credential to up-date my knowledge and to improve my job rating. [Head librarian, school district]

The part-time field for "untrained" WASPish middle aged social workers seemed to be drying up—had wanted to get MSW for many years. [Part-time clinical social worker, received MSW in 1974]

Spanish language associated with my job—non-degree. [U.S. State Department employee]

Only a minority of the reentrants to the work force undertook preparatory studies. Instead, most resumed employment on the basis of their experience and qualifications. Two returnees who did pursue further credentials commented:

Still "hung up" from Dean Gildersleeve's admonition to Barnard girls about using their "trained brains," I guess! [Ph.D. in physics 1970, Assistant Professor]

Had expected to need additional income and felt new field of paralegal not only more interesting to me than original field of economics but also easier, by far, than updating in economics. [Pre-1963 M.A.]

And a reentrant who had received teaching certification in 1967, but whose last job was terminated in 1973, checked "wish to enter field with better job opportunities," as her reason for her recent studies. Next to it she wrote "Joke."

A few of the women who had not been employed at all between 1963 and 1974 had undertaken courses of study, although in only one case was this a degree program: an M.A. in chemistry who was in library school and who commented: "The library field *may* have better job opportunities than the field of organic chemistry for the 'mature woman' returning to the labor force. [I] would prefer chemistry."

Another long-time non-worker with an M.S. in public health education looked forward to preparing for elementary school teaching: "Having felt that in a few years I would like to return to education to meet a challenge I feel to help provide a concerned prepared teacher for children."

One explanation for the apparent lack of a felt need for further education by most of the returnees may be the fact that many of them had graduate credentials in occupations that could readily be resumed because of their earlier professional training and experience. In addition, superior qualifications alone probably placed some of these women at an advantage in the job search relative to other middle-aged female job seekers.

Reentry to the Labor Force

Among the 173 workers whose 1974 occupations were described in Chapter 4, were 34 women who had not been at work in January 1963. Twelve women who also had not been employed at the earlier date had reentered the labor force thereafter but were not working in December 1974. These 46 women were not the only returnees to the labor force since there were also reentrants who had resumed work before 1963. Since the data are most comprehensive for the 1963–74 period and since reentry following a prolonged absence from the work force occurred more frequently during these years, this section is devoted primarily to women who resumed gainful employment after 1962.

An examination of the reentrants' job search provides some idea of the way in which well qualified women who were otherwise engaged for extended periods were able to renew their ties to the world of work. Answers to two questions supplied information on this point: work histories which indicated how all respondents had learned about each of their jobs from 1963 to date; and an inquiry to the respondents who had *ever* returned to work after an absence of three or more years about how they had obtained their initial job after their most recent period of temporary retirement.

For those who resumed work after 1962, the most successful results of the job search were achieved through contacts with former employers, colleagues, or teachers (44 percent). Next in order of frequency was personal assistance of other types (28 percent). Other methods of obtaining jobs—employment agencies, want ads, personal application, and specific job offers—led to initial placement for the remaining returnees.

Among the specific methods of getting hired for their first reentry job were the following:

A woman with an M.S. in public health education, whose last paid employment in 1957 had been as a junior high school science teacher, had spent three hours per week in 1971–72 as a volunteer parent aide serving as a science tutor. In 1972 she became a paid employee of the same school system as a 30-hour a week teacher aide in math and science, taking this position when the "principal of the school called me."

An M.S. in journalism who had left a job as a reporter in 1949 and returned to the labor force in 1968 similarly capitalized on her volunteer experience. While serving as a volunteer she had learned of her reentry job in which she served as secretary of a hospital volunteer department and editor of the hospital newspaper.

A biostatistician, whose last employment had been in 1955, found government work in the same field in 1969 "by telephoning various people in statistical sections of several agencies."

After a Ph.D. in geology had completed an assignment involving the organization of a technical library in 1958, she withdrew from the labor force until 1965 when she became an associate professor at a foreign university which had just hired her husband. She learned of the job through "correspondence with fellow-stamp-collector who held the job and was leaving it."

A social science researcher with an M.A. in economics became employed after a seven-year absence when her "former boss called me to work with him" as a research associate engaged in an evaluation of a government program. Another respondent with a master's in economics who had left a government position as an economist in 1952, was hired by a university as a research assistant in 1967 after learning of the job "through husband, a university professor, and personal contact."

These comments are quite representative and many of them demonstrate how important the right contacts can be. It is "know-who" perhaps even more than know-how that represents the difference between the job search of a woman with high qualifications in both the educational and socioeconomic sense, and that of individuals of lower status.

Of the total number of respondents, 103 (46 percent) had returned to the labor force at one time or another after an absence of three years or more. Thus, the group who had reentered work after 1962 represented less than half of all returnees, although they commonly had spent more time as non-workers. Table 6.4 shows how all reentrants with a hiatus of three or more years from work obtained their first jobs.

One option offered in the question, "Response to your want ad" was never cited. "Personal application" was not on the checklist but was noted by a sufficient number of women to warrant inclusion in the table.

Although former employers or colleagues were the most common sources of assistance received by returnees after 1962, for all women who had *ever* reentered the labor force, other contacts were more productive. Information from the latter group was provided in response to a checklist while the information about the methods used by reentrants between 1963 and 1974 came from their written comments. Since the term "personal contact" is subject to varying interpretations, it is reasonable to use it to encompass all assistance by acquaintances, regardless of their identity, and to conclude that it was not only recent returnees but all respondents who had ever temporarily retired from work who found their most productive way back to the labor force was facilitated by people they knew rather than by formal structures and processes.

A few of the 46 respondents who were not employed in January 1963 but who worked afterward had not left careers primarily to devote themselves to homemaking. These exceptions were a junior high school teacher who left that job in 1962 due to ill health (after one month's

Table 6.4   Method of Obtaining Most Recent Reenty Job

Method	Percent
Personal contact (other than those listed below)	42
Former employer or colleague	21
Personal application	11
Acquaintance in field	9
Response to employer's ad	5
University placement office	5
Former teacher	3
Private employment agency	2
Public employment agency	2
Total percent	100

Number = 95
Other or NA = 8
Not Applicable = 123

employment), and who reentered the labor market in September 1963 as a university language instructor; a college history instructor who changed from part-time work to full-time study when her youngest child entered first grade in the fall of 1961 and who earned a Ph.D. in 1966; and a research physicist who had received an 18-month maternity leave of absence from her part-time job in an industrial laboratory in 1961, but found when she was ready to resume work that a new management opposed her part-time arrangement. She unsuccessfully sought other part-time work and then decided to undertake doctoral studies, receiving her Ph.D. in 1970.

Finally, among the group of women who cannot be classifed as former homemakers who returned to employment, was a respondent who was technically out of the labor force in 1963, insofar as she had been serving as the unpaid editor of a magazine devoted to the arts since 1959, as well as writing fiction and criticism. She kept her editorial position until 1966 when she entered gainful employment. During her tenure as magazine editor she had supported herself and her four children on alimony provided by her ex-husband from whom she had been divorced in 1956.

In addition, there were some women who had left full-time jobs at the time of marriage, pregnancy, or the birth of their first child, and who later had entered part-time employment from which they eventually exited from the labor force. For example, a caseworker left a 40-hour-a-week job in 1953 when she was pregnant and returned to an eight-hour-a-week job as an interviewer for a neighborhood improvement project nine years and three children later. After the project ended five months later, she was not employed again for eight years.

A college English instructor after marriage to a professor in 1957, spent many of the subsequent years teaching for three hours weekly as an adjunct professor at the same institution that employed her husband until the birth of a child in 1961.

The manager of promotion and production for a book publisher left a 32-hour-a-week job in 1960 when her first child was born, but for a year between 1961 and 1962, she was a free-lance proofreader, indexer, and copywriter for another publisher until her second child arrived. She then stayed out of the labor market until 1973.

An example of multiple retirement was provided by a woman who left a hospital position as a child psychologist in 1949 when she married and moved to a new location. The following year she had a one-day-a-week job, also as a psychologist, which she left when she became pregnant. In 1953, after she had given birth to her second child, she took a half-time job in the same field because she "could not afford household help without working part-time." The family moved again the next year and she stayed out of the labor force until 1966.

There were several similar cases, some involving an exit, followed by a return to part-time work and then another exit, usually for a longer period; others consisting of a change from full- to part-time or free-lance work before a prolonged departure from the labor force. The first of these patterns appears to have been the result of a realization that return was premature and could not be handled satisfactorily. The second was more typical of women who were reluctant to completely detach themselves from work and hoped in vain that part-time work would provide a modus operandi whereby they could maintain their ties to work rather than cut them. Most reentrants to the labor force after 1962 were either women who had made clean breaks from employment at some time before 1963, or those who had made unsuccessful attempts to continue or resume work before 1963.

Almost half (47 percent) of the returnees had had five to nine years of work experience prior to their last departure from the labor force; about one-quarter had worked only two to four years; the pre-1963 employment experience of the remainder had ranged from 10 to 17 years.

Three out of five of the reentrants to work after 1962 had withdrawn from the labor force ten or more years prior to their return; one-quarter of this group had been absent for at least 15 years. Only seven percent of the reentrants had been out of the labor force for as long as 20 years.

The master's was the highest degree in 1963 of about four out of five women who had left the labor force for homemaking and who later returned to work. Almost a third of all M.A.'s in the liberal arts had exited from the labor force prior to 1963. Among reentrants were 57 percent of all M.A.'s in the social sciences, alone. In no other field of study, with the exceptions of journalism and business, did reentrants represent more than 40 percent of the total.

For the most part, the jobs held by reentrants at the time of their exit from the labor force were in occupational fields that were similar to the subjects they had studied in graduate school. While hardly any exiters had achieved a position on or near the upper rungs of the career ladder, many had made some progress prior to quitting employment, and had achieved a certain amount of seniority in their occupations. These included women in such occupations as teacher below the college level; newspaper reporter; government economist; foreign affairs analyst; biostatistician; attorney; biochemist; accountant and social worker. A few reentrants never had been employed after receiving their graduate degrees, although they had some prior work experience; others had been underemployed in relation to their educational attainment. The underemployed included a substitute teacher with a master's in social work; a two-hour-a-week math tutor with an M.A.; a legal secretary and a bookkeeper both with graduate degrees in accounting; and a part-time science librarian with a Ph.D. Three women had left faculty positions in higher education, but none of them had a doctorate and therefore could not contemplate promotion.

Many of the women who had temporarily retired from the labor force and who had returned to work between 1963 and 1974 were in occupations where the need to remain *au courant* with technological or other developments or new methodologies is not as essential as in others. These included schoolteaching, social work, library science, and journalism. This is not to suggest that changes may not have occurred in these fields during this period, but that work that essentially utilizes the basic competencies acquired in graduate training can be performed adequately, and any updating can be easily accomplished on the job. In addition, many such professions are female dominated occupations in which periodicity of employment is built into the employment structure and/or there is a relatively flat hierarchy. It is easier to leave and return to these fields without too great a cost in terms of progress—although loss of seniority and income are inevitable.

The women with M.A.'s and ABD's in the arts and sciences, who had a large representation among the reentrants, were different from the foregoing group insofar as their educational status had a less distinct vocational cast. Their degrees might have placed them in preferred positions to compete for a variety of jobs with holders of the baccalaureate, but they were likely to be at a disadvantage in relation to women with doctorates or with master's degrees in professional fields. In academe, the Master of Arts is generally viewed as a way station to the doctorate and, when that terminus is not reached, it often leaves an individual vocationally high and dry. Although a few of these women had left jobs that held possibilities of upward mobility, most had either a succession of miscellaneous jobs, many of which had only a tenuous relation to their educational qualifications, or they had held one position of fairly long standing but of little promise.

Women who did not leave the labor force when they had children were more likely to have been in positions that encouraged them to believe that further advancement would be their lot. Most of those with Ph.D.'s were employed in higher education when their children arrived and many continued working without interruption. For example, a Ph.D. in history joined a university faculty after completing graduate school in 1948 and continued teaching through the births of two children in 1958 and 1961. In 1963, she was an associate professor, and by 1974 she was chairman of her department.

A lawyer stopped working for one year when she had her first child in 1948, but did not discontinue practicing when her second child was born in 1950. In 1963, she was working both in her own legal practice and as an assistant attorney general, and by 1974 she had become a judge.

A physician with four children never ceased working. Her first two children were born during her internship and residency in 1951 and 1953; her last two in 1957 and 1960. After that she became an associate in her specialty at a VA hospital. By 1963, she was a department chairman at a large general hospital, a position she maintained through 1974.

While the status of one's career at the time of marriage and, more particularly, of childbirth appears to have had a strong influence upon a respondent's decision to abandon her work role, the nature of her training appears to have had an even greater impact upon her behavior at that stage of her life. Women with lengthy and intensive graduate and professional preparation were far more reluctant to abandon the fruits of their labor than those who had been involved in less rigorous educational programs, probably because the former women were much more likely to have obtained the kind of work opportunities they had anticipated and because the cost of temporary retirement is often high— not only in terms of lost earnings, but also in terms of stale skills and outdated knowledge.

Yet, it is impossible to ignore the possibility that the decision to leave the work force had its basis in attitudes formed prior to graduate school. No woman is likely to embark upon training for a field that requires constant dedication to work if she is inclined to feel that full-time child care must take precedence over career goals. Some women may change their minds about this issue as they proceed in school and work; there were mothers with master's degrees who worked steadily and those with doctorates and first professional degrees who did not. But generally, despite the implied commitment we have ascribed to graduate education, the respondents' careers took many courses, only one of which was straight and unimpeded.

The median age of reentrants after 1962 was 42 years. Only one woman returned to work after the age of 49. The reentry employment of more than three out of five was part-time, and most entered the same occupational field that they had left prior to 1963.

Instances of changed occupations include college instructors who returned to work as schoolteachers; a former reporter who reentered the labor force as a high school English teacher; a government administrative assistant who resumed work as a public relations copywriter; and a woman who left secretarial work and later became a high school commercial teacher. Many of these changes were not too far removed from the women's original occupations. In most cases, radical change involved further education.

Almost half the reentry jobs were in government; a third were in non-profit institutions; 12 percent were in profit-making organizations; and the remaining 7 percent of the reentrants were self-employed. Two out of five of the reentrants employed by the government were in higher education and approximately one-third were in schools below the college level. Thus, while government was the principal employer of the returnees, it was primarily government as represented by public educational institutions, that is, state, county, or local government.

The job setting of nearly one-third of the reentrants was public or private higher education. Social agencies were the next most common places of reentry work, and these, along with hospitals, membership organizations and the like, comprised 26 percent of the total reentry settings. The remaining reentry jobs were scattered among public administrative agencies, business or professional firms, and self-employment.

Teaching was the principal job activity of the largest group of returnees (43 percent). Most of the teachers were either college instructors in the humanities or were teaching miscellaneous subjects in schools below the college level. The major job functions of the remaining returnees were as follows, in order of frequency: professional service (17 percent), writing and editing (13 percent), research (11 percent), administration (9 percent), and clerical (7 percent).

More than three-quarters of the reentrants initially obtained staff positions; only five women (11 percent) obtained supervisory jobs. The latter included marketing director for a book publisher; director of a federal cultural program; two casework supervisors; and a community college department head. Three women returned as self-employed professionals; a free-lance newspaper writer; an antiques dealer; and a piano teacher.

The 13 returnees whose initial reentry jobs were in academe were primarily hired as instructors or lecturers (39 percent) or in research or administration (31 percent). Only two women entered regular faculty positions above the level of assistant professor (another woman became a part-time adjunct professor). One was a woman with an ABD in English and nine years of varied employment prior to 1960, primarily teaching at higher and lower levels and in personnel work, who was hired by a community college as an associate professor and director of English as a second language. The other was a Ph.D. in the physical sciences who was hired by a foreign university as an associate professor.

There were two other Ph.D.'s among the returnees. One earned her degree in 1966, thereupon becoming an assistant professor of history at a coordinate woman's college of a state university where she had previously served as an instructor between 1953 and 1961. In her case it had not been family responsibilities that caused her to leave the labor force since she had worked part-time despite the presence of three young children. Rather it was the relief from many of those responsibilities when her youngest child entered first grade that persuaded her to abandon her part-time employment for full-time study.

In the other instance, a woman who had earned a master's in physics in the late 1940s and had acquired a Ph.D. in 1970, five years after the start of her doctoral studies, reentered the labor force as a part-time teaching fellow that spring and became a visiting part-time instructor at a four year college in the fall.

Seven of the 13 reentrants who became employed in academe had not proceeded beyond the master's degree. Five of these women were hired as junior or senior college instructors, primarily as adjunct and/or part-time faculty; one became a research assistant, and the other a part-time psychologist in a medical school.

As noted earlier, 34 of the 46 reentrants to the labor force after 1962 were working in 1974. Over one-third of the 34 had been back in the labor force for more than five years. Thus, in most cases, there had been sufficient work experience to permit an analysis of renewed employment histories.

The reentrants tended to increase their hours of work as their years of employment lengthened. The number of part-time workers dropped from 21 to 14 and the working hours of four of the latter had increased. There were few changes in job setting between the reentry position and 1974; most of the women remained in the same type of workplace and with the same class of employer. Among those who did change settings after reentry were an accountant who had been initially self-employed and was working in the same capacity for a business firm in 1974; a school librarian who later switched to work in a public library; a high school English teacher who became a college journalism instructor for a short while and was a free-lance journalist in 1974; and an eighth-grade English teacher who left this job when her husband was relocated, but later took a part-time teaching position in a job training program.

In most instances, the 1974 occupational fields of reentrants were the same as their reentry occupations. No worker who was not in the labor force in 1963 was in a current occupation that was radically different from her first reentry occupation.

Although extended absence from the labor force tended to place reentrants at a disadvantage relative to women who had taken little or no time out from work, there were exceptional cases. Possibly the most striking illustration of a returnee who reentered the work force after 1962 and proceeded to move rapidly upward is that of a woman with an M.S. in journalism who had nine years of work experience, primarily in the federal government, prior to leaving the work force in 1955, when her husband changed jobs and left Washington. In 1964 when she resumed employment because of financial need arising from an impending divorce, she had three children, aged 6, 10, and 12. The rest of her story has been pieced together from her own words:

This [divorce] propelled me back into a career sooner than I would have planned. And the need to provide most of the support for my family motivated me to make the most of my talents and experience. My M.S. from Columbia and my nine years of experience in Washington over-qualified me for most available positions. I knew I would have to undergo some retraining for the job market. And I knew I did not want to commute. It took from January until May 1964 for me to find my first job teaching in N—— [a neighboring suburb]. It paid all of $125 a week. And when I began working as a free lancer on PR accounts for a local ad agency, I was paid $2.50 an hour or about $75.00 a week for 30 hours of work. Thirty dollars of that went to a lovely grandmother-type I was fortunate to find to keep things going at home. Both of us needed more money and that led to the R—— job [an electronics manufacturer].

Perhaps I should have asked more than $7,500 a year in 1965 to write and edit (and do photography for) the R—— magazine. It was only a little more than I had earned nine years before; I failed to allow for inflation. But it got me "in." And once inside the working world, there was opportunity for growth. Within a year I was asked to write trade publicity and soon consumer publicity. In a major reorganization by the parent company, my boss was terminated and I was given his job. The office was small [and] this forced—or allowed—me to learn public relations by doing almost every aspect of it myself. I produced newspaper columns of publicity easily worth a million dollars a year if measured in advertising dollars.

I was very happy at R—— and I was given almost free rein to "do my thing." Salary increases, while regular, were modest. When I was given full responsibility for the company's public relations, I thought I would be paid at least $10,000. But they gave me a healthy 15% increase instead, which brought the total to something over $9,000, about half of the $18,000 my predecessor had been earning.

During the winter of 1972, at a meeting, I asked the vice-president of Human Resources of our parent company how many women he had interviewed for the position of vice-president. And he said, "None. On the other hand, no one has presented herself." I decided the next day to "present myself" for the position of Director of Public Relations for R__, a step up the ladder that didn't exist. I pulled together my qualifications and my achievements, sent them to my boss with copies to Personnel, the President, and the VP from the parent company . . . and never heard one word from anybody! A woman friend in the personnel office told me later that the men had a good chuckle over it: I had the top PR job, was doing a good job, what more did I want? I was so dumbstruck by their apparent unwillingness to discuss my career aspirations that I failed to follow up the memo.

The next summer I chanced to tell this tale to T__ who was writing a book about women in business. She asked for my resumé, so I pulled out the above memo and sent it along. In September [1973] she called to say she had recommended me for the top PR position at G__ a textile manufacturer. When she said the salary range was $35,000 to $50,000 I couldn't believe it. I decided that at least I could go for interviews.

So I met all the top executives and looked over the town. To my surprise, the people matched the high caliber individuals I felt so comfortable with at R__. The business was three times as large as R__ and new responsibilities would really stretch me. But I knew I could handle them. If G__ made me an offer I could comfortably accept. If they didn't, I still had R__.

Well, the offer came—an offer I couldn't refuse: $35,000 to start, more than double what I was making. My friends at R__ were pleased for me and even paid me the honor of saying they might have tried to match $25,000, but $35,000 was more than all but the President and Vice-President were making.

G__ has been good to me. I've had two salary increases and am due for another. I work 60 hours a week easily and I travel a great deal, and this I like. I'm one of two female representatives in the PR section of the industry's trade association. I supervise the preparation and dissemination of all press releases and oversee publication of the company newspaper. So life has come almost full circle in the past ten years. From the depths of despair, I've come to sitting on top of the world.

Few respondents, regardless of the course they took, provided so detailed a report of their career progress. Other women also had top jobs, but only a handful of those who had taken extended absences from the labor force came close to matching this woman's performance over so short a span of time. She provides an extreme example of careers that received their initial impetus from the dissolution of a marriage.

The 1974 earnings distribution of reentrants differed considerably from that of women who had been in the work force in 1963. At the two upper ranges, the percentages of 1963 workers with earnings of $30,000 or more, and of those earning a minimum of $20,000, were triple those of reentrants (7 percent and 18 percent, respectively). At the bottom, the proportion of reentrants who earned under $12,500 (44 percent) was four times higher than that of other workers. Much of this difference is due to differences in working time, part-time workers being one-and-a-half times more prevalent among reentrants. When the earnings of reentrants working full time were compared with those of women who were full-time workers in both years, the proportion of the latter earning $20,000 or more (62 percent) was two and a half times that of reentrants. Recent returnees obviously had a way to go in trying to catch up with women with lengthier employment experience.

Non-workers

Fifty-three respondents were not employed in 1974. These included 16 women who had retired upon becoming eligible for benefits or because of disability; five non-retirees who had been employed in 1963; 12 women who had not been employed in 1963 but who worked at some later period; and 20 women who were out of the labor force throughout the entire period between January 1963 and December 1974.

The women who had retired for reasons other than health had been in top jobs in their fields when they left the labor force: they included four full professors at state universities; two supervisory librarians; a social service administrator; a school district director of instruction; a physician who had been a regional director of a state health department; and a deputy director of an office in the federal government. Most of the retired women had spent all of their adult lives in the work force; seven of the ten had never married and none had children.

There were also three retirees who were part-time workers in 1974: a college librarian who continued working part-time, a former college department chairman serving elsewhere as a visiting professor, and an ex-associate professor of English who spent four hours a week as a librarian.

Not all of the retired women were over the age of 65. Six out of the 13 (workers and non-workers) were below the age of 65. These were primarily employees of government agencies or other public non-academic institutions who were eligible for retirement after a specific number of years of employment. In addition to the three employed retirees were three other non-retired workers aged 65 years or older.

The women who were forced to retire for reasons of health also had reached top positions. Among them were a former hospital director, a university department chairman, and college professors.

The five non-retirees who had been employed at the start of 1963 but not at the end of 1974 gave assorted reasons: job termination; husband's job relocation; full-time study; an employer move; an employer closing. The two women who lost their jobs because of the last two circumstances had been out of work for only a short time. The student was the chemist who had decided to attend library school. Job termination applied to the director of a day-care training project who was 62 years old in 1974 and was interested in obtaining part-time employment.

The last of this group had an exceedingly diversified work history. Between 1963 and 1974 she had seven jobs primarily as a part-time modern language instructor at three colleges where she had been hired to fill in for absent faculty. She had also tutored privately and had done translations, her last assignment having been completed in 1972. The mother of four children over 17, she had been widowed in 1974. She was seeking part-time employment but said, "If the emphasis is on *preference*, I would *prefer* not to have to undertake any paid employment. Present situation makes it imperative to try to do so."

The majority of non-workers in both 1963 and 1974 who had been in the labor force at some time between those dates, had left work voluntarily after less than three years of employment. Their reasons included: preference for volunteer work; a husband's job move or sabbatical; and family responsibilities. Some explained their decisions. A respondent had left a one-year position as visiting associate professor of law at a university in the southwest in 1970 because she "didn't enjoy the low caliber of students and fellow teachers. Wasn't worth my time. I took the position because I was intrigued with the idea of teaching law in the manner I was exposed to from the greats at Columbia Law School. Boy did I bomb!" She was not regularly employed in 1974 but she occasionally served as a part-time consultant.

A former college lecturer taught history in high school for one year—1965–66—but left because of "inadequate domestic help—at any price!" A respondent with an M.S. in mathematics tutored at the eighth-grade level for one semester. She noted that "except for tutoring I no longer feel qualified for interesting employment."

There were also reentrants with longer spells of employment after their return who were not employed in 1974. For example, in 1974, a social worker and mother of a 17 year old, who had been intermittently employed throughout the sixties and early seventies

moved to accommodate husband and new locale too far to job sites. Working at home not feasible as too remote. Also, small earnings, on top of husband's salary, wiped out by income tax. Also, am well known in community as husband is a judge and am criticized for competing with young therapists for dollars they are desperate for. Also, I'm tired and somewhat demoralized! Would like to work, but have to be on tap for family emergencies even tho' these are not frequent.

A social scientist who had worked part-time for several periods from 1963 to 1971 lamented:

> I really thought that at this stage of my life—with my children 15 and 18—I would be at work not merely part-time, but easily into virtual full-time employment in my field of training. I am quite disappointed to find that health can be such a disrupter of plans! I have developed some problems which leave me with limited energy so I seriously doubt I could manage paid employment in the near future—even on a half-time basis. Luckily, my financial situation is such that I do not *have* to work so I can use my limited energy resources for myself, my husband and my children—but I do hope to be at work again!

Three reentrants had lost their last jobs: a visiting college instructor, a teacher, and a social researcher. The first two were actively seeking employment in 1974; the last woman had developed health problems and was currently unable to work. Reentrants who had voluntarily left jobs after a period of employment were not necessarily averse to reemployment. In fact, one of them indicated that, after 1974, she returned to the employer she had left in 1971, the year she decided to concentrate upon political campaigning as an unpaid volunteer.

Child care responsibilities were cited most frequently as the explanation for not working at all between 1963 and 1974; of the 20 respondents who had been out of the labor force during these years, this reason was noted by 14. Such responsibilities, in conjunction with a preference for other activities—noted by 13 of the 20—overshadowed all other reasons given for lack of gainful employment during this period. Only five women claimed that they were complying with their husbands' preference, and very few cited lack of jobs, demands of elderly family members, poor health, or retirement (noted by one premature retiree).

Citation of child care as the preeminent reason for lack of recent employment was an echo of the past, since such responsibilities caused most of the mothers to decide to take time off from their careers. The majority, however, had returned to the labor force by 1974. Of the 14 women who gave child care obligations as a reason for not working between 1963 and 1974, ten had pre-school children during part of this period, but virtually all of these children had come of school age before 1974.

The second most common reason for absence from gainful employment—personal preference—usually was linked with child care. Hence, it seems reasonable to infer that child care often was the initial stimulus for an absence from paid work that became sufficiently satisfying to discourage the thought of a return to the labor force.

Among other reasons for a prolonged period at home was that of a 53-year-old librarian who lived in a college community and had not worked for 25 years.

Attempted to secure full or part-time work in both 1964 and 1970 as professional librarian but found that my paid work experience (1943–49) was not considered recent enough. Have not given up thought of working in the field, however. Hope for more opportunities when we move to another area after husband's retirement. [He was in his late fifties.]

With a few exceptions, the women who were not employed after 1962 had relatively short work histories and had not abandoned jobs that were anywhere close to the top. A far higher proportion (75 percent) had master's degrees than of all respondents (48 percent) and, while ex-students in all subject fields, except medicine and the sciences, were represented, librarians predominated (a quarter of the total; a third of the master's). While this has little significance in view of the small size of the group, it points up the popularity of the library degree as a contingency credential.*

There were four doctorates and one ABD among the women who had not been employed between 1963 and 1974. Two of the doctorates had prolonged absences from work for reasons of health and both were in their sixties. A third woman had 20 years of work experience primarily as a teacher of physiology, but she stopped work in 1961 when her husband relocated his legal practice. At the time she exited, her two children were 11 and 3 years old. Her reasons for her continuing absence from the labor force follow:

I feel that I made a significant contribution 1) to my students as a teacher, 2) to my chosen field, as a researcher and an editor, and 3) to the status of women in my field, by my example. I stayed in my field so long as I really enjoyed it. But there were many other things I wanted to do and I couldn't do justice to a career and do all these other things, too. I feel very fortunate to have contributed significantly to the education of hundreds of students, to have enjoyed a very satisfying career, to have a great family and still have had the satisfaction of using my talents and abilities in several other areas, too. And I'm still enjoying my life. . . .

Obviously, she thought that she had had the best of two possible worlds—a design for living that is likely to be envied by many males as well as females. What she had done was to reverse the pattern of many of her peers: her career came before, not after, concentration on other concerns. While she seemed deeply satisfied with her decision, she had

---

*This may be a presumption of the past, however, since new technologies have caused major changes in library science that may bar return without retraining.

left the labor force when she was a part-time assistant professor so that, in objective terms, she had not approached the peak of her profession.

The fourth Ph.D. without gainful employment during this period was a social scientist who had achieved distinction in her field despite only minimal paid work experience. She had primarily engaged in full-time independent research and writing, and had received a small intermittent income from occasional consultation and royalties. She was childless and had often collaborated with her husband who was in the same field. Among her comments about her career were the following:

> We have sufficient income from my husband's salary. If I took a paid full-time job I would have obligations that would interfere with my research, writing, and training programs. The fact that I have chosen not to take a salaried job gives me flexibility and the opportunity to take on obligations that interest me. I do not think that a woman must earn a salary in order to be "respectable." The fact that I am unpaid has not affected my professional status and has given me a freedom that would not be possible otherwise. Consequently, I'm not particularly sympathetic to couples who insist that both must have salaried jobs unless there is a financial problem of an unusual type.

In essence, this is a woman who has had all the trappings of a successful career, except monetary rewards. She was highly productive, having been the author, co-author, translator and editor of several books, as well as the writer of numerous articles, and she had received awards in recognition of her contributions to her field. Her career is an illustration, albeit an extreme one, of deceptions that can result from the customary method of defining labor force participation. There are many women, including other respondents, who perform unpaid professional work, but for most it is a temporary expedient while simultaneously fulfilling family obligations. Nevertheless, it may be a mistake to conclude that this type of career is so aberrant as to have no general relevance. Kahane suggests, on the contrary, that it may be increasing in frequency:

> The growing numbers of educated persons with interests relating to their education, the tight labor market for professonal activities and the sometime disaffection of persons for career ladders as the appropriate environment for doing their serious work combine in a way to reinforce the need to think more thoroughly about the implications of a possible disjunction between jobs and all of the kinds of unpaid work that men and women do:[2]

Also of note in this respect are the remarks of a professor's wife who left the labor force in 1960 after seven years of employment in university libraries. She had cited both child care and her husband's preference as the reason for not working thereafter.

> It all depends on your husband and what his attitudes and actions are . . . I have found that the assistance I give him in his writing, editing and teaching are very satisfying for me. Most people do not know that I am thus "employed" however, so I get no recognition for it. Nowadays a woman does not rate very high (except with her family) for an arrangement like mine. If recognition is important, better arrange to receive a salary.

Another woman with an M.A. in English who had worked full-time in the past three years on unpaid research and volunteer work commented that she had "contributed in many indirect ways to my husband's recognition as an outstanding environmentalist." And an M.S.W. with minimal paid work experience was the president of the board of directors of a social service agency to which she devoted 30 hours a week. She remarked: "My husband's work [playwright and producer] is such that my working would have been a strain. It was *my* decision not to work and I have not regretted it so far." Many of the remaining long-term non-employed were also spending some amount of time volunteering, taking courses, or engaging in creative arts.

About half of the women with master's degrees who had not been paid workers in recent years expressed the desire to return to work, primarily to part-time or free-lance employment. A former librarian who wanted part-time work remarked: "If I suddenly received an offer of employment, I would be overjoyed to accept it. Chronological age and lack of recent experience are deterrents." A journalist who had not been employed since 1962 commented:

> Would like to do a bit of journalism, but not keep hours; however, this desire is tenuous enough that I do not actually follow up and seek such employment. Having sunk into middle-aged comfort, I find I do not think "career" very often or very strongly. If there were greater need for me to participate in earning family income, I can imagine becoming motivated and enjoying working again.

If non-retired respondents who were not working in 1974 but who expressed an intent or desire to resume employment actually realized this goal, the labor force participation rate of the respondents (given continuing work participation of the remainder) would be at least ten points higher than the current rate of 77 percent. Information post-dating December 1974 indicates that some of these women had already obtained employment, but these were women with relatively recent work experience. Several of the women who had hopes of returning to paid work had been out of the labor force for more than 20 years. Whether they could obtain jobs without retraining is moot, especially at a time when the supply of highly qualified workers exceeds the demand in many of their occupational fields.

Summary

Most of the respondents had some volunteer experience and many had devoted considerable amounts of time to this type of activity, particularly those who had spent periods out of the labor force. While resumption of employment usually resulted in a decrease of volunteer involvement, it did not always signify abandonment of such interests, and some mothers substituted a heightened volunteer commitment for paid work as their children grew older.

Reentrants to the labor force who had engaged in volunteer work while out of the labor force usually felt that it had made a positive contribution to their resumed careers. Most commonly, this contribution was in the form of improved personal growth and self-confidence; for many women, volunteer experience also had served to maintain, improve or develop their career skills.

Several respondents pursued additional studies between 1963 and 1974, but relatively few had undertaken degree programs. Instead, they had taken work-related courses primarily in order to update skills, enhance promotional opportunities, or to meet employer requirements.

Most reentrants to the labor force after 1962 did not return to school prior to resuming employment, presumably because their qualifications and early work experience were sufficient to enable them to obtain acceptable jobs. The reentry job search was usually facilitated by personal contacts; professional women seem to know the right people and therefore are in a preferred position to secure the right positions.

Very few job exiters before 1963 had been well advanced in the occupational hierarchy when they withdrew from the labor force, although many had achieved a fair amount of seniority. The exit jobs of a large number had been in predominantly female professions in which flexibility of labor force participation is not uncommon.

Mothers who did not exit from the labor force were more likely to have been in positions with substantial potential for upward mobility when their first child was born than were those who left their jobs at that time.

The majority of returnees to the labor force between 1963 and 1974 were women in their early forties whose first reentry employment consisted of a part-time job in their previous occupation. As time passed, they tended to increase their hours of work so that, by 1974, most employed reentrants were working full-time. However, their earnings distribution did not approach that of respondents who had been in the work force in January 1963.

Non-workers in 1974 were not employed for a variety of reasons including retirement, ill health, job termination, relocation and personal preference. Some of these women had been employed in 1963; others were reentrants who had voluntarily or involuntarily reexited; still others had not engaged in any paid work between 1963 and 1974. The women with extended absences from the labor force primarily attributed their non-work status to child care responsibilities. Most of this group had minimal work experience after completing their education.

A few non-workers had achieved most of the concomitants of a professional career save financial compensation. The possibility of accomplishment in an independent non-market career; as a husband's unpaid partner; or as a full-time volunteer is probably confined to women with superior qualifications and high family income. Such women must also be willing to accept non-monetary tokens of recognition for their work or, in some cases, no concrete recognition at all. It is doubtful whether this type of behavior will be emulated with any frequency in the future since it is likely to be in conflict with the feminist goal of achieving equal footing with men.

Notes

1. Marnie W. Mueller, "Economic Determinants of Volunteer Work by Women," *Signs*, I, 2 (Winter, 1975), p. 334.

2. Hilda Kahne, "Economic Perspectives on the Roles of Women in the American Economy," *Journal of Economic Literature*, XIII, 4 (December 1975), p. 1277.

7] OCCUPATIONAL ACHIEVEMENT

The preceding chapters have examined distinct aspects of the respondents' employment. It is the aim of this chapter to present appraisals of the women's overall occupational achievement based upon the success attained within specific fields of work. These assessments provide a view of the career progress of women with different work histories and avoid comparisons among occupations. The use of objective evaluations permits judgments to be made about the degree to which these highly qualified women have been able to fulfill their early promise.

Six criteria were utilized to estimate each respondent's career: earnings, rank or job title, job responsibilities, professional reputation, quality of employing institution, and productivity. This information was derived from the respondents' job descriptions and other data in their questionnaires. Not in every case was each criterion available or relevant to a respondent's job, but there were sufficient data to permit evaluations of the achievement of all respondents with a body of recent work experience. The standards used were similar to those employed in the prior study. The following extract from *Life Styles of Educated Women* provides a detailed example of how one standard, earnings, was handled:

> In establishing cut-off points for a fourfold category scheme consisting of high, good, fair, and low achievement levels, we took into account differences in salary levels in various types of employing institutions, such as

government and business and differences in prestige of employing institutions. For example, a full professorship at a small teachers' college has less prestige than an associate professorship at a major university. Furthermore, different vocations command different rewards. A successful librarian rarely receives the same salary as a successful lawyer.[1]

As a general rule, assignment to an achievement level was based upon the importance, responsibility, and rewards associated with the job, in light of hierarchical structures and income ranges within different occupations and employment settings. Certain criteria were applied only when relevant to a particular job, e.g., publications in academic occupations.

Women whose achievement was judged to be high were employed in superior positions in their occupations and received commensurate earnings. Those whose achievement was rated as good had made progress in their occupations but their employment status lacked certain of the attributes of maximum achievement. Fair achievers were making use of their training in subordinate positions, and women whose achievement was judged to be poor were engaged in work below the level of competence associated with their educational background.

Obviously, any procedure that involves assessing performance is subject to grader bias, but this possibility was minimized by having two independent appraisals of the progress of each respondent, followed by reevaluation in instances of disagreement.

To provide a better understanding of the achievement classifications, some illustrations of women placed in various categories and of changes over time are presented below.

Among respondents at the high level was a physician and chairman of the department of medicine at a university medical center whose annual salary was more than $30,000; a professor of physics at the main campus of a large state university whose earnings were between $20,000 and $29,999 a year; and the director of volunteers and communications at a community hospital in a small city who described herself as being "responsible for services of 350 volunteers; operation of switchboard, info desk, mailroom, coffee and giftshop; editor of hospital newspaper and supervisor of 22 employees." Her salary was in the $15,000 to $19,999 range.

Respondents whose achievement was estimated as "good" included an associate professor of sociology at a territorial university whose earnings were between $15,000 and $20,000; a managing editor of an encyclopedia whose salary was between $12,500 and $15,000; and a supervisor of paraprofessional social workers for a county health department who earned $12,000 a year.

The "fair" category included a part-time associate professor of mathematics at a state university who received a salary in the $7,500-

$10,000 range; a part-time caseworker earning between $7,500 and $10,000 yearly; and a physician, employed part-time by an insurance company, whose annual salary was somewhere between $15,000 and $20,000.

A part-time librarian in a community facility who received $2,500 to $5,000 was in the "low" category; as was a woman who spent an average of 4 to 6 hours weekly as a member of the board of advisers of a charitable trust fund for which she received between $5,000 and $7,500 per annum; and a free-lance newspaper article writer whose annual income from her work was under $2,500.

Examples of changes in achievement level between 1963 and 1974 include a respondent whose self-employment as a part-time piano teacher with a weekly income of approximately $18 was deemed "low" in 1963 who had become a "fair" achiever in 1974 as an assistant professor of English at a state college where she was earning between $12,500 and $15,000 a year. A health education consultant for the U.S. Public Health Service who had an annual salary of $10,000 in 1963 and was given a "good" achievement rating had risen to the top level by 1974 as a health education adviser in the same agency. Her earnings were in the $20,000 to $30,000 range.

The non-worker in 1963 who reentered the labor force in 1964 after a hiatus of nine years and by 1974 was the director of public relations for a major corporation at an annual salary of more than $30,000 was in the high achievement category. A teacher-librarian in a junior high school whose salary was $9,100 per annum in 1963 was placed in the fair achievement level for that year. Her status rose to the high level in 1974 because she had become head school district librarian and media specialist, earning between $15,000 and $20,000 a year. A similar rise from "fair" to "high" achiever was exemplified by an attorney who was a part-time worker on the legal staff of a non-profit agency paid on the basis of $3.85 an hour in 1963, and in 1974 was a partner in a major law firm, earning more than $30,000 annually.

One respondent who remained with the same employer, a state college, and had a fair achievement rating in 1963 as an assistant professor of music education, earning $7,300, was at the "good" level in 1974 since she had become an associate professor with various supervisory responsibilities and was earning between $15,000 and $20,000 annually.

An overview of the respondents' achievement in 1963 and 1974 is shown in Table 7.1

There was a strong advance in occupational achievement between January 1963 and December 1974; the proportion of high achievers rose by more than 200 percent. While more than half of the women were classified as fair or low achievers in 1963, half were in the highest category alone in 1974. In addition, the accomplishments of more

Table 7.1   Achievement Levels 1963 and 1974[a]

	1963	1974
Achievement Level	Percent	Percent
High	16	50
Good	31	32
Fair	36	12
Low	17	6
Total percent	100	100
Total number	(168)	(194)
Not appropriate	(58)	(32)

[a] Excludes 58 non-workers in 1963 and 32 in 1974 who had insufficient work experience to permit assessment. Retirees were evaluated on the basis of their last regular employment.

women were evaluated in 1974 than in 1963 because of the larger number who had amassed an appraisable amount of employment by 1974.

Among the 168 women whose achievement was assessed in 1963, about 30 percent were at the same level in both survey years and in only two cases was there a regression to a lower level by 1974. Improvements in achievement were related to the 1963 level of accomplishment. Thus, four out of five respondents who were classified as good achievers in 1963 were at the high achievement level in 1974, but only one out of 28 women who were in the lowest classification in 1963 had reached the top level by 1974 (Table 7.2).

Of special interest is the 1974 achievement of women who had too short a work history to warrant evaluation of achievement in 1963 but who had acquired sufficient subsequent work experience to permit assessment in 1974. These women were generally more successful by 1974 than those employed in both years who had a low level of achievement in 1963. This finding suggests that a longer worklife, by itself, is no guarantee of occupational progress. A reentrant, through perseverance, talent or luck, separately or in combination, was sometimes able to surpass the accomplishment of a woman with more work experience, who either may have deliberately chosen a long-standing peripheral attachment to the work force or who may have been unable to overcome obstacles to career progress.

Despite adjustments for income differentials among occupations, there was a strong positive correlation between earnings and achievement which is shown in Table 7.3.

The table excludes 24 respondents whose achievement levels are included on other tabulations; while they had accumulated sufficient

Table 7.2   Achievement Level 1974 by Achievement Level 1963

	Achievement 1963 (percent)				
Achievement 1974	High	Good	Fair	Low	Minimal Work
High	93	79	46	4	9
Good	7	21	42	36	53
Fair	—	—	12	36	22
Low	—	—	—	24	16
Total percent	100	100	100	100	100

Number = 194
Achievement not rated 1974 = 32

work experience to permit evaluation, they were not employed in 1974. These included 13 retirees for age, three of whom were employed part-time in 1974 but who were judged on the basis of their pre-retirement position; and 11 other women who were not working in 1974 for various reasons but who had lengthy careers which warranted consideration. More than half of these women were in the high achievement category; a third were good achievers; and the remainder were placed at the low level. Most of the retirees were in the top group.

Only about 7 percent of the women who earned less than $15,000 in 1974 were assessed as high achievers, in contrast to 100 percent of the respondents earning $30,000 or more. Nevertheless, the fact that the estimate of some women's achievement was above or below the norm for their earnings range indicates that while earnings played a major role in judging achievement, other factors were also influential.

Two principal determinants of the respondents' occupational

Table 7.3   Achievement Level by 1974 Earnings[a]

	1974 Earnings (percent)				
Achievement Level, 1974	under $12,500	$12,500-$14,999	$15,000-$19,999	$20,000-$29,999	$30,000 or over
High	9	5	30	78	100
Good	15	71	67	22	—
Fair	52	24	3	—	—
Low	24	—	—	—	—
Total percent	100	100	100	100	100
Total number	(33)	(21)	(36)	(49)	(31)

[a]Non-earners in 1974 = 56.

Table 7.4   Achievement Level 1974[a] by Proportion of Years with Work Experience and Proportion of Full-Time, Full-Year Work Experience, B.A.-1974

Achievement Level 1974	% years worked			% years worked full-time, full-year		
	100	76-99	less than 76	100	76-99	less than 76
High	70	54	18	74	65	27
Good	28	28	44	26	27	40
Fair	1	13	25	—	6	22
Low	1	5	13	—	2	11
Total percent	100	100	100	100	100	100
Total number =	(76)	(63)	(55)	(43)	(63)	(88)
Not appropriate = 32						

[a]Excludes respondents without achievement ratings—1974.

achievement were the duration and continuity of labor force participation. Table 7.4 shows how the proportion of adult years in the work force and of full-time, full-year work experience were associated with the level of career achievement.

Those respondents who had worked full-time full-year for 100 percent of their adult lives included the largest proportion of high achievers. Conversely, the group that had spent the smallest proportion of their lives in the labor force, with some amount of work experience in three-quarters or fewer of the years after college, included the smallest proportion of high achievers (18 percent). The achievement of every continuous full-time worker was good or high; almost two out of five of the women with the most discontinuous work experience were fair or low achievers. The probability that a continuous worker would reach a high level of occupational achievement was about four times greater than that of a woman who had been employed for some period in 75 percent or fewer of her adult years.

Women of high achievement were the least likely to have spent any time in part-time employment (not shown). In fact, the lower one's achievement level, the more extensive her part-time work experience. Nevertheless, almost 30 percent of the high achievers had spent some of their lives working part-time but, in the majority of instances, their years of part-time employment comprised less than 20 percent of their total worklives.

Continuity of employment prior to 1963 was closely related to 1974 achievement. Seven out of ten of the women who had worked in every year prior to 1963 and at least 50 percent of the years thereafter were high achievers by the end of the latter period, but fewer than two out of five of those with proportionately less work experience in the earlier period had similar ratings in 1974, even if they had been continuously employed after 1963. This should not be interpreted to mean that broken early patterns of employment usually barred access to the top, but that it took a fair amount of time to accumulate sufficient experience in resumed careers to retrieve lost standing resulting from career neglect.

In addition to the impact of employment stability upon achievement, total years in the work force also were associated with successful careers. For example, the proportion of high achievers among women who had work experience in more than 20 of the years after college (62 percent) was more than double the rate of high achievers among those who spent fewer years in the work force (28 percent). A comparison of full-year, full-time employment reveals a similar difference: 69 percent versus 30 percent. The combination of extensive and continuous employment was almost a guarantee of success. Of 98 respondents with more than 20 years in the work force, 89 had been employed full-time, full-year for at least 80 percent of this time, and 65 were high achievers. Of 88 respondents with 20 or fewer years of work experience, only seven had been employed full-time, full-year for a minimum of 80 percent of the time, and just five were high achievers.

Since age was related to time spent in the labor force, it was also associated with achievement. Rated as high achievers were three out of five respondents aged 55 years or older; about half of the women between 50 and 54 years; and less than two out of five under the age of 50.

Recent increases in the extent of employment were associated with heightened achievement. In 1963, 70 percent of the high achievers had worked full-time throughout each year since college. In 1974, on the other hand, only a third of those at the top had such extensive full-time experience. Seven out of ten of the high achievers in 1974, however, had worked full time throughout every year after 1962. Thus many respondents had been able to compensate for arrested occupational progress by more diligent attention to their careers in recent years. Despite the strong relationship between both length and continuity of labor force participation and occupational achievement, breaks in employment did not always preclude eventual career success.

There was a close association between achievement and satisfaction with one's current schedule of activities. Only among high achievers was the desire to maintain the status quo with respect to the allocation of their time more common than the yen for change. The proportion of women at the top achievement level who were satisfied with the way things were was double the percentage who wished to make modifications in their weekly schedules. In contrast, the percentage of women at lower achievement levels who hoped for change in their schedules was over three times greater than the proportion who were content. This would appear to validate the classifications since it is not surprising to find an expression of interest in altering modes of life among those who may believe they have something significant to gain.

Women with doctorates or first professional degrees were more successful than those who had earned other graduate credentials (Table 7.5). Yet, the gap between the achievement of women with different academic qualifications, although large, had narrowed between 1963 and 1974. The proportion of women with master's degrees whose 1974 achievement was classified as high or good (73 percent) represented a quadrupling of the proportion at these levels in 1963. Nevertheless, even in the earlier year, almost three-quarters of the women with degrees higher than the master's were at the two top levels.

Women with the highest academic credentials have already been shown to have had the most stable and extensive employment. Therefore, the fact that they had attained higher levels of achievement than other respondents was to be expected. Even when the proportion of years with work experience is held constant, however, differences in achievement by highest degree persist. Table 7.6 shows the distribution of high achievers who had spent similar proportions of time at work but had earned dissimilar degrees.

The percentage of high achievers in each educational group dropped as work experience decreased, although the careers of members of the more highly credentialed group were not as harmed by discontinuities as were those of women with less schooling. Regardless of similarity in the proportion of years at work, women with doctorates or first professional degrees were more successful than those with other degrees.

Differences in the proportions of high achievers among women with

Table 7.5   Occupational Achievement 1974, by Highest Earned Degree

Achievement Level, 1974	Doctorate (percent)	First Professional (percent)	Other[a] (percent)
High	64	85	31
Good	28	11	42
Fair	7	4	17
Low	1	—	10
Total percent	100	100	100
Total number	(69)	(26)	(99)

[a]ABD, masters, B.A.

Excludes 32 women with no 1974 achievement rating.

Table 7.6 Percentage of Respondents at High Achievement Level in 1974, by Educational Attainment and Proportion of Years Worked to 1974

Highest Degree	Years Worked by High Achievers (percent)		
	100 percent	80-99 percent	less than 80 percent
Doctorate or FPG	76	73	44
Other[a]	59	35	11

N = 96.
Not appropriate = 130.

[a]ABD, masters, or B.A.

different scholastic credentials also obtained when high achievement was analyzed with respect to full-time, full-year employment. Similarly, a comparison of achievement based upon the absolute number of years worked separated the doctorates and FPG's from the others. For example, four out of five women with the higher degrees and more than 25 years of full-time, full-year work were high achievers compared with slightly more than half of those with other credentials and the same amount of steady, full-time employment.

One must conclude that credentials had an independent influence upon achievement apart from length and stability of work experience. The progress of women with academic doctorates or first professional degrees who had some career interruptions was much less likely to have been retarded than was that of women with master's degrees who had breaks in employment. In fact, a short period out of the labor force for doctorates or FPGs, as Table 7.6 indicates, had practically no detrimental impact upon achievement. Employers seem to have been more likely to overlook brief periods of retirement by women who had earned the highest academic or professional credentials than by those with less prestigious degrees.

In large part, it was the profession behind the degree rather than the degree itself, that was associated with differential career success. Women who aspired to be physicians or lawyers, for example, had to aim for first professional degrees, but for those who desired careers in such fields as social work or library science, a master's degree sufficed as a professional prerequisite and only a handful of these women obtained doctorates. Credentials alone were most likely to have impeded the progress of women who had been graduate students in the arts or sciences but who did not earn a doctorate. Such respondents represented less than three out of ten of the women without doctorates or first professional degrees.

Although an M.A. in the arts and sciences probably had more cachet a generation ago than today, it did not have the vocational implications of other graduate or professional degrees.

To determine whether grouping together all recipients of master's degrees obscured differences between women with a master of arts and those with a master's in pre-professional fields, the achievement of the two groups was compared. Respondents who had received their degrees in pre-professional subjects were twice as likely to be at the high achievement level than those with a master's in the liberal arts. While 31 percent of all women who had not gone beyond the master's degree were high achievers in 1974 (Table 7.5), this was true for 36 percent of those in pre-professional fields but for only 19 percent of respondents with a master's in the liberal arts. Moreover, while 18 percent of respondents with a pre-professional degree had insufficient work experience in 1974 to permit evaluation of their career accomplishments, 27 percent of the M.A.'s were in that position.

Even grouping the pre-professional and liberal arts graduates separately masks certain differences in achievement by specific field of study. We have already noted that the M.D.'s included the largest proportion of highly successful women (87 percent). Next in order of percent of high achievers were Ph.D.'s in the social sciences and women with law degrees (each 67 percent), followed by doctorates in education (64 percent) and Ph.D.'s in the sciences (61 percent). There were no high achievers, on the other hand, among women with master's degrees in science or the humanities. And less than a quarter of the respondents who had earned a master's in education or in journalism were at the top level.

In three of the four general areas of most of the doctorates (humanities, social sciences, science, education), more than three women out of five were high achievers, humanities being the exception; but the achievement of women with the master's in the same areas was far below the norm. Moreover, a disproportionate number of women with a master's in the three liberal arts areas—humanities, science and social science—had minimal work experience. These findings suggest that the biggest losers in career terms were former liberal arts students who had concluded their graduate studies without receiving a doctorate.

Of course, not everyone was currently employed in an occupation related to her field of graduate study, although few women had made drastic changes in their occupational pursuits (Chapter 4). Although achievement was found to be related to education, it was measured with reference to the respondents' current or most recent fields of employment. The relation between the sex composition of employment in the respondents' current or last occupation and their achievement is shown in Table 7.7.

Table 7.7   Achievement Level 1974 by Percentage of Women in Occupation

Level	(underrepresented) 1-25% female	(well represented) 25-45% female	(overrepresented) 45% or more female
High	64%	42%	41%
Good	25	32	42
Fair	10	15	12
Low	1	11	5
Total percent	100	100	100
Number	(74)	(62)	(57)
Not appropriate = 33			

A greater percentage of women who were employed in occupations in which females are underrepresented were at the high achievement level than those whose fields of work employ larger proportions of women.

Respondents in predominantly male occupations had higher graduate degrees and tended to have spent more of their lives at full-time, full-year work than those in fields less dominated by males (Chapter 4). Both characteristics—extensive employment and superior credentials— were associated with high achievement. When full-time work was held constant, however, women with master's degrees employed in female-dominated occupations who had worked full-time every year were the most likely to be high achievers (86 percent), compared with 75 percent of respondents in fields in which females are underrepresented, many of whom had doctorates or first professional degrees. But only about one in ten women in traditional female occupations did work full-time consistently in contrast to more than one in three of those employed in predominantly male fields.

In occupations where women represent between 25 and 45 percent of employment, continuous work attachment produced the smallest proportion of high achievers—60 percent. Here, too, there were few continuous workers (16 percent) and a possible explanation for their inferior progress relative to continuously employed professionals in female fields may be found in differences in types of employer. Respondents in occupations with fairly equal sex ratios were more likely to be in business employment than were women in predominantly female fields and, as shall subsequently be shown, sex discrimination was most common in the profit sector.

Since these comparisons relate solely to the achievement of different groups of respondents, inferences about these women's success relative to that of males cannot be supported. Nevertheless, Galenson's conclusion that "women are more nearly equal in the professions calling for high skill and training than in the lower-level [professional] jobs," may be applicable to the respondents.[2] Although Laws has described traditional female occupations as those where "the debilitating sex-role conflict is minimized, and the achievement motive is given full rein," our findings do not sustain this characterization.[3] Instead, they imply that women who choose to enter such fields may not place a high value upon the "achievement motive." To the extent that occupational choice is a product of self-imposed role differentiation, women who deliberately sought to work in disproportionately female fields may have desired to play a more passive work role than those who opted to enter male-dominated occupations. Moreover, female occupations tend to cast women in conventional sex roles by providing opportunities for entry and reentry and for flexible work schedules. Women who take advantage of these opportunities may lose out to men in advancing to the top.

In terms of class of employer, government had the highest proportion of top achievers in 1974 (53 percent). Non-profit employment (46 percent) and self-employment followed closely (40 percent), with the private sector far behind (21 percent). At the other end of the scale, 6 percent of the women in the first three of these categories were low achievers, compared with 39 percent of the respondents in the employ of business firms.

Since vocational success was linked to the respondents' lifetime labor force participation, it was also associated with their family status, which has been shown to have strongly influenced the women's work decisions (Table 7.8).

This table includes women whose 1974 achievement was not graded due to insufficient employment in order to indicate how family status affected the total career position of each subgroup.

The similarity between the 1974 achievement levels of childless

Table 7.8   Achievement Level 1974 by Marital and Maternal Status
(percentage distribution)

Achievement Level	Never Married	No children	1 child	2 children	3 or more children
High	65	61	61	30	21
Good	26	35	27	23	31
Fair	5	—	4	18	15
Low	2	—	—	11	6
Not rated	2	4	8	18	27
Total percent	100	100	100	100	100
Number	(55)	(23)	(26)	(56)	(67)

Table 7.9   Percent High Achievers 1963 and 1974 by Marital and Maternal Status in
Each Year

Family Status	% High Achievement 1963	% High Achievement 1974
Never married	25	67
Ever married	12	43
No children	22	64
One child	15	67
Two children	8	37
Three or more children	7	29
Number =	27	96
Not appropriate =	199	130

women and of mothers with one child was a relatively recent
phenomenon, since the 1963 achievement of mothers of one had not
been on a par with that of women without children. In fact, only 9
percent of all mothers were high achievers in 1963; by 1974, this
proportion had risen to almost one-third (Table 7.9).

Only mothers who had limited their families to a single child had
been able to compensate fully for any disadvantages incurred due to a
period of absence from the labor force. They spent shorter periods in
temporary retirement and a greater proportion of their time in full-time,
full-year work than mothers of two or more children.

It was not the presence of children, per se, but the absence from the
labor force they occasioned that led to the lower achievement of mothers.
When the progress of mothers who worked during almost every year was
compared with that of childless women with worklives of similar
duration there was little difference: more than 60 percent of each group
was at the top achievement level.

Summary

More than four out of five of the respondents whose career achievement
was assessed were rated as good or high achievers. Those at the top level
alone represented 43 percent of all respondents, and 50 percent of those
with a sufficient body of work experience to permit career evaluation. In
other words, from an objective viewpoint, seven out of ten of all
respondents had made at least adequate use of their skills, and four out of
ten had reached a superior position on the career ladder. The remainder
as yet had been unable or unwilling to fulfill the career expectations
associated with their advanced training.

There was an increase of more than 200 percent in the proportion of
women at the high achievement level between 1963 and 1974. This rise

was the result of progress in both established and resumed careers. Although extensive continuous employment was most likely to have led to high achievement, discontinuity was not an inevitable impediment to advancement; several women with breaks in their early work histories had attained the top achievement level by 1974.

A composite portrait of the typical high achiever looks something like this: a recipient of a first professional degree or of the Ph.D. in a social science who had always worked full-time, full-year; was earning more than $20,000 a year in public employment in a male-dominated occupation; and who had either never married or, if married, had borne no more than one child.

Workers with the lowest level of achievement are typified by an M.A. in science or the humanities who had spent less than three-fourths of her life in the labor force; was earning under $15,000 per annum working for a business firm in an occupation in which female employees are well- or overrepresented; and who had a minimum of three children.

Notes

1. Eli Ginzberg, I.E. Berg, C. A. Brown, J. L. Herma, A. M. Yohalem, and S. Gorelick, *Life Styles of Educated Women*, (New York: Columbia University Press, 1971), p. 98.

2. Marjorie Galenson, *Women and Work*, ILR Paperback, No. 13 (Ithaca, N.Y.: New York State School of Industrial and Labor Relations, Cornell University, 1973), p. 24.

3. Judith Long Laws, "Work Aspirations of Women: False Leads and New Starts," *Signs*, I, 3, Part 2 (Spring, 1976), p. 47.

8] EMPLOYMENT DISCRIMINATION

The existence of sex discrimination in the labor market is generally acknowledged and a considerable body of research deals with its causes, incidence, and manifestations. Because this study is confined to women alone, it cannot provide objective evidence of differences between the career progress of the respondents and that of their male peers. The women did offer their personal judgments about their treatment in the work force compared with that of men who had similar qualifications and experience, however. Although subjective perceptions of discrimination may misrepresent the true state of affairs when lack of awareness or self-deception block recognition of discrimination, or where hypersensitivity or unrealistic expectations lead to unjustifiable grievances, these women's impressions should not be disregarded. Since apprehension of discrimination must precede the search for proof, an examination of the respondents' opinions can identify likely foci of attempts to rectify inequities and can suggest possible reasons for differences in perceptions.

In addition to scrutinizing the respondents' views on discrimination, this chapter discusses the types of employment discrimination that the women said they had encountered, and the effects of recent political and social developments upon different aspects of their employment.

Equal Treatment

In response to the question, "Do you think that your treatment as a woman has been at least equal to that accorded males with similar

Table 8.1   Perception of Employment Discrimination by 1974 Achievement Level

Treatment as	Achievement Level (percent)		
Worker	High	Good	Fair or Low
Equal	40	51	59
Unequal	60	49	41
Total percent	100	100	100
Number	(96)	(63)	(32)
NA = 3			
Achievement not assessed = 32			

qualifications and experience?'' 53 percent of the respondents who had been employed between 1963 and 1974 replied in the negative. While a 47 percent positive response rate may imply to some persons that sex discrimination is not as rampant as generally proclaimed, to others, the answer of the majority may serve as additional confirmation of the pervasiveness of sexual inequality in employment. The fact that more than half of a group of women with high qualifications and strong career motivation declare that they have not received equal treatment as workers would appear to be more a cause for alarm than for celebration.

One respondent, a retired professor of speech, remarked: ''I, like so many other women, experienced years of humiliating, overt and subtle 'put-downs.' Any woman who has not experienced this has been living in a 'doll's house' sheltered by her ignorance.''

Some of the women noted that their negative response to the question about equal treatment referred to past rather than to current employment discrimination. ''No—in the 50's and 60's. Yes today,'' said a government foreign policy analyst, and a state government bureau chief commented, ''Yes now—but long time in coming.''

Analysis of the response to this question revealed a seeming paradox—successful workers were more likely to have reported discriminatory treatment in the labor market than women with lesser occupational attainment (Table 8.1).

The perceptions of the high achievers were the reverse of those of respondents with fair or low achievement. One reading of this finding would suggest that attainment of a high measure of success often required the ability and willingness to persevere through adversity. Since the question referred to discrimination at any point in the women's worklives, such an interpretation seems sound.

In addition, the women's career choices, which have already been shown to be associated with their achievement, were also associated with perception of employer bias. For example, the extent of occupational segregation not only differentiated achievement levels, but also correlated with reports of employment discrimination (Table 8.2).

The proportion of women reporting discriminatory experiences who were in occupations with male majorities was approximately double the proportion of respondents in fields in which females are in or close to the majority. Only in the latter occupations was equal treatment reported by most women.

Since the question pertaining to equal treatment in the labor market asked for the respondents' *perceptions*, not proof, their replies support the inference that women who are relatively few among many may be more sensitive to differences in treatment between the sexes than women who work with a paucity of male associates.* Where there are large numbers of men in a work setting, it is probably easier for a female employee to measure her relative progress than in settings where women are in the great majority. The accuracy of the perceptions of women in female fields, however, is subject to question in view of the preferential treatment that the male minority is wont to receive. Personnel practices in education, for example, result in a disproportion of male administrators in settings that are overwhelmingly female.[1] And, "in spite of the rapid movement of women into the library profession, the highest paid administrative positions in larger libraries have very much remained a male domain."[2]

Although the respondents' occupations were fairly evenly divided among fields with different proportions of female employment, the overrepresentation of women in certain types of jobs is the salient characteristic of the total female work force. Respondents in occupations with a disproportion of women workers resemble the typical

---

*Although data on occupational segregation pertain to the most recent job while discrimination experience covers a total worklife, relatively few women made radical career changes and those who did virtually always moved to an occupation with a similar range of female representation. Therefore, this analysis has long-term validity.

Table 8.2   Perception of Treatment in Employment by Occupational Sex Ratio

Treatment in Employment	Female Ratio in Occupation (percent)		
	1-25% female	25-45% female	45-99% female
Equal	36	40	69
Unequal	64	60	31
Total percent	100	100	100

Number = 199
NA = 7
No work 1963-74 = 20

female professional. The relatively low rate at which this group reported discriminatory treatment may imply reluctance to admit that sex discrimination exists, or disinclination to compete with their male colleagues. Pinder's comment about English women may be equally applicable to Americans: "Women are in general treated as an auxiliary element in the labour force. . . . And, since society expects it of them, the majority acquiesce in this assessment of their role."[3] Males and females who enter traditional female professions may have such divergent goals that they do not see themselves as rivals, although objective evidence may demonstrate differential outcomes that strongly hint of sex discrimination.

The perception of discriminatory treatment by women in occupations with different ratios of male and female employment was associated with career achievement. At the highest achievement level, in occupations of each type, there was a larger proportion of women who reported unequal treatment than at lower levels of progress. This may have a self-congratulatory ring but it may also depict exactly what happened. Perseverance may have been rewarded; the less competitive were satisfied with less or, at least, may have realized that some roadblocks were self-constructs. Of course tokenism cannot be ruled out as an explanation for success in some instances.

The gross division of occupations according to female representation conceals some interesting differences among specific occupations. For example, while most physicians felt that they had not always been treated equally, the majority of lawyers disagreed, possibly because of the greater availability of less competitive work settings which offered them some measure of protection against discriminatory employer policies. As one lawyer remarked: "I've stayed out of certain areas of the law—private law firms, corporations, labor unions—and stayed in government because it was always clear that women were at such a disadvantage in those other areas."

Physical and biological scientists were more than one-and-a-half times as likely to have noted discriminatory experiences as social scientists, and about twice as likely as women in the arts or humanities. This finding correlates with sex ratios in these fields; the first of these groups employs the smallest percentage of females. Women in the field of education were evenly divided between those who did and did not charge discrimination, but this masks the fact that the majority were on college or university faculties. More than four-fifths of teachers and other school employees below the college level felt they had been treated fairly.

Most academics, at all job levels, believed they had been the victims of bias. Their widely held view that they had been victims of sex discrimination echoes assertions of faculty women throughout academia. Juanita Kreps once asserted: "The universities have been the worst offenders [because they] are dealing with highly intelligent people, highly motivated professional women, so there was no excuse."[4]

Since the work experience of each respondent had been substantially confined to a single job setting and class of employer, these aspects of employment were examined in relation to reports of discrimination. More than nine out of ten of those who were currently employed in business or professional firms reported discrimination in employment as did three out of five women whose current or most recent employment was in higher education, hospitals, and government agencies. In contrast, half or more of the respondents working in schools below the college level, social agencies, voluntary membership organizations and libraries were inclined to believe that they had been treated equally. In the last setting, this opinion was unanimous.

When setting and employer were examined jointly, business still held its ground as the king of the discriminators. Private colleges and universities followed closely; 72 percent of their employees charged discriminatory treatment, in contrast to 59 percent of workers in public institutions of higher learning. The jobs of each respondent in academic employment had not always been in institutions under the same form of control and, as noted in Chapter 4, most change was in the direction of publicly sponsored colleges and universities, which may have been due in part to differences in the treatment of women.

The proportion of workers in government administration who felt they had been subject to discrimination was similar to that in governmentally controlled colleges and universities. With the exception of public schools below the college level, there were no differences in the perceptions of employees in other types of setting—welfare agencies, libraries, research organizations, etc.—according to class of employer. About three-fifths of workers in these settings, under either public or private auspices, felt they had been dealt with fairly.

If business turned out to be the biggest culprit, public education below the college level was viewed as the most benign employer—93 percent of employees believed they had received equal treatment. But before the applause breaks out, it is best to take a closer look backstage where, as noted earlier, one often finds that there is a tracking system among school employees similar to that operating among pupils: among employees, however, the tracking is done on the basis of sex. Since this has been standard operating procedure in schools for a long time, one must infer that women who entered teaching were fully aware of their opportunities and chose this career without consideration of advancement potential. Hence, expected treatment amounted to equal treatment.

Women with doctorates were much more likely to feel that they had been subject to discriminatory personnel practices than those with master's degrees (70 percent and 40 percent, respectively). Slightly more than half of the women with first professional degrees also reported experiencing unequal treatment. Since most doctorates and all FPG's were in predominantly male fields, the differences in their perceptions suggest that there were other factors at play. The most obvious is employment setting: doctorates were largely academics; although some FPG's had teaching appointments, these were in medical schools rather than traditional academic settings. This is further testimony to the university's reluctance to perform the role of equal opportunity employer.

The duration of time spent in the labor force, both on full-time, full-year schedules, and on any time schedules, was not related to the women's perceptions of equal treatment. This finding has particular interest because explanations of sex differences in career progress have often focused upon differences in lifetime labor force participation.[5] The fact that respondents with continuous full-time work experience were as likely to report discrimination as those with breaks in their work histories suggests that anticipated female behavior, rather than actual behavior, may often be responsible for discriminatory employment practices.

Most of the factors that have been customarily offered as rationales for sex differentials in employment outcomes do not apply to the majority of respondents who claim to have been treated unequally in the labor market. This group was principally composed of workers in male dominated fields and neither their education, occupational choice, weekly hours of work, nor total work experience conformed to traditional sex-linked conduct.

Marital status was associated with perceptions of equal treatment insofar as women whose marriages had been broken by divorce or widowhood were considerably more likely to say they had been victims of discriminatory policies than women who had never married or those who were still married to their first husbands. Two-thirds of the women who had been widows or divorcees at some period thought they had been treated unfairly compared with about half of the remaining women.

Since marital disruption often results in the pressing need of former wives to improve their financial position, this finding suggests that these women may have found themselves at a particular disadvantage when changed circumstances either compelled reentry into the labor force or prompted job holders to seek more lucrative employment. Although some divorcees and widows may have cushions in the form of alimony, child care support, or bequests, the income of many of them is frequently insufficient to provide adequate living standards. Thus, many women who had previously been content to concentrate upon

Table 8.3 Dimensions of Employment in which Respondents Experienced Sex Discrimination

Aspect of Employment	Percent[a] Not treated equally	Percent[a] Not cited
Salary	74	26
Promotion	61	39
Responsibility	30	70
Assignment of duties	28	72
Hiring	25	75
Tenure	16	84
Grants	8	92

NA = 9
Equal treatment = 95
No work 1963-74 = 20

[a]Based on N = 102

homemaking or other non-market activities or who had willingly assumed the role of secondary wage earner, may have found that necessity bred the motivation for career success. Exigency coupled with an abrupt change in direction may have sharpened their awareness of disabilities imposed upon women in the labor market.

The women who reported that they had been subject to unequal treatment in employment were requested to use a checklist to note those dimensions of employment in which they believed sex discrimination had affected their jobs. Salary and promotion were the most commonly cited foci of unequal treatment (Table 8.3).

All aspects of employment on the list are not of the same order as an employment component nor is each one relevant to every job. Some have to do with functions; others with rewards. Some are applicable to all types of employment; others, such as tenure and grants, pertain to academic employment primarily. But all areas of employment discrimination are essentially interrelated, and it may be presumed that the respondents specified those areas in which discrimination had the greatest personal impact. For instance, although discriminatory hiring is usually the precursor of discriminatory promotion opportunities, the latter area was cited more often, and while inequality in promotion was mentioned with less frequency than salary bias, the relationship between the two, as the Malkiels found, is generally one of cause and effect. The reason for professional salary differentials between the sexes is that "women with the same training, experience etc. as men tend to be assigned to lower job levels."[6] Since the corollary to this finding was that women and men who are in the same professional jobs do receive equal pay, most respondents who mentioned salary, alone, may be presumed to have also suffered from inequitable promotion policies. Or, they may have been promoted, but to different jobs from those of their male peers, thereby precluding strict earnings comparisons.

Among respondents claiming unequal treatment, women aged 55 years and over were much more likely to have experienced discrimination in hiring than younger women. In contrast, a disproportionately large number of young women complained of inequity in promotion. There were no striking age differences with respect to other aspects of discrimination, but these specific differences alone suggest that any improvement in hiring policies in recent years has not extended beyond the entry level. This may be related to the fact that older and younger respondents were seeking jobs in different social environments. Many older women looked for work during the Depression, when male preference was the rule in contrast to the somewhat more favorable hiring situation that confronted postwar female job aspirants. The responses in Table 8.3 support Brown's conclusions that "it is advancement on the job and movement up the job ladder which contributes most to the additional earnings derived from investment in human capital, continuity of employment, and experience."[7]

In the two areas most frequently cited as sources of discrimination—promotion and salary—there were interesting findings which were related to various respondent characteristics. Differences associated with size of current earnings were slight—37 percent of all women who had full-time earnings of $30,000 or more in 1974 claimed to have experienced salary discrimination compared with 44 percent in the lowest earnings range (under $15,000). Some of this difference may be due to rectification of earlier inequities among those at higher salary levels. In other cases, respondents' expectations may have differed depending on experience and weekly hours of work.

Occupational sex ratios, however, were related to the respondents' reports of salary and promotion inequities (Table 8.4).

Inequity in salary was noted more frequently by women who had received unequal treatment in fields in which females were underrepresented or well represented than in occupations in which females had a larger representation. Workers in occupations with male majorities tended to earn more than women in predominantly female fields, yet they apparently were more aggrieved about their relative earnings status. It is possible that their grievances referred to past salary discrimination that had later been rectified, but one may also speculate that, since women in male-dominated occupations had the most career continuity, they possibly had anticipated higher rewards. While their earnings were greater than those of women in occupations with higher

Table 8.4   Reports of Discrimination in Salary and Promotion By Occupational Sex
Ratios

Salary Discrimination	Females Underrepresented	Females Well represented	Females Overrepresented
Yes	77%	73%	58%
Salary not mentioned	23	27	42
Total percent	100	100	100
Promotion Discrimination			
Yes	63	51	68
Promotion not mentioned	37	49	32
Total percent	100	100	100
Number	(48)	(37)	(19)

NA = 7
No unequal treatment = 95
No work 1963-1974 = 20

proportions of females they may have been lower than those of male co-workers of similar background.

Unlike the other groups, a smaller proportion of workers in female dominated occupations mentioned discrimination in earnings than in promotion. In many of the predominantly female fields, there may have been few men, if any, with whom to compare earnings so that salary discrimination would be more difficult to assert than inequity in advancement. The fact that these women's earnings tended to be lower than those of other respondents partially reflects the general earnings distribution in female occupations. The other women had higher earnings but they had plenty of males whose salaries could be used as points of reference and, having done so, they apparently felt that they had been relatively deprived.

Several women enlarged upon their responses to this question. The following quotation illustrates a combination of sex and age discrimination since the job search described occurred at age 54:

> . . . in 1972–73 when I was working on my dissertation and looking for employment in the health care field . . . as a woman with considerable experience and about to obtain a Ph.D. in Health Organizational Research, I found myself being interviewed by men of lesser academic background *and* experience and they wanted no part of me!

This woman eventually obtained a position as a professor in a state university 500 miles from her home and she commuted weekly.

Some women supported their assertion of discriminatory treatment by summarizing their accomplishments. A former professor and department head, retired for reasons of health, commented:

> Even though I had developed innovative Masters and Doctoral programs in art ed., published textbooks, was speaker at nat'l conventions; men who had done none of these things were promoted before me and paid higher.

Other respondents felt they had been subject to deliberate administrative sabotage. A teacher specialist in health education reported:

> I was in line for promotion to a higher position, and highly recommended. An incoming male eliminated the job rather than give it to a female. If he reinstates the position, I plan to get it or make complaints through the proper official channels and/or courts.

There were also cases in which prejudice against women influenced the choice of employment setting. A private medical practitioner noted that "sex discrimination at higher academic levels (advancement on the faculty) made me go into private practice in 1956."

A manpower specialist believed that the question about equal treatment was "hard to answer—! Yes! if my work history alone is considered. No, if you take into account some of the unequal treatment earlier that obviated certain career lines."

A librarian employed in the children's department noted differences based upon the nature of one's clientele:

> Lack of discrimination was due primarily to my work assignment. *Other* women on the staff were discriminated against in hiring, promotion, responsibility and assignment of duties.

Presumably these others were librarians who dealt with adults. Her comment is consistent with the hypothesis which posits that the presence of sex differentials in employment is related to discrimination by customers.[8] Although libraries are often public facilities and government employment tends to be least affected by consumer preferences, they are also public services which ordinarily are locally controlled and therefore are unlikely to differ substantially from private firms in this respect.

There were also women who attributed salary differentials to their role as wives, such as a lawyer who felt that she had "always been treated equally with men in work assignments and responsibility," and that the "only discrimination was remuneration basically because I was not a family breadwinner." Similarly, a professor of physiology asserted that salary discrimination was "usually rationalized because I was married to a salaried professor."

Academicians occasionally referred to an atmosphere of prejudice. "The informal discrimination was overwhelming," said an anthropologist. "One just had to grit one's teeth and hang in. When I became a department chairman my dean said, 'What's a little girl like you doing as a department chairman?' " But she *did* become chairman, one is constrained to observe.

A sociologist regretted that she had "not been included in 2 seminars and other activities relevant to my qualifications and interests." And a classicist wryly observed that "in the first few years I was never appointed to a committee but now increasingly so—in fact too much!"

There were a few instances in which respondents reasoned that discriminatory policies resulted from their preference for part-time employment. A social science researcher asserted: "I am sure . . . if I could have worked full-time I would have been listed as co-author on some of the books and pamphlets I worked on."

A part-time adjunct professor of English at a private college opined:

> Without there being any diabolical plot, I think college administrators find it handy to have a few talented women hanging around to fill in the gaps in curriculum. A man or an autonomous woman would not remain available for part-time work over so long a period of time.

A psychologist and director of special services for a school system said:

> I was told at hiring that I was willing to work for less hours and therefore less money than any male did . . . I must add that I was always given special privileges as well. I could leave easily if I had no baby sitter coverage and that kind of thing.

Finally, a federal bureau chief who thought she had received equal treatment gave the following reasons for her view:

> If I had been a man, I would not opt for time to drive car pools, etc.; and would doubtless have eagerly increased overtime and responsibilities. I have been treated according to my options, not my sex as such, and my options have curtailed any increase of responsibility.

This is a case of self-imposed, rather than employer-inflicted, differential treatment. Yet while "sex as such" may not have been a consideration in the treatment accorded her, to the extent that the options that caused her to behave differently from men were sex specific, sex was indeed a factor in any differential results.

Recent Changes

In addition to providing information about employment discrimination, the respondents supplied information in response to a question asking whether recent governmental and social pressures against sex discrimination in employment had any effects upon various aspects of their jobs. Table 8.5 presents the responses to this question.

Table 8.5 Anti-Discrimination Action on Aspects of Employment

Was Action Taken?	Aspect of Employment (percent)			
	Own Job	Employer Policies	Attitudes of Male Colleagues	Relations with Students, Clients, etc.
Yes	26	38	31	35
No	20	36	48	58
No action needed	44	11	13	5
Action needed	7	12	6	2
Reactive	3	3	2	—
Total percent	100	100	100	100
Number	(186)	(187)	(187)	(186)
Not applicable	(30)	(29)	(29)	(30)

The meaning of a response of "no" was often unclear since it could be interpreted as meaning either that no action was necessary or that it was needed but not taken. Many respondents clarified their answer, thereby permitting the breakdown used in Table 8.5. Despite this ambiguity, if attention is directed primarily to the "yes" replies, it is clear that only a minority of current employees noted employment-related effects from recent efforts to improve female opportunities. Although positive action affecting the respondent's own job was mentioned least, it is the area in which the least necessity for action was indicated. While improvement in employer policies was mentioned more than any other aspect of employment, it apparently was not always related to improvement in a respondent's own status, possibly because her own lot was seen as less of a personal than an institutional problem, or because her status was not viewed as being linked to recent developments.

The finding that close to half of the employed respondents thought no action was needed with respect to their own job status may be seen as a measure of job satisfaction. If this group is viewed in combination with those whose employment conditions had been improved as a result of some type of positive action, it may be concluded that seven out of ten of the respondents who had been in the labor force at some time after 1963 had no grievance in connection with the terms of their employment.

The respondents who stated that their own jobs had been affected by recent efforts to provide equal opportunity were asked to explain their answers. Several of those who had responded "no" also provided explanations of their replies. From these remarks, it was possible to define those areas of employment that had been affected.

Most frequently mentioned as an element of improvement in their own employment were salary, status, hiring, and promotion. Some women also noted increased consideration for assignments and functions that had previously been exclusively performed by males. In addition, a few of the respondents had successfully challenged their employers' policies on their own behalf.

There was a close correlation between the women's reports about changes in their jobs and employer discrimination throughout their careers. Of those who noted recent positive changes in their job conditions, more than three-quarters had claimed to have been affected by unequal treatment in the labor market; of those who said that no action was needed, only 16 percent had reported employer bias. Every respondent who felt that needed action was not taken had indicated exposure to employment inequities.

Women who noted positive improvement in their employment status due to pressures for equal opportunities were more likely to be at the high achievement level than those who gave other responses. Almost two-thirds of the former were top achievers, compared with 45 percent of the women who specifically stated that no action was needed, and 43 percent of those who simply noted that there had been no effect upon their own jobs as a result of such recent efforts.

Among academics, the highest degree of positive change was reported by women employed by private universities (62 percent). Half of those at public universities, and only one-third employed by 2- or 4-year colleges, reported improvement. At least half of the workers in government agencies, research organizations, business and professional firms had felt a positive impact from efforts to improve women's status. Only 6 percent of workers in schools below the college level said the same, but over three-quarters of them thought no change was needed, a sentiment that was echoed by all workers in hospitals, libraries, and voluntary membership organizations. Objective inferiority of job status had no necessary relation to the views of individual job holders.

Comments about salary increases included:

In general, women in editorial jobs used to receive less pay than men—as federally sponsored center, K__ had to equalize these." [Employee of scientific research center]

My salary was *abysmal* (under $10,000/year) for creation of & teaching of graduate courses & supervision of *all* M. A. students—2 dozen+—in our college in Child Development until Affirmative Action got strong on campus & a *slight* upward adjustment began to be made. [Assistant professor at private university]

Salary increase of 25% subsequent to letter from women employees to Institute regarding possibility of discrimination. [Geneticist employed by a research institute]

Additional remarks about other aspects of positive change include those of a federal government research analyst who attributed improvement in her position to the fact that "federal officials are under direct pressure to justify failure to give women equal opportunity and rewards." A physician and public health official said: "I think it is particularly true in government that management positions are being offered to qualified women to meet Affirmative Action, etc."

A professor of social work declared that she had begun to receive "more recognition and status from university administration," but that "both required constant effort on my own part." Another faculty member at a prestigious coed college noted change but related that "refusal of departmental chairmanship brought issues into open." And the chairman of a department at a university medical center attributed her appointment to "pressure to recruit women."

A social scientist remarked on changed attitudes toward nepotism in describing her experience with a "university seeking top women and willing to appoint [me] to same department as spouse—would NOT have occurred a decade ago." A professor of chemistry attributed her improved conditions of work to "consciousness raising." "I demand more," she wrote, "and they feel they owe me equal treatment."

A social worker who returned to the labor force after her husband's death remarked that her "supervisor is a 32-year-old single, career-oriented woman who states she will never marry," and who "seems 'liberated' in sense that my status as widow, older woman, etc., did not deter her from hiring."

One respondent, an associate professor of anatomy at a medical school, supplied the details of her complaint of discrimination against her employer, including transcripts of official findings and newspaper reports. "This portion of my answer need *NOT* be kept confidential," she wrote. "It may help other women to know that it *is* possible to fight for their rights."

In brief, she related that in 1972, with more years as an associate professor than any male at the New Jersey Medical School of the College of Medicine and Dentistry of New Jersey, and "having watched males with qualifications no better or poorer than mine being promoted to full professor after relatively few years in lower ranks," she brought a complaint with the State Division of Civil Rights against the medical school charging sex discrimination. The Division issued a finding of probable cause and, after fruitless attempts at conciliation and six days of public hearings, directed the College to pay her salary owed retroactive to June 1972, to promote her "forthwith," and ordered it to engage in "reportable affirmative action." This order was appealed by the College, but in March 1976 the Appellate Division of the Supreme Court of New Jersey delivered a unanimous decision in favor of her sex discrimination complaint. The decision also established the right of the

Division on Civil Rights to mandate "affirmative recruitment, hiring and promotion of qualified women" and the establishment and maintenance of "policies which will insure salary equity between comparable male and female faculty members in the future."

A subsequent complaint filed by the respondent charged that, as a result of her sex discrimination suit, the college and chairman of the anatomy department had shifted her teaching responsibilities from medical to dental students so that she was excluded from teaching embryology, her area of expertise, and from the laboratory teaching of medical students. At hearings before the state Division on Civil Rights, faculty members testified to the more challenging and prestigious character of the medical anatomy program. In addition, many of them supported the allegations. The official record quotes a male colleague's description of the complainant as "a fantastic teacher who loves teaching," and he goes on to say, "this is a way to punish her."

A finding that probable cause existed to support the charge of reprisal was made in April 1976, but the school refused to sign a consent agreement. In June 1977, after several days of public hearings, the president of the college signed substantially the same document he had previously rejected. This agreement guaranteed the respondent fair treatment in the department and a return to a primary teaching assignment with medical students. With the settlement, the respondent was at last "free of the tension of the 5 year fight [which] points up the inadequacies of our Civil Rights enforcement procedures."

This case is an illustration of the kind of perseverance and tenacity that is often required of a woman who decides to challenge discriminatory practices. It also demonstrates the kind of employer intransigence that still confronts highly qualified women of all ages, this respondent having been 63 years old when her case was finally resolved.

The second part of the question about the effects of pressures for non-discriminatory policies concerned employer policies in general.

Those who described positive developments in employer policy most frequently mentioned efforts to recruit and hire women; actions to step up promotions and tenure for females; and the general institution of more equitable courses of action.

Among the remarks about employer policy were the following:

Women now in jobs that were all male 3 years ago—copy desk, sports reporting, picture desk—paper looking for woman photographer. Still no women editors except women's page. [Newspaper reporter]

Women professors are now hired in equal numbers & at equal salaries to male professors. Their duties are now the same. [Professor of chemistry at state university]

Shift in recruitment from dominant attention to males toward significant attention to female candidates. [Professor of English, private four-year college]

Generalized non-specific reaction that more opportunities should be made available to female physicians. [Associate director of radiology, voluntary hospital]

College administration is being *very* careful about both women and minorities. I am convinced that I got the job as Associate Dean without significance that I was a woman; I was there. But I will be replaced by a woman because she's a woman. [Executive dean, community college]

Definitely more awareness of the potential women candidates for high positions—but *Also*—an uneasy sense that a woman or minority member should be chosen when not always the best person. There has been an *increase* in prejudice against white males. [Caseworker supervisor, voluntary hospital]

There is a great increase in *consideration for jobs* of women candidates. I am asked more frequently to recommend and I write many more letters, but this does not result in more placement of women in tenure slots. They are mostly in a revolving door situation. [Professor of art history, private university]

The respondents were also requested to note whether there had been changes in the attitudes of their male supervisors and colleagues. Women who reported positive changes among their male fellow workers most frequently cited greater respect, sensitivity, and awareness of women's needs. Some women declared that they had never found the men they worked with or worked under to be discriminatory, and a few others noted that they had no male colleagues. Negative comments primarily referred to surface changes, attitudes of reluctant non-discrimination in fear of penalties, and the continuation of traditional male attitudes often characterized as chauvinistic and defensive.

Here are some of their comments in regard to fellow employees.

They take women in science slightly more seriously. [Assistant professor of astronomy at a public university]

I notice increasing sensitivity of male educators to needs and desires and problems peculiar to women. [Teacher and reading specialist, large urban school system]

There has been an increase in the number of women in supervisory and administrative positions in the school district no doubt because of social pressure and this has resulted in more respect for opinions and word of women psychologists also.

I find men whom I direct more unselfconscious about a woman boss than 10 years ago. [Bureau director, state department of public welfare]

They considered W[omen's] L[ib] a big joke at first but more are willing to admit to sex discrimination in employment and to consult with the women employees. However, they still expect the secretaries to carry their coffee to them; and in the competition for a higher position would give the break to the male on the basis that the female didn't have the necessary experience to handle the increased responsibilities. [Foreign exchange and investment analyst for oil company]

Defensiveness and lack of sensitivity were also noted as either continuing or having been newly engendered by the Women's Rights Movement.

They make self-conscious jokes—they are concerned about inequities. Some are hiding their male chauvinism. On the surface, few differences, except an increase in nervous laughter and occasional angry disputes. [Professor of sociology]

There is a degree of antagonism which was not present before. [Professor of history]

I do not think "the movement" changed any minds or attitudes. Good work was rewarded with more work to do, and I was given much responsibility, if not the top title. [Retired federal administrator]

In regard to relations with clients, students, customers, patients, etc., fewer respondents enlarged upon their answers. Among the women who did so, several wrote about the new emphasis they themselves were giving to women's problems in their work. Others mentioned giving specific encouragement to women and their consciousness of serving as models. Some teachers described their female students as being more self-confident and aspiring. A few noted greater receptivity towards women professionals on the part of those they dealt with in their work and more regard for women from women. Some of their remarks about this particular aspect of their employment follow.

In the South, student awareness of sex discrimination is light years ahead of the entrenched academic bureaucracy and the full professors. [Writer and lecturer]

. . . women's lib has made more clients feel that female social workers can offer as much in some cases as male psychologists, social workers or psychiatrists. [Part-time caseworker]

We deal with physicians in our writing and in the past we were considered "the girls" even though we were handling their professional public relations—they often called us by our first names but usually expected us to call them "Dr." This has eased up quite a bit in the past few years. [Writer/editor, all-female public relations firm]

One problem has developed which I had not anticipated—the negative ways students *still* react to women professors. . . . Women professors are perceived by students as being the motherly or the overaggressive type. There are no "distinguished" women professors at our institution. Of course we are beginning to work on this problem, but it's extremely frustrating. [Assistant professor of education and department chairman, private college]

Awareness of these trends has been part of my work in therapy. Just as I have been buoyed by such gains, I help others to become aware and/or involved. [Psychologist]

Summary

High qualifications were no bar to sex discrimination. Slightly more than half of the respondents claimed to have experienced discriminatory treatment during the course of their careers, although some stipulated that this claim referred to past, not present, employment.

Women whose career performance had been assessed as superior expressed the belief that they had been victims of sex discrimination more frequently than those lower on the scale of achievement. The high achievers typically demonstrated strong career commitment primarily in fields requiring rigorous preparation and consistent dedication and which have a dearth of female employment. Hence they epitomized the women Pinder describes in the following observation: "Except where there is an absolute sex bar, the outstanding woman can and will get the job she wants though it will take her longer than it would a man of comparable ability."[9]

Salary and promotion were the two aspects of employment in which discriminatory treatment was cited most often. Hiring was cited with much less frequency, indicating that unequal treatment did not customarily begin until after a woman established an employment relationship. In other words, able women could make their way *in* readily but had difficulty in making their way *up*.

About one-third of the respondents declared that recent pressures against sex discrimination in employment had influenced positive changes in one or more aspects of their employment, but only about one-quarter noted direct job benefits. Almost half, however, indicated that no change was required in respect to their own jobs. Nevertheless, it was apparent from their comments that many women felt that there was still plenty of room for improvement. Some had challenged discriminatory treatment and others had taken action in support of colleagues. However, fighting for one's rights is a costly battle, which would be unnecessary if there were universal compliance with anti-discrimination laws and regulations.

Bella Abzug once remarked: "Our struggle today is not to get an Einstein appointed as assistant professor. It is for a woman schlemiel to get as quickly promoted as a male schlemiel."[10] The respondents were women of high promise, yet many of their careers were injured by bias. If many of *them* couldn't make it, pity the poor schlemiel!

Notes

1. G. Niedermeyer and V. W. Kramer, *Women in Education: Administrative Positions in Public Education: A Position Paper* (Philadelphia: Recruitment and Training Institute, 1974).

2. Rudolph C. Blitz, "Women in the Professions, 1870-1920," *Monthly Labor Review*, XCVII, 5 (May, 1974), p. 36.

3. Pauline Pinder, *Women at Work*, Vol. XXXV, Broadsheet 512 (London: PEP, May, 1969), p. 628.

4. Leonard Silk, "A Candid Academic at Commerce," *The New York Times*, May 8, 1977, p. F9.

5. See, for example, *Economic Report of the President*, transmitted to the Congress February 1974 (Washington, D.C.: U.S. Government Printing Office, 1974), p. 154 ff.

6. Burton G. Malkiel and Judith A. Malkiel, "Male-Female Pay Differentials in Professional Employment," *American Economic Review*, LXIII, 4 (September, 1973), p. 704.

7. Gary D. Brown, "How Type of Employment Affects Earnings Differences by Sex," *Monthly Labor Review*, XCIX, 7 (July, 1976), p. 29.

8. Victor R. Fuchs, "Differences in Hourly Earnings Between Men and Women," *Monthly Labor Review*, XCIV, 5 May, 1971, p. 11.

9. Pinder, *op. cit.*, p. 554.

10. *The New York Times*, March 31, 1976, p. A22.

9] ASSENT AND DISSENT

Statistical analyses cannot do full justice to individual differences and a sampling of the many perceptive observations made by respondents serves to add illumination to our narrative. Most of the remarks quoted in the preceding chapters were supplied as addenda to short answers. There were additional responses, however, that were in reply to questions which asked for views on certain subjects.

Respondents were asked in one question to offer advice to able young women undergraduates about three courses of action: combining family and career; attending graduate or professional school; and entering their field of graduate study. Replies to the first part of this question have already been discussed in Chapter 3. This chapter deals with the other topics.

In addition, no inquiry of this kind could afford to neglect consideration of the women's movement. The preceding chapter has discussed the respondents' employment relationships in terms of recent active attention to women's opportunities in the labor market. The final section of this chapter is devoted to a description of the effects of the women's movement upon other facets of their lives.

Advice About Graduate Education

The preceding discussion, in effect, has recounted the contributions of graduate or professional training to the worklives of the respondents. Since one aim of this research has been to provide data to inform the vocational decisions of young women of high ability, the respondents

162

were specifically requested to offer them advice about the value of advanced training. It was anticipated that older women of high ability would provide many useful insights based upon their own experiences and observations.

When asked what advice they would give to an able young undergraduate about attending graduate or professional school, only one respondent expressed blanket opposition to schooling beyond the baccalaureate. This view came from the head librarian of a school district who dissented in these terms:

> Forget that—and find some kind of trade or skill that is in demand. Apprentice as a plumber or electrician. Try computer programming.

This woman also expressed the opinion that library work is enjoyable "if jobs are available." She was a supervisor with relatively high earnings for her occupation ($19,790), although she complained about being in the same salary grade as her assistant. One may infer that her stricture was based upon pessimism about job opportunities for women with graduate education rather than upon her own experience.

While there were other respondents who recognized problems confronting highly qualified women in the current labor market, more than three out of five of the answers to this question unreservedly endorsed the notion of graduate or professional training. The rest either expressed certain qualifications or felt this decision was up to the individual. The following are typical of the remarks of the enthusiasts, many of whom were especially sensitive to problems faced by women.

> By all means. Take yourself seriously as a person. So, it's harder if you're female, but being female can't be helped. And culturally imposed complications can't be helped. [Assistant professor of astronomy]

> Become a specialist early, so that your skills can be recognized in a competitive field and recognized by men who still dominate the market. [Professor of anatomy]

> To compete with men, women have to have greater competence and better credentials. See yourself as part of the larger system; make your areas of interest and skills broader than you expect to need, so you can roll with the punches and take advantage of the opportunities. [Program specialist, federal government]

> Highly desirable to pursue vocation which will help to reassure woman that she merely has to interrupt her career for a relatively short time if she has children. If she merely gets an A.B. and no further training she may well need considerably more training before she can work in profession she wants. [Professor of education, 28 years employment; 5 years home]

One type of qualification conditioned approval of graduate school upon the existence of material or other resources.

If you can afford it, do it, realizing that, in most fields, it's only a beginning.

By all means if she has the physical stamina, and the natural resources to do so successfully (not to mention the financial resources!) in order to pursue an independent career, and if she has the desire to be regarded as a person in her own right, rather than as an appendage to another person. A higher degree of professional preparation is one safeguard against being forced to work below her abilities, whether full or part-time.

Several respondents thought that further education should be pursued as soon as possible after college. Others specified that it should take place before assuming family responsibilities.

One woman who had accumulated half the credits toward a doctorate but never attained the degree recommended that a young woman

Do this while one is young and still used to the routine of studying, doing research—and while *without* responsibility of husband and/or family.

A social worker who herself had spent one year working in that field before attending graduate school commented:

While some prefer to defer such training, I would advise this only if it is impossible to make career decisions without some further exploring of possibilities.

In a piece of advice that urged both immediacy and high goals, a woman with a master's in public health education said the idea of graduate school was "Great! Get that PhD as soon as you can."

The recommendation of a respondent who had received her graduate degree in 1950, the year of her marriage, and who had left her only job in 1951 during her first pregnancy was "to attend before marriage—also to work for several years before marriage if possible."

In contrast to the foregoing advice were suggestions that further education be postponed until after a period of work or other activities. A writer who had entered graduate school immediately after college advised:

Get as much education as possible. However, if "stale" from the education grind, take a year off for foreign travel (work as a stewardess on a ship or something of the kind) and return to school.

A retired professor of library science who had taught history in a high school for 17 years after college, during which time she received an M.A., and who then changed careers, acquiring a graduate library degree in 1947 at the age of 41, remarked:

An able woman should go on to graduate and/or professional school, though perhaps not immediately after Bachelor's degree. I believe work experience is very helpful before selecting graduate field, or at least before continuing to doctoral study.

A health education officer who had worked as a laboratory technician for nine years between college and graduate school recommended graduate school with

> No hesitation, if she knows what she wants to do. Otherwise, work a year or so in field of greatest interest to test degree of interest and need for further study.

From the dean of students at a woman's college who probably was often faced with similar questions, came the following advice:

> I believe this should be a deliberate choice to fulfill a particular goal. If that goal is not clear at the end of undergraduate work I would encourage the taking of at least a year or more to explore options, by way of employment or travel, volunteer work (if that can be afforded). I would suggest the advantages of being well into graduate work before starting a family, however.

While several of these comments seem to have been based on personal experience, either confirming or repenting past decisions, some respondents explicitly referred to their own careers, or lack thereof.

A four-hour-a-week free-lance journalist with minimal work experience said: "If you can afford it, do it for pleasure. In my case, the monetary rewards are negligible."

Another former journalism student, currently in public relations declared:

> I can only speak for journalism—it's not really necessary or helpful but it's interesting and good for future contacts—certainly not important academically.

A political science M.A. who had been out of the labor force for twenty years had this to say:

> If it seems likely that she will use the training and it can be provided without serious sacrifice—by all means go on. However, based on my own experience, I have to admit that judging the girl's likelihood of using this training is very hard.

A more positive note in this regard was struck by the technical director of a blood bank:

> Degrees are important in scientific fields. Knowledge is expanding so rapidly, continuing education is extremely important.

If the respondents' advice to the younger generation is seen as a reflection of their own experiences, it is patent that they did not regret their attendance at graduate or professional school. Taken at face value, there is no question that they would recommend that scholastically able young women go and do likewise.

There was a higher degree of unqualified endorsement of graduate

Table 9.1   Should an Able Young Woman Enter the Same Field of Study as Yours?

Respondents' Views	Percent
Yes, without reservation	45
Yes, with reservations	20
Depends on individual talents, qualifications, etc.	12
No, with qualifications	9
No	7
Right for some, wrong for respondent	4
Unsure	3
Total percent	100
Total number = 187	
NA = 39	

education, per se, than of graduate education in the respondents' own fields of study. Table 9.1 summarizes their views in this regard.

In general, the women's opinions about the value of graduate studies in their own major were based on one of two considerations: their own experiences in the occupations for which they had trained, or their readings of current and future job opportunities in these occupations. In other words, the women answered this question in the main with reference to their fields of work since their occupations largely corresponded to their fields of study.

Respondents who were unreserved in recommending that young women follow their example often supplied reasons for their recommendation. In many instances, their reasons concerned advantages specifically related to women's concerns. For example, flexibility of scheduling or ease of reentry were frequently cited to support endorsements of various graduate disciplines. The following sample of comments illustrates these views:

My field is fantastically interesting. It also provides summer vacations and a working day geared to school age children. [School psychology]

I could not recommend social work highly enough as a satisfying and flexible career for anyone, male or female, if their desire to earn a lot of money is not a priority.

Medical practice can be made flexible enough to meet family demands, and it is a field in which women can find great satisfaction.

Law is a very flexible career and flexibility is very important in these times.

It is an excellent field for a woman because it can be utilized at all times more readily than some. One can make her own opportunities in it to a degree. [Music]

One of the better ones for keeping a hand in while raising a family—for moving in and out of without losing touch. [Journalism]

Although I have made little use of my library degree so far, it has been a wonderful insurance policy, and the time may come when my husband has retired and all my children have left home, when I will want to reenter the labor force. I am glad I got the degree, and I would urge others to do the same.

Some fields were given high marks because they provided many opportunities for employment and/or advancement for women.

Has excellent opportunities. I entered the field in 1945 when very few women were attempting to become CPA's and we paved the way for wide acceptance of women in this field. Lends itself to working only part of the year which I prefer to a part-time weekly schedule.

There are some disadvantages—especially in terms of field work and travel— but with the women's lib movement, women are now sought after for geological jobs.

The male still dominates but there are a few signs of change. Now and then a woman is listed among the officers of a corporation, or is promoted to a middle-management position. The trend, I believe, will accelerate, and the younger, educated woman will find many more opportunities for advancement than at present.

A very good field for women. Less discrimination in my own discipline (even many years ago) than most. [Sociology]

Social work has always been an acceptable field for women—though many administrators are now male—if a woman wishes to devote the time to it, she can certainly be a leader in this field.

Some respondents praised their field for a variety of career options.

Law opens many doors. I heartily endorse the utility of a legal education.

If the person is interested in math, the field of health statistics is challenging, worthwhile, and has opportunities available for choices in jobs.

The field is concerned with fundamental problems in biology, is "fundable," offers a number of options (teaching, research, combination). [Genetics]

Know all the options, possibilities and varieties. It's a great field for free lancing and part-time work. [Journalism]

The most frequent type of endorsement was one that mentioned personal satisfactions derived from pursuing particular professions.

Student personnel is a very varied field and offers many satisfactions for those who relate easily to other people, have the capacity to listen well, enjoy planning and programming, and have some administrative sense. At the top there is considerable responsibility for administration and the satisfaction of being able to work to correct some of the institutional weaknesses which can impair the successful delivery of student services. I recommend it with enthusiasm to those whom I think have the right qualities.

Librarianship is an exciting field, particularly in the field of reader services and the relatively new computerized technology as applied to technical services (cataloguing and order work). There are challenging possibilities in service to readers and administration. Be prepared for changing ideas.

I encourage it whenever I can. If I were given the opportunity to relive my life, I'd choose the same field, the same school. And since I'd know I would go into the correctional field, I'd add the study of law. [Social work]

It's a deeply rewarding field if you enjoy students and research. It could be a wonderful experience if all administrators left it. There will be discrimination against you because you are a woman but you can help change that. [Anatomy]

Among the most frequent reasons for the reservations of those whose basic advice was "Yes, but . . . ," or "No, unless . . . ," or simply "No" was a lack of job opportunities.

Well, not now (not my particular field, astronomy) unless that is your only interest. The job market is terrible. And if you think you might follow a husband you would be happier with a more portable field of expertise.

With the current retrenchment in foreign languages, a career in teaching French literature cannot be enthusiastically endorsed.

Of course, today, no one with her eyes open is going into public school teaching unless in special ed or some of the other specialized fields that are still in demand.

In recent years, I know from placement pleas that School of Journalism grads (men and women) are finding the field very nearly closed. Thirty years ago, I thought journalism opportunities were attractive and varied, but not so today.

While it offers opportunity to women, the field is overcrowded and should be entered with caution by either men or women. [Law]

There were also alarms raised about difficulties encountered because of sex discrimination:

I would encourage a woman to enter archeology, but warn her that some prejudice exists. I do not believe that it is stronger than in law, medicine or other fields of natural and physical science. I also think that the situation is better now than when I began.

If you really like physical science, yes. But it still is a field where it's difficult for a woman to get ahead. I also feel that to do well in the physical sciences does require full-time effort, i.e., children would be difficult.

State Department as yet does not encourage women for career posts above the clerical level. God knows we need Sinologists and women in diplomacy.

She should know that "entry positions" are easily obtainable but the chances of ever obtaining "top level" positions are minimal. [Guidance and counseling]

It is like breaking into an exclusive private club. One may be tolerated, but not welcomed; in but not "In." It takes a very able, highly motivated and a self-assured woman to reach the highest echelons under these circumstances. [Geology]

Another caveat about some occupations referred to the demands of the field.

Teaching is a satisfying, rewarding career but not easy. Be prepared for violence, indolence, a lot of beautiful happenings, and endless frustration.

Competition in school supervisory positions in many places has become very intense and public pressure is unremitting. A woman with children will need physical and emotional stability to a large degree to work many years in educational supervision. The job is essentially as demanding as any professional educational position a man can hold, and dedication to the job should be total.

I consider my field difficult and would not encourage anyone to enter it unless they have a real passion for wishing to enter it. [Architecture]

Yes, if she reckoned with the demands of social work and could balance the investment of self in a not always rewarding field with other interests or avocations that make less severe demands on self.

A physician in private practice who recommended medicine as being "tough but satisfying" went on to describe problems in her specialty:

Chances of more women entering internal medicine (a field in which we *need* more physicians) are still low—because of a) long training; b) inhuman working hours; c) wide and intensive responsibilities; d) unrealistic image and demands by society.

A number of respondents specified conditions for successful pursuit of careers in their occupations; conditions which not all of them had met themselves. For example, a college modern language instructor who had terminated her doctoral studies before obtaining a degree said:

Don't do it unless you really *love* to teach, unless you're willing to go on to get a PhD *immediately* and unless you're ready to fight for tenure (and accept the possibility of failure).

Among other comments of a similar nature was that of an accounting graduate employed as a part-time auditor and bookkeeper who remarked: "Good career—but get the CPA (I did not)."

Similarly, a supervisory social worker with a master's degree recommended her field "If willing to work for doctorate and *not* concerned re financial rewards . . . otherwise would choose another field with more remuneration." She earned between $20,000 and $30,000 in 1974.

A health educator with an M.S. suggested that the young woman in question "go for the M.D. or the top of the line, whatever your sphere of interest."

In a slightly different vein, a former librarian asserted: "I loved school library work, but if I were doing it over, I would enter industrial library work because of the chances to advance." An M.A. in economics warned: "Only should enter economics these days if [she] has interest or ability in mathematics."

Another conditional recommendation by a librarian was: "Only as a *first* choice. There are opportunities for able and committed librarians but for too many persons it is a second choice career."

Several respondents felt their choice of graduate study had been a mistake and they gave diverse reasons for this conclusion. In some cases, they conceded that their reaction was personal and would not necessarily apply to everyone. In other instances, they recognized that the younger generation was less likely to confront conditions they had encountered. Here are some responses of this type.

> My field was law. A mistake for me many years ago—too difficult for women to get a good job unless they were absolutely top drawer. Perhaps times have changed—the new women's lib movement makes employers hesitate to turn away *all* women.

> I chose graduate rather than law school because of discrimination. Now would go to law school in preference to graduate work. [M.A. in history]

> Teaching is a rewarding field. I'm just not suited for it. Maybe she is.

> I consider "my" field, political science, as a fuzzy-wuzzy, and would urge economics or intellectual history as better substitutes providing sharper tools and more solid intellectual discipline and training. [Federal bureau chief]

> Have mixed feelings about social work and "helping" professions in general.

Further illustrations of the views of respondents toward aspects of their career fields were the following:

> Some years ago this would have been encouraged without hesitation. The field is now undergoing some chaos, uncertainty about values connected with levels of training, roles of professional staff and the place of social work for meeting today's needs. Jobs and funding are not secure.

> This field of study is interesting, but no more than other fields. However, being a PhD in an MD dominated field is not the most desirable situation. [Anatomy]

She should by all means *avoid* the liberal arts fields, unless she wishes to be underpaid throughout her career, or unless she has an independent income, or does not care about material well-being beyond a certain point. She will probably do better financially if she enters a professional or technical field.

One respondent took a different approach which was less concerned with the pros and cons of her field than with the desirability of recruiting women for it.

Depends on students—and again, era—in past, had to urge bright students to think about a career in sociology—nowadays problem has shifted—how to tell women students they are NOT good potential for careers in sociology— Expanded career horizons of women recently means many with little going for them are seeking careers in fields they have little aptitude for—just as men have always done.

It must be evident from the foregoing quotations that thumbs up from one woman was often countered by thumbs down from a member of the same profession. Here are two examples of such contrary opinions:

By all means. Philosophy would be better off for having more women working in the field!

versus

Don't enter it unless you find that you cannot stay away from it.

and

The opportunities couldn't be greater. [Physics]

versus

Job opportunities not good—but always possible for excellent people.

While some fields received a higher degree of endorsement as desirable subject areas for graduate study than others, it would be incorrect to make inferences about career satisfaction on this basis because of the dual threads of advice, one reflecting personal experiences and the other, perceptions of the future. A school teacher with nothing but pleasant memories of her worklife could not recommend her field because of a dearth of jobs, while a lawyer who recalled professional hardships and frustration recommended her field because of improved opportunities for women.

In general, the respondents seemed cognizant of current and prospective occupational opportunities, and many who had no regrets about their career choice tempered their enthusiasm in light of changed realities. Despite the fact that their advice was often based upon many considerations, the percentage of respondents in each field of study who unqualifiedly recommended their fields to the younger generation is of interest. (Table 9.2).

Table 9.2   Unqualified Recommendations to Enter Field of Study by Field of Most Recent Graduate Study

Field	Percentage Giving Unqualified Recommendation
Medicine	79
Journalism	73
Business	67
Library science	62
Law	60
Social science	45
Public health	43
Science	42
Social work	35
Education	29
Humanities	18

Number = 85
NA = 39
Not applicable = 102

If journalism is viewed in the wider context of communications, then the three most highly endorsed areas of study are fields with relatively bright outlooks for females seeking careers. In fact, in September 1977, the Columbia University Graduate School of Journalism for the first time in its 65 years of existence, enrolled more women than men.[1] Library science may seem misplaced in so high a spot but, as some respondents noted, new and improved technologies and other developments have resulted in an increased demand for librarians with special skills. On the other hand, science seems lower than one would have anticipated if not forewarned by comments about persisting sex discrimination.

The low degree of enthusiasm for the humanities and education also is in accord with conventional wisdom in the mid-1970's. In fact, to the extent that the women's advice was based upon predictions for the future and to the extent that such predictions have validity, the order in which the various fields obtained favorable assessments marks the respondents as fairly astute observers of the opportunity structure.

Women's Rights

Thus far, the question of women's rights has been limited to consideration of the treatment respondents had received in the labor market and to recent changes in employment conditions resulting from intensified activity for equal opportunities. The focus was on changes in the ways employers, colleagues, and clients dealt with women, not with changes that may have taken place in the women themselves. Yet, no examination of women's careers between 1963 and 1974 can afford to ignore subjective consequences of the women's movement since these were as likely to have employment implications as were changes brought about by administrative or legislative fiat.

While it is clear that middle-aged and older women do not have as much leeway for taking action to alter their circumstances as younger women because they are more likely to feel constrained by longstanding commitments, it was precisely for this reason that an inquiry about changed perceptions and behavior seemed worthwhile. The real test of a movement for change is its ability to affect the hard cases, and while the respondents weren't the hardest cases because their superior qualifications often served as a counterweight to their advanced age, younger women have generally been hailed as the iconoclasts who would lead the attack against tradition and who would win the spoils of victory.

But most of the respondents had miles to go before reaching senior citizenship and were in positions to benefit from their own changed perceptions as well as from changes in the larger society. While many of them had been pacesetters for the new feminists, others had lowered their sights rather than do battle with their antagonists. Whether respondents were premature women's liberationists or had settled for more traditional roles, the manner in which the emerging self-consciousness of women impinged upon their lives permitted a view of the ability of the women's movement to move an elite sector of the female population whose support and assistance can be invaluable.

The respondents were asked the following question: "Apart from employment-related concerns already noted, in what ways have recent efforts to improve the status of women had any effect upon your own attitudes, relationships, self-image, activities, etc.?"

Of the 226 respondents, 183 either provided one or more examples of ways in which these or other aspects of their lives had been affected by the women's movement; specifically claimed no impact on certain facets of their lives from the pressures for women's rights; or declared that in certain respects their liberation was antecedent to the new feminism. In addition, many women volunteered opinions of the women's movement. Reports of the effects of the women's movement on their own lives precedes a discussion of their views of the movement.

Effects of the Women's Movement

Table 9.3 indicates respondents' perceptions of the influence of pressures for women's rights on various aspects of their personal lives. Almost half of the women who answered this question reported positive

Table 9.3   Effects of Women's Rights Movement[a]

Nature of Effect	Aspect of Life Affected (percent)				
	Attitudes	Relationships	Self-Image	Activities	Behavior
Positive	32%	33%	36%	29%	39%
Always Liberated	21	13	18	1	7
Mixed or Unsure	12	6	5	–	2
Negative	1	1	3	1	1
Little or No Effect (specified)	34	47	38	69	51
Total percent	100	100	100	100	100
Number	(129)	(100)	(122)	(76)	(97)

[a]Other than employment-related effects.

changes in at least one area of their lives.* The term "always liberated" describes recollections of past actions that accord with current feminist precepts. Included among "mixed effects" are responses detailing both good and bad results or equivocal results. Also in this category are expressions of regret at losses incurred because women had not taken concerted action earlier. Claims of little or no effect were sometimes unclear; they seem to have meant either that these respondents could discern no effects, or that they saw no need for change.

Among positive effects, those involving behavior were cited most frequently, while participation in activities related to the women's movement was least commonly noted. If a liberated prior stance and positive change are combined however, the aspects of the respondents' lives which were most commonly affected affirmatively were self-image (54 percent) and attitudes (53 percent).

Almost a third of the responses indicated active participation in efforts to advance women's rights, a slightly higher percentage than that reported in a 1974 study of female doctorates, only a quarter of whom devoted some amount of time to such activities.[2]

A change of attitudes was most frequently described in terms of improved understanding of the reasons underlying women's traditional roles but, as the following comments indicate, it involved other subjects as well.

A reentrant who worked as a substitute teacher in 1974 said: "I've

*"Positive" is used to describe the value placed on the change by the women themselves.

become more aware of the need for independence, of becoming a 'contributing' member of society (in an economic sense), of the joys of being paid for my labor."

A part-time librarian, also a reentrant to the labor force, declared that the activities of the women's movement "have made me more aware of the lack of opportunity for many women and their poor self-image compared to that of men, but they have had little effect upon my own life except to make me understand in retrospect many dissatisfactions with my life when my children were very young and my activities limited."

A professor of education remarked:

> Perhaps changes in day care provisions in this country is one way I have found myself altering my thinking. Children can be cared for, even quite young children, by surrogate mothers very adequately. I see the lack of provision for adequate day care for working mothers as one of the most discriminatory practices in our country. . . . Until effective alternatives for child care other than present day care in most of the country can be implemented, I do not see a conscientious working mother ever being able to work *and* seek an effective uninterrupted career on the same basis as a man.

A social worker who said she "never felt disadvantaged in dealing with my world because I am a woman," also acknowledged that "recent efforts on behalf of women have made me more conscious of the subtle and overt obstacles to women's freedom to operate in a society with equal options to men."

A professor of astronomy declared

> I was startled to find that the movement increased my awareness of ways in which women treat themselves and other women as the second sex. I had thought I knew it all, but I'm still noticing ways in which I have been disadvantaged not by discrimination but by culture—and also seeing ways in which even a feminist mother can help to transmit this culture to a daughter.

Of special interest are the words of a social worker:

> As a black woman, racial aspects rather than those of sex have been of primary concern to me. Only very, very recently in connections with the health activities of the women's movement have I begun to develop a beginning interest in issues regarding the status of women.*

An attitude contrary to the foregoing statements was that of a teacher who said

> Some recent efforts to improve the status of women have made me convinced that I am no women's libber. I feel that every individual deserves respect and dignity. I feel also that there are roles for males and roles for females and vive la difference!

*There were five black women among the respondents, only two of whom made specific reference to their race in *any* context.

Among assertions of liberated attitudes prior to the new wave of feminism was this one from a professor of public health.

> I came from a family who took the view that both boys and girls should be educated to their capabilities so recent efforts may foster new attitudes among many people but to me they merely reinforce the attitudes of the family in which I was born and reared.

A writer hailed

> great personal reinforcement from the Women's Movement, and strong validation of my own ideas and feelings which were scorned by my colleagues (men) when I was younger.

While age was no bar to changed attitudes, the older women were more likely than their juniors to describe themselves as having long been liberated. This statement from a retired professor is typical of the remarks of many women over the age of 60:

> My career was closing about the time others felt the effect of Women's Liberation. My attitudes did not change, because I had fought for 40 years for recognition of equal rights.

It may be that these older women had confronted many more career barriers than their younger counterparts, and that strong convictions about sex equality were a necessary condition for surmounting these obstacles.

The following remarks of a non-worker illustrate a mixture of attitudes arising out of the women's rights movement:

> I do not in any way consider myself a "women's libber" (the closest I come is being a member of the League of Women Voters) and do not care for the strident voice of most women's lib organizations; however, I get tired of condescending advertisements and *a bit* riled whenever old acquaintances and even friends deride the whole movement. Equal work for equal pay and the same privileges for public office, etc. are the basic contributions of such groups.

Notes of effects of the women's movement on relationships primarily referred to three types of bonds: with other women; with men in general; and with husbands (and other family members) in particular.

A sociologist stated that the women's movement had made her "more friendly, less competitive with females . . . more relaxed sexually, more able to initiate relationships—less convention bound."

A psychologist remarked:

> I feel much more comfortable in my relationships with men and in male-oriented activities. I have always had a "drive" to do what (and act as) I wanted to do regardless of sex-role type, always with some degree of "unsureness." Now I feel more comfortable and certainly pleased with the

status of women. I also think men are more comfortable and less defensive so that it is surely a 2-way improvement in most cases. There is still a long way to go.

A college dean declared: "I sense in myself and other women less competition with each other, more easily shared concerns, more self-esteem and self-confidence, less compulsion to act, talk, look in prescribed ways."

A physician married to a business executive noted "major effects on marriage—husband now more contributory to previous 'female chores.' "

A professor of home economics, wife of a psychology professor, and mother of two said that the women's movement "probably made me more assertive in my marriage—more aware of being 'used' as a mother or wife and I've had to rethink that this is what I want to do. My family takes my work for granted now as women are 'supposed' to achieve."

The social worker wife of another professor asserted, "I no longer feel slightly guilty about letting my husband do a good many household chores so as to give me more free time for my writing and study."

The respondents roamed freely in their expositions of what women's liberation had done to or for their self-image. A social worker remarked that "as attention has focussed on the rights of women, the right to be married or single has been reinforced. This has been salutary to me as an inveterate single woman." A recently divorced librarian stated that she had been "given confidence as a single woman after 23 years of marriage." And an editor confirmed that the women's movement "made me realize how dependent I am on women—especially since I've been a widow."

A business research analyst gave the women's movement credit for helping her "self-image more than anything else. In the early years of my career I often had guilt feelings about being tied to a job and not always available to play the more traditional wife's roles."

A college dean, who had left an instructorship after 1963 in order to complete her doctorate, remarked: "I have a great deal more self-confidence than I had in 1963, and I have turned a job into a career."

A college librarian reported that her association with a college women's center "has made me recognize a number of early life decisions as feminist decisions (and others quite the opposite!). I can see myself now as a member of the generation brainwashed by the 'feminine mystique'—and by and large I think I've overcome it pretty well."

The remarks of a journalist exemplify those of the "prematurely" liberated with respect to their views of themselves.

When I went back to work leaving infants with a sitter 15 or 16 years ago, I was regarded as an odd ball. Now I'm regarded as a pioneer. The same thing applies to attitudes towards my going out of town on assignments. Because I did these things, I am less restless, less concerned with being my own person now, than many of my friends.

A pragmatic note was struck by a social scientist:

I always considered myself to be "emancipated." Of course it is clear to me now that my generation's view of freedom was quite limited. We thought we could play all the roles simultaneously and superbly. For me, the result seems to be a little like Dr. Johnson's dog that walked on its hind legs—it is not remarkable that it's badly done, but rather that it's done at all. . . . It is too late to struggle for more. I am accustomed to my life and in most ways it could not be improved. It's all a matter of 'compared to what'—and in my case, I feel reasonably content compared to my generation.

Negative psychological effects from the new pressures for equal rights were remarked by a respondent with minimal work experience:

I am glad for the gains made; I believe opportunities should be equal. I resent being made to feel guilty for choosing not to work outside the home, however; I think my own self-image has probably suffered as a result of the women's movement. But I am glad I have resisted the pressure to look for a job I didn't really want.

Another non-worker who was currently studying in a new field after spending many years at home commented: "I'm afraid they have made me dissatisfied with what I have done with the talents I have/had."

Involvement in activities specifically related to equal rights for women were mentioned by some respondents. In a few cases, these were job-related, as the following report from a professor:

In 1973 I was active in founding a Women's Coalition at R__College. This is a group representing all employed women on campus, from maids through administrators. I was active in an ad hoc committee on campus studying the status of women and I became a member of the __Association's Commission on the Status of Women. Next year I will be co-chairing the Commission.

The activities of a non-working teacher illustrate another form of involvement.

Because I am not employed at present, I have been able to participate very actively in the women's movement. Most of my efforts have been devoted to working for ERA. I have lobbied, participated in debates, presented programs on ERA to public and private schools, been taped for radio presentation, co-sponsored and participated in workshops on women's rights.

Another form of active response to the women's movement was reported by a public health official who said she had "hired several women 'managers' into good positions in the department." She went on to say that she had become "much more conscious of role as woman professional than previously."

A professor of education declared

I have become very aware of the bias in our language. I have taken an active interest in combatting this through workshops and lectures—and through weeding such expressions out of my own language.

A sour note was struck by some respondents who resented assignments as token females. The plaint of a professor of medicine that she had "been appointed to University committees as a WOMAN—and much of this is a waste of time" was echoed by several other women. In some cases it was unclear whether the women were critical of the utility of the committees or of the tokenism. Their disinclination to assume certain masculine prerogatives, however, should be heeded by those who advocate full participation of women in all activities formerly barred to them, without any assessment of value. Who knows but that a boycott of redundant practices may be salutary for both males and females!

The last set of comments refers to changes in the respondents' behavior as a result of the women's movement. A state bureau chief noted that she now had "fewer inhibitions in participating, stating opinions in all areas of my life." She went on to say, "I guess the only inhibition I still have is that I have access to the executive restroom but choose not to use it."

A physician who was the associate director of a hospital department declared

I had waged my own quiet war of liberation (successfully); now I am more vociferous. I felt I had to stand *against* society to achieve my goal of being a whole person, not just a biological thing. Now I know that the real goal is not that—the goal is to change society!"

A professor of art reported

Since 1968 I've shared my home with a female colleague—we are equal partners in ownership of property, etc. She is enthusiastically feminist and has encouraged me to be even more aggressive in pursuing my rights. At present, we're engaged in combatting a case of discrimination against us in the matter of an insurance policy.

Changes in the behavior of a professor of speech were directly related to her work. "I have concentrated on encouraging women students to attain distinction in undergraduate studies and activities," she reported, and "I have become more out-spoken in defense of women colleagues."

A former university officer who left this position in 1975 in order to become a private consultant confessed that she "got the nerve to shake loose from the establishment and go into self-employment which I find really exhilarating."

A professor and mother of two who had worked continuously said

I have done more soul-searching, have a better opinion of myself and demand better treatment from others. I don't have the need to constantly justify my behavior to myself and others.

Among the comments with respect to the behavior of the "always liberated" were "Others are catching up with my way of life," from a physicist, and "I find that I now share my views more freely and enjoy more positive responses than previously," from a social worker.

An advertising agency vice-president acknowledged

I'm slightly more aggressive than I was but I was never a shrinking violet. I was raised by a father who suggested I try to become a doctor (never a nurse) and it never occurred to me that being a woman held me back from becoming anything at all—one was limited only by one's abilities. I wanted to be a Marcel Proust—it was not society's fault that I never made it, believe me.

There were also retrospective evaluations of past conduct.

A health education officer admitted

I have greater understanding that I was in fact discriminated against in employment most often subtly and that I conformed in some ways (i.e. didn't act too aggressive) and evaded (without challenge, because men knew what *they* had done) tasks I didn't want to do. I ducked seeking administrative leadership roles and chose program assignments.

A retired professor of education also had misgivings about her earlier behavior:

Recent events have made me realize that I was a victim of injustice in my job and that the only way to get justice is to *fight* for it. I have never been a fighter, so . . .

Several respondents offered an inventory of various types of effects they had observed in their own lives as a result of the movement to advance the cause of female equality.

A grade school teacher remarked

I welcome the "equal rights" aspects and have been "awakened" to the inequities of past systems. My relationship to my husband has subtly changed and we share the housework now. Perhaps I would have followed a male-oriented career, like medicine, married later, spent more time on my music instead of my children if I had been born later. I feel more assertive but also sentiments of regret and dissatisfaction arise from thoughts of what might have been—feelings which I consider to be destructive in terms of self-image.

Another account of multifold effects came from a social science professor.

More retrospective resentment that the "sharing" profile I thought characterized my own marriage re home and children was so far from real sharing. Efforts to implement more are difficult once a relationship has jelled over so many years—Also retrospective resentment at the degree to which one's self-confidence is routinely undermined by men, so that no matter what one achieves as a woman, there is a deep-seated rankling that says it isn't as good as some think, or that one may not be able to do a thing one sets out to do in research or writing. There are limits to the extent one can change such basic aspects of self in the middle years—so one learns to live with it.

The following report was also provided by a professor:

The first way in which the movement(s) to improve the status of women has affected my self-image is to make me realize that the problems I had faced throughout my life were not due to some failure or weakness in myself as a person or as a professional woman but were reflections of the general attitude towards women who did not conform to the accepted norm. In a sense this awareness has complicated my relationship with men including my husband. I see such relationships very differently. Where previously I was willing to accept, for the sake of conformity, the "woman's role," I now refuse and demand equal status. I assert myself without too much concern for "male" susceptibilities. Inwardly I always felt I should. In my relations with women there's greater understanding with some, less with others. Since I am trying to maintain a balance between the extreme feminists and those who reject the latter's outlook, I often find myself damned by both groups.

A returnee employed as a reading specialist in public schools reflected

I grew up to be rather passive, but finally I'm learning to be confident enough to have opinions of my own and to assert my feelings, especially when I feel my needs are being ignored or violated. My husband and I have a better—but not smoother—relationship because of this. I am probably less religious than in my youth because I cannot find a congenial niche in the male-dominated organized church to which I belong. . . . For me the most difficult task has been to free myself physically and psychologically from the morass of domestic activity that a family expects or desires from a wife and mother . . . somehow I am dogged by guilt if everything is not ship-shape for them.

A reentrant currently employed as an administrator and married to a business executive reported

Certainly made me personally more *aware* of our status; contributed to a mutual interest with our two daughters; encouraged me in my effort to hold onto my most recent career despite its meaning living apart weekdays from my husband (he commutes from another town weekends).

There were other expressions of resentment, ambivalence, complaint, some of which included a note of pride at having achieved despite obstacles. The following comment was made by a government administrator:

They [efforts on women's behalf] have permitted me a great feeling of arrogance—that I *made* it, with my mind, personality, high energy and perseverance, with (or despite) my sex and marital peregrinations. I also feel, like a Victorian, driven to lean over backwards *not* to be pushy, to act entitled or abusive, and to proceed in social or professional relationships on the merits without the distraction of consideration for my sex.

A professor of biology and mother of one child who confessed that the women's movement had forced her to realize that she "had been discriminated against many times," also had the following complaint to make:

I have an awareness of myself as a woman in the career field now, whereas before I considered myself a scientist. This has its uncomfortable aspects. Where previously I was recognized as a scientist primarily, now I have the extra label of woman . . . and I resent [it]. . . . I achieved my present status on my own initiative, hard work, some sacrifice of personal comfort and a larger family, development of a competence, etc., without the help of Affirmative Action and I feel an impatience with most women's movements.

Among women who saw no real change in their lives as a result of the women's movement was an ABD, mother of five and currently separated from her husband, who had not worked since 1947.

All the organized public soul-searching going on now I had already endured privately years ago, as I'm sure most thinking women have ever since the division of labor forced women into a subordinate position in the power structure. My day-to-day activities have not changed because the circumstances of my life have not changed to a degree significant enough to affect my day-to-day responsibilities. . . . Legally my status has improved in part because California has enacted an expanded community property law, giving the wife the right to *control* as well as ownership. This has not, however, changed anything within my family. . . . Affecting my life-style significantly requires a far more profound and complex change in our whole social system than can be achieved in the foreseeable future by these recent efforts no matter how dedicated.

Among the few women who described only negative effects on their lives as a result of the women's movement was a professor:

I have been personally hurt by stress on women's rights. . . . My oldest son (a white male) Natl. Merit Scholar etc. was really told he would have gotten scholarship help if he were a girl—all he got was an "honor," so I am forced to work extra hard to provide the quality education he and his brother need and deserve—this is the backlash women don't see. Also, my husband [also a professor] has not had the employment offers I have had as he is a man. I would prefer to be more of a wife and less a career person but I cannot afford to.

This report of the vicarious effects of a presumed "backlash" directed against a son and husband contrasts with a warning by a history professor about another kind of backlash:

In my own field the changes in the position and role of women during the past few years have been unprecedented. But much remains to be done. A backlash is developing among men which could have serious consequences both on a personal and professional basis. . . . We have merely uncovered the tip of the iceberg that is the position of educated women in a society which is most reluctant to recognize their existence and to grant them equal status.

Opinions of the Women's Movement

The foregoing quotations largely describe specific effects of the women's movement upon aspects of the respondents' lives. As mentioned earlier, many women responded to this question in terms of the way they felt about the movement rather than, or in addition to, describing its actual impact upon their own lives. Ninety-seven respondents stated specific views of the women's movement. More than two-thirds of this group expressed positive opinions; 22 percent had mixed reactions and 9 percent had only unfavorable views about efforts to improve the status of women.

There was little difference in the views of respondents having different educational credentials, but women in predominantly female occupations were more inclined to oppose the women's movement than those in occupations employing higher proportions of males. Possibly women in female professions foresaw more competition with males or, more likely, these women are more tradition bound. There were no other characteristics by which enthusiasts could easily be distinguished from respondents with mixed or negative feelings about the women's movement.

Elaborations of affirmative views were rare. Women with misgivings were much more likely to amplify their position. Among the supporting statements were the following:

I think the women's movement is one of the half dozen or so more important intellectual developments in the last 200 years, and as such it causes one to think a great deal about the lasting implications and consequences. [Professor of English]

The National Organization for Women and the Women's Movement are the greatest inventions since sex. They have done more to advance women in business, education, and social development in the last 5 years than has been done since 1776. Whatever mistakes have been or will be made, educated women have a moral obligation to advance the women's movement, to help other women. [Sales executive]

I've always thought women were beautiful (in the sense that black is) and I reject the notion that a successful career woman is some kind of superwoman.

I think our society does women an injustice by not having very high expectations of us. [Lawyer]

I think one of the best things to come out of the "women's movement" is the change in men's attitudes—especially young men. I think that men now and in the future will encourage and at least respect women's desires to pursue their own interests, intellectual or whatever. [Mathematician]

Mixed views often were on the order of "I'm all for equal pay and equal opportunity but. . . ." Among the variations on this theme and on others were the following remarks:

I object to the defensiveness of much of the women's movement although to the extent it has encouraged more young women toward professional attainment, it has been worthwhile. I am, however, concerned about the effect on child rearing and worry about the children of mothers who today strike me as quite self-centered. [Lawyer]

I think most of the women's lib business is "media-fodder." I think the only substantial issues are equal pay and equal opportunity—absolutely just and important—but unfortunately the effort to achieve these ends are, in my opinion, mixed up with a great deal of unseemly nonsense and breeding all sorts of unfortunate "asides"—Erica Jong is a very good example, a two-bit no-talent and humanly the size of the TV screen. Do you think Margaret Mead is in the least impeded by being female or that any of the women's lib business had had any effect on her life and achievement? . . . No woman of real stature, achievement and "grace" that I can think of has been affected by women's lib's endeavors in areas of importance. [Business administrator]

Except for equal pay for equal work I think Women's Lib is for the birds. I wish I had never heard of it. [Librarian]

Although on one hand there is now greater pressure to be employed for pay and "do" something . . . I think now there is greater acceptance of a *variety* of life styles, enabling women to have a greater choice and comfort in that choice! [Non-worker]

The theme of most of the wholly negative comments about the women's rights movement largely emphasized style and attitude rather than substance. Some of them also included opposition to substantive issues, as the following examples demonstrate:

I really come through antediluvian here—I have never when working or "unemployed" felt discriminated against as a female. . . . In many ways, I think the women's movement has come on too strong. I think it would be sad if a young educated girl was made to feel guilty because she chose to remain at home or raise children. [M.S. in journalism—home since 1953]

My attitude is and always has been that a woman who is willing to work for *anything* can have it. She shouldn't expect special concessions because she's a woman; and she shouldn't expect to be treated like a man unless she's willing to guarantee that she'll never revert to being a woman! [Non-worker; former college professor]

Programs such as improving status of women have caused many of my coworkers to become dissatisfied shrews with low productivity, a centering on self to the detriment of their jobs, and an exalted opinion of their own worth in professional spheres. Many are acting like spoiled brats rather than true professionals. [Statistician]

I have been disgusted by the extremes to which these movements have gone, particularly in wishing to change nomenclature such as chairman to chairperson, etc. I am also disgusted at the "equal opportunity" extremes for women (or men?)!! Mortar Board loses its identity, for example. And although I am not a champion of Greek sororities and fraternities, I was amazed at the effort to break them up. I still believe that there are certain courtesies that a "lady" likes to have shown to her; I think there are certain occupations (requiring physical abilities beyond her) that a woman should not try to enter. [Professor of romance languages]

I do not see that the current modifications in family mores are any more successful or satisfactory to individual women than the pattern of the so-called traditional or nuclear family. In this I seem to be at odds with the majority of educated and supposedly liberal-minded women particularly the activists of the women's movement. It seems to me that they are far less perceptive than were the emancipated women of the 19th and early 20th century, and have thus far achieved little beyond what their earlier leaders accomplished. I am discouraged and saddened to find that I am so far out of touch with what seems to be the avant-garde of women's liberation. [Non-worker—former language instructor]

I object very much to being referred to as "Ms." . . . I am very proud of the designation "Mrs." and have been for 28 years. The blanket bestowal of "Ms." on *every* woman seems very highhanded to me. I am an individual, not one of a group . . . the use of "Ms." seems to me to be an uncalled for, personally unasked for, unfavorable comment on and subtle criticism against marriage. I am *not,* of course, against the use of "Ms." by those who choose to be so referred to. But women should be asked their preference. Don't assume. [Former librarian, not employed since 1949]

I feel "women's libbery" is most pertinent for mediocre-calibre women of very moderate ambition, whose attitudes as "good little girls" coupled with limited talents have kept them otherwise from achieving the visibility necessary for some levels and types of advancement [Federal administrator]

In addition to assessments of various goals of the women's rights movement were some comments that were not so much critiques of feminism as suggestions for new emphases or were simply musings about present or future implications.

For example, a psychologist pinpointed what she thought was insufficiently stressed by the movement.

> The big area which still needs work is in the cultural expectations of woman as wife and mother. I think that while employment opportunities, pay, status in jobs etc. has shown the biggest gains there is still the male feeling that women can now do whatever they wish to do and are qualified for *as long as* they do the laundry, get dinner, etc. etc. While these factors are lessening, there is necessary a concerted educational drive beginning in pre-school to change expectations and to ensure shared responsibilities between men and women particularly in family situations.

A speech professor referred to the need for equal status in the family.

> The status of women will not improve (in my opinion) so long as educated women do not demand intellectual equality in the home for themselves or girl children. Men reflect their wives' attitudes in dealing with other women. No amount of Women's Lib demonstrations will substitute for the learning which is neglected in the home in early childhood.

A part-time professor of chemistry brought up an aspect of the problems faced by women who wish to continue family and career.

> Although I wholeheartedly support all efforts on the part of women for equal recognition as reward for their work, I also feel that special consideration should be given to women who want to divide their efforts between family and career for a part of their lives. It is important for those women to have an opportunity to combine working in their field, albeit part-time, accruing experience and seniority until such time as they want to re-enter full time.

There were two themes in the additional remarks of a social worker. One concerned relationships with men; the other was addressed to the female opponents of women's liberation:

> Our true success is in the re-educating of men. This can be hopeless in some cases. In other cases, men will experience relief and freedom as women become people instead of feminine objects inclined to the "poor little weak defenseless me"—Men have overtly seemed to like this role but deeply they resent the obligations it places on them. Also, beware of the vociferous *anti* liberation woman. The woman most threatened by this movement is the woman who has *achieved* the most by the subtle use of her family to bolster dependency needs. She sees the movement as destroying these roles—her husband in the kitchen displaces the maid she fought hard to get, etc. etc. She doesn't want it to come easy to other women either. She is more a victim of the system than those able to fight it.

The mother of five children, a non-worker since graduate school, ascribed recent progress in the career status of "the younger generation of educated women" not to the women's movement but to the "unprecedented degree of control over their reproductive function, giving them the freedom to beat on the doors to the (business and professional) world and to devote their time single-mindedly to professional success, as a man may."

The remarks of a consultant in the area of career development dealt with observations arising from her work.

> The idea of "equality to men" has been applied far enough to show that women and men alike suffer inequities that must be corrected. The fact that women *have* to be there to deal with these conditions along with men is the great step forward . . .

It should come as no surprise that the respondents, whose earlier behavior ran counter to the norm, should give a ringing endorsement to the goals of the women's rights movement. Nor should some amount of indifference have been unexpected since many of these women had themselves anticipated the new feminism and had long ago fought the same battles. That not every respondent would be favorably affected or impressed with efforts to improve women's status was also predictable. Gross similarities in school attainment are unlikely to erase differential absorption of prevailing attitudes and social expectations, since this depends on a host of factors antedating and subsequent to education.

In the main, the responses convey the impression that women who had wholly or partially avoided filling conventional female roles welcomed the emergence of a widely shared recognition of common problems. The changes cited by some of the respondents who had exhibited the most dedicated career commitment testify to the power that social controls had been able to exert on the lives of even the most emancipated women. Moreover, very few of the women claimed that they were too old to feel the impact of the women's movement in the present or in the future. In fact, if the respondents' reactions to efforts to strengthen women's status are compared with the findings of a 1974 national poll, the percentage of unconditional support among the respondents is about the same as that of the 18 to 29 year old women who were polled.[3] College women in the national survey showed the same degree of support as the respondents but that classification covered all age groups. While this suggests that the respondents were young in spirit if not in body, what it probably means is that the relatively extensive work experience of mature women who had graduate training provided them with more accurate information about the need for concerted action to achieve equal rights and opportunities than is available to women who spend much of their lives away from the workplace.

Notes

1. *New York Times,* September 12, 1977, p. 27.

2. John A. Centra, *Women, Men, and the Doctorate* (Princeton, N.J.: Educational Testing Service, 1974), p. 133.

3. *The Virginia Slims American Women's Opinion Poll,* Volume III, The Roper Organization (no publ. date), p. 3.

10] SYNOPSIS AND EPILOGUE

The premise underlying this research was that degree programs beyond the baccalaureate constitute the highest level of vocational training and that a woman's decision to undertake advanced studies is an implied commitment to a career in the professions or in occupations of corresponding prestige. Unlike undergraduate education whose goals are so ambiguous that the lack of a relationship between college studies and subsequent pursuits is generally regarded with indifference, most graduate training is viewed as the prelude to the pursuit of specific types of high status market work. The argument that vicarious achievement from presumptive contributions to the success of husbands and children is sufficient justification for educating women at the college level is not applicable to female graduate education, according to Cross:

> Few would maintain that a master's degree in any field is necessary or even desirable for women who expect to live out their lives as wives and mothers, and many people would argue that a Ph.D. is a downright disadvantage.[1]

The fact that a woman's professional commitment can be altered at will reflects the ambivalence of society, and of the woman herself, about the proper feminine role; it does not negate the import of her training.

This study of the careers of a group of women of superior scholastic aptitude who pursued advanced education has demonstrated how their professional skills were utilized over time. Most of the respondents were in their late thirties or early forties when initially surveyed in 1963, at which time they were either employed at various levels of an occupational ladder, or were out of the labor force attending to home, family and other non-market concerns.

The updated view of their careers through 1974 has provided an opportunity to examine their work histories since leaving college, with special attention to developments during midlife.

This concluding chapter summarizes the major findings about the work decisions of these women. It also discusses some implications of the research in light of recent trends in female behavior and offers recommendations for interventions to support and encourage the expansion of opportunities for the utilization of the skills of highly qualified women. Since this research has looked backward into the lives of women who commenced their career preparation a generation ago, the report concludes with speculations about the status of their successors a generation hence.

Findings

The key finding of the research was that the career commitment of this group of women was variable in intensity, but was rarely extinguished. Relatively few of the respondents prepared for careers that never materialized. Although the attention that many of the women paid to their professions wavered or ceased at times, only a handful of the women remained preoccupied with family and leisure activities to the exclusion of gainful employment during most of their adult lives.

In economic terms, the educational investment of the few women with limited worklives had a much lower pay-off than of those who were gainfully employed throughout most of their adult lives. But the women who chose to derive their gratifications outside of the labor market did not have to think in terms of pay-offs because they had husbands who provided adequate family support. As long as women are not charges upon the public treasury, they are free to spend their time as they choose. When they need public assistance, indifference is supplanted by inducements to enter the work force, regardless of job qualifications or family responsibilities.[2] This type of differential treatment means that pressures for female labor force participation turn out to be, in effect, inversely related to the magnitude of human capital investment.

While no social stigma attached to the lack of utilization of these women's professional expertise, the finding that most of the respondents had worked during the bulk of their adult years, regardless of financial need, attests to their desire to realize their early career goals. Those who dropped out of the labor force in order to fulfill maternal responsibilities may have made more conventional choices than women who never married or the mothers who never left employment, but withdrawal was usually temporary. Careers had not been relinquished but recessed. Reentry to the labor force which was a highlight of the follow-up period commonly resulted in the resumption of an earlier career or the pursuit of a new career option, on a continuing basis.

The presence of a disproportionate representation of never married women among the respondents contributed to the high degree of career continuity exhibited by the group. Relatively few married women remained childless and it was primarily the presence of children that acted as a brake upon careers.

Husbands' attitudes alone rarely inhibited wives' employment, presumably because withdrawal from the labor market was a mutual decision. Moreover, these women had married highly educated men who largely were sympathetic to their wives' career aspirations. Nevertheless, precedence was given to husbands' careers by many wives who left employment to follow their spouses to new job locations. However, the willingness to subordinate their own career goals did not permanently retard these women's progress, possibly because their high qualifications facilitated placement after relocation.

Loss of a husband acted to propel non-workers into the labor force and to spur career progress. Separation and divorce, in particular, created an incentive for earned income and possibly also a psychological need for occupational success to compensate for failed marriages.

Among mothers, size of family was found to be a crucial determinant of labor force continuity. Never married women, childless women, and mothers of one child demonstrated the greatest career attachment, and this group comprised almost half of all respondents. Many women may have intentionally shunned responsibilities that ordinarily distract females from careers. That children are such distractions was clear since the birth of each successive child had the effect of shortening a mother's worklife.

The negative influence of multi-child families and of young children on maternal labor force participation was modified, however, among women with academic doctorates and first professional degrees, most of whom prepared for non-traditional careers. This finding indicated an interrelationship between career choice and career commitment independent of family composition. The decision to pursue careers requiring extended and rigorous training connoted a strong initial work orientation which led to a more persistent professional attachment than that demonstrated by mothers of families of similar size who had made a smaller investment in career preparation.

Many respondents were found to have maintained their hold on their careers by means of part-time employment. Reduced work schedules made it possible for such women to continue to pursue their careers while simultaneously attending to home-based duties. An interpretation that translates the recourse to part-time work into a dilution of

career commitment—because women with objectively similar responsibilities remained on full-time work schedules—disregards the fact that
all occupations do not invoke similar penalties for occasional, or even
extended, part-time employment. Many women who had a considerable
amount of part-time work experience were eventually able to approach
and even to equal the achievement of continuous full-time workers in
their fields; others seemed more interested in the opportunity to devote
some time to their professions than in attaining top jobs.

Concentration upon professional tasks at a high level of competence
is more appealing to many individuals than advancement to
administrative positions which require the abandonment of functions
that originally attracted them to their fields, such as teaching, patient
care, research. Since part-time employment permitted continued
professional activity, it was often a satisfactory resolution to periodic
conflicts between career and family demands. Part-time work was often
indicative of career dedication in the face of circumstances that in other
cases resulted in departure from the labor force.

The level of career achievement attained by the respondents was
judged to be quite high in terms of rank, rewards, responsibilities, and
productivity. The majority of the women had made at least adequate use
of their skills and almost half of them had reached superior positions
within their occupations.

Since this study did not make comparisons between the sexes, the view
of these women's progress had to be from the perspective of what they
were able to achieve within the constraints set by the larger society rather
than with reference to the achievements of their male peers. In these
terms, many of them did very well and some were able to make
extraordinary use of their talents.

In general, the proportion of women in predominantly male
professions who had attained top employment status was greater than in
fields with larger proportions of female employment. Although the
psychosocial aspects of career choice were not an element in this
investigation, it is possible to conjecture that women who were
numbered among the very few admitted to training in male dominated
professions between 1945 and 1951 demonstrated a presumptive
willingness to compete with the male majority. In Horner's terms, they
were the exceptional women who did not fear success. Instead, they may
have actively sought it, and many of them achieved it.

Professions dominated by women were found to lend themselves more
readily to the realization of the conventional female role, but the
relatively few women who demonstrated an uninterrupted commitment
to these fields were often able to attain high status in their occupations.
As a rule, however, the choice of a career in a field with a high ratio of

female employment appeared to have either a cause or effect relationship to broken patterns of labor force participation.

Being a member of the educated elite was found to have been no protection against inequitable treatment from those in control of the portals to career mobility. Claims of merit often had to give way before claims for male preference. The majority of respondents felt they had been subject to sex discrimination in employment, although some of them stipulated that they had not had to contend with prejudicial treatment in recent years. This change may be seen either as a sign of the times or as a tribute to their persistence in surmounting obstacles to advancement.

Discrimination with respect to salaries and promotional opportunities was reported with greater frequency than employment inequity in such areas as hiring and assignment of duties. Respondents appeared to have had less difficulty in securing employment than in progressing at a pace equal to that of their male peers. Superior qualifications may have enhanced their chances of being hired but were of less benefit in competing for higher positions.

The perception of discrimination was not related to continuity of employment. Women who had pursued continuous full-time employment were as likely to report having experienced unequal treatment in the labor force as those with similar training and employment characteristics but less consistent career commitment. Thus, these women provided no support to the common attribution of female work discontinuity to explain sex differentials in employment status and salaries.

Colleges and universities were found to be a major locus of discrimination. Academic women did reach high ranks but primarily in institutions of lower prestige than would be considered acceptable by males who had earned doctorates from a prestigious university, confirming Sandler's assertion that "Somehow women who are qualified to receive Ph.D.'s at our major institutions are unqualified to teach at the upper ranks of those same institutions."[3] Many academic women emulated the pattern of work of their male colleagues, but this was apparently no assurance of equal treatment.

The assault against affirmative action by male academics which appeared to rival in intensity the opposition of other segments of society was a curious reaction from those who might be expected to be women's close allies. Rossi sees this stance as not so much antiwoman as a reaction to a contracting academic labor market:

The readiness with which academic men translate the "goals" of affirmative action into "quotas" should be seen as nervous confusion as they face an uncertain future unlike their own past, and not simply as resistance to the legitimate claims of academic women. . . . We are placing sharp demands on academic institutions in a period when the best will in the world will not yield easily to them.[4]

This explanation might be more convincing if there were evidence that academic men had shown "the best will in the world" when faculty jobs were more plentiful and women were therefore less of a threat. Little evidence of this sort was presented in the survey. Instead, most successful women, academics and non-academics, seem to have advanced despite male obstructiveness rather than because of male assistance.

Recent measures against sex discrimination in employment had directly affected the job status of a quarter of current or recent workers. Since almost half of the women expressed no complaints about their relative treatment in the labor market throughout their careers, there appears to have been a fair amount of improvement where improvement was believed to have been indicated.

Many respondents who had contended with employer discrimination had nonetheless been able to become well established in their careers prior to the onset of accelerated activities on behalf of working women. Others found their age to be a handicap in seeking equal treatment; younger women were reaping the benefits of equal opportunity and affirmative action efforts. In these cases, age had supplanted or accompanied sex as a cause of discrimination.

There was little evidence of pronounced conflict between the demands of career and family. Most of the mothers were satisfied with the way they had allocated their time. It is possible that the ability of many reentrants to the labor force to compensate for career breaks was a factor in the expression of eventual satisfaction with earlier labor market decisions. Among the minority of mothers who did have reservations, remorse about insufficient dedication to careers was expressed more frequently than regrets about inadequate time spent on family concerns.

The frequency with which mothers temporarily abandoned their careers to concentrate upon family concerns for a period of time indicated that women who had behaved unconventionally by seeking high credentials during a family oriented era were unable or unwilling to fully free themselves from all social restraints. Childbearing was unlikely to have been an unplanned event among this group; although they may have been reluctant to renounce careers in favor of motherhood, they were equally unwilling to do the reverse. But careers can be neglected more readily than children, and there were few mothers who were both willing and able to follow a course that enabled them to handle these responsibilities simultaneously. Since society offers neither the approval nor the instrumentalities to facilitate combined attention to career and family, it was not surprising to find such a pattern to be exceptional.

A period of withdrawal from the employment arena usually did not mean a retreat from all career interests. Many respondents were heavily involved in volunteer activities at such times. Mueller's finding that the respondents' volunteer work prior to 1963 was a means of maintaining their marketability while out of the labor force was substantiated by the subsequent finding that this aim had largely been fulfilled.[5] In some cases respondents pursued non-market careers as permanent involvements which completely replaced gainful employment as the means of realizing their professional aims. Such a course can only be followed by women with alternative sources of income and most of the married respondents had such a source in the person of high earning husbands. Nevertheless, relatively few women appeared willing to consider focusing on non-market careers over the long term.

Reentry to the labor force after a prolonged intermission was not found to have been a particularly difficult process for the respondents. The job search was simplified because they had maintained or renewed professional contacts or had influential friends. Formal retraining was rare; updating of skills was apparently accomplished on the job. Only in a few cases where women decided to change careers or to acquire additional credentials were educational programs undertaken prior to reentry.

A measure of these women's attachment to their professions was demonstrated by their choice of options for the years after age 65. Relatively few of them wanted to enter retirement at that time. Instead, the most frequent preference for their old age was part-time employment, often in conjunction with independent professional activities. The desire to continue working was expressed by women with discontinuous work patterns, in particular, and appeared to indicate their reluctance to relinquish holds upon revived careers.

Finally, the study demonstrated that women in their middle and late years were not immune to the virus of Women's Liberation. The women's movement received substantial endorsement and many respondents noted various changes in their own attitudes and behavior as a result of the recent stress on women's rights. Several were self-proclaimed premature liberationists, some of whom, by acting against the social grain, had incurred a heavy toll in guilt. Those who had compromised their earlier goals while not necessarily regretful were often envious of the greater freedom of action available to their younger counterparts.

Implications of the Findings

Although the respondents were provided with the opportunity to develop their potential in the training place, society was laggard in providing them with a support system to enable them to use their skills in the workplace. Their education may have appeared to put them on an equal footing with males, but this was an illusion. It was the women who were expected to provide most of the support system to enable men to remain preoccupied with their careers. High qualifications were rarely a sufficient excuse for a wife to be similarly preoccupied, especially if she had children.

In essence, sex discrimination in employment flows from different expectations for men and women. It is, at the least, an unconscious expression of the belief that a woman's place is in the home while her children are in the home, and that she serves her husband best by freeing him for his work responsibilities and by doing what she can to foster his career. Some of the respondents had exceptional husbands who aided and abetted their wives' careers, but most mothers took time out to attend to their families' needs because they either thought there was no other way to satisfactorily fulfill their maternal responsibilities or they found no acceptable alternative.

That relatively few mothers regretted these decisions must be viewed in light of their time and possible inclinations. The employment of middle class mothers was treated as aberrant behavior in the years when these women were raising their children. Mothers who insisted upon their right to work were much more iconoclastic than are mothers today who feel the same way but have considerably greater backing.

Highly educated females recently have been challenging the validity of many of the proscriptions and prescriptions of the past that acted to modify or stifle the commitment of highly qualified women. Perhaps the most striking inference to be drawn from a conjoint examination of the behavior of the respondents and of trends among their younger counterparts is that the atypical respondent is becoming the prevailing model for professional women.

The atypical respondents were those who either abstained from marriage, who remained childless, or who limited their families to one child. As a consequence, they were able to retain an enduring career commitment. Today, an increased tendency among young professional women to depart from the conventional nuptial and childbearing timetable may result in more extensive emulation of the male model of continuous work attachment.

Respondents normally had broken patterns of work participation due to periods of withdrawal from the labor force to fulfill family responsibilities. Delayed family formation among the younger generation is likely to reduce the time spent out of the labor force, for postponement of childbirth should enable many women to attain secure professional status before they have children. Reluctance to forfeit present advantages and presumptive future gains may encourage them to limit their absences from the work force or even to eschew extended absences, a reasonable possibility for women with superior earned income.

Moreover, the finding that some respondents were able to discharge career and family responsibilities by working part-time may take on added attraction as a substitute for terminating employment as more employers are persuaded to adapt their schedules to the needs of preferred workers.

If women do maintain closer ties to their careers throughout their lives, the volunteer activities that played a significant role for many respondents during periods out of the labor force may no longer be an attractive substitute for paid work. The pressure is for equal pay for equal work. No pay for equal work hardly seems to answer the same need, despite the existence of alternative sources of income.

The choice of nontraditional professions was relatively infrequent at the time the respondents undertook their graduate training, both because few women chose them and few were chosen; today, growing numbers of women are enrolling in hitherto predominantly male fields. In general, respondents who entered male occupations were more objectively successful than those in fields with larger proportions of female employment, but the introduction of more women to male fields may have equivocal effects. Heretofore, the few females in male occupations were generally superior to the male norm because that was the basis of their selection. As women increase their representation in these fields, the possibility of the development of a two-track system to assure higher status to men cannot be disregarded.

Despite pressures to change young women's view of their future role, much early conditioning and treatment of the sexes remains unequal, if not separate. Notwithstanding the rising rate of women in nontraditional professions, there has been no equivalent increase in male representation in female fields. The larger pool of females who are opting for advanced education is supplying a relatively unchanging representation of women to female occupations in addition to a new female component to male fields.

Underlying the choice of a female profession is often recognition of the ease with which these occupations lend themselves to adjustment and modification during periods when home responsibilities are heavy. Acceptable flexibility of labor force participation may be a more attractive career attribute than earnings maximization for many highly educated women who can anticipate marrying men with superior income prospects. Yet, coming generations of women who choose fields in which women are preponderant may become sufficiently influenced by the women's movement to seek continuous careers and to challenge the hold of the male minority upon the top positions.

Anti-discrimination regulations were introduced long after the respondents had entered the labor force. Women who obtain high educational credentials today start out with the knowledge that they have legal claims to equal consideration. While such claims often have not been honored, women with superior qualifications are in preferred positions to challenge discriminatory actions because they generally have a clearer understanding of their rights and a greater ability to seek redress than females with less schooling and financial resources.

It is important to point out that the careers of the respondents came to fruition or were usually resumed during a period when economic conditions favored their employment and advancement. The outlook for professional women—and many professional men—may not be as rosy today or tomorrow as it was yesterday.

The question of future job opportunities for the growing number of highly educated women was addressed by one of the respondents, a social worker and ex-economist.

> Will we be continuing to have a growth economy with more jobs available? If not—what will it do to employment for women? Can one continue to keep everyone employed at the kind of jobs they wish to have? I grew to maturity in an expanding economy which made a difference in what was open to me and the choices I had. Will this generation have similar options, more or less?

This is, of course, a problem of the first order. The opening of doors that were previously only slightly ajar has coincided with a shrinkage of job opportunities in many fields, and this will heighten job competition between women and men, as well as between women and minorities. Under such circumstances, it is unlikely that women who are at last gaining a piece of the action will docilely revert to their traditional peripheral work roles in order to insure that men have first claim on a diminishing pool of jobs. On the other hand, males are still the gatekeepers to most employment, and they will surely try to rationalize the rights of men to job preference.

Surface changes often conceal the strength of tradition as it acts to frustrate new modes of behavior, and there is customarily a considerable lag between advocacy and actualization. Highly educated young women are still confronted with the need to reconcile conflicting personal and social expectations and to combat discriminatory forces in and out of the labor market. This study has identified specific problems associated with the fulfillment of professional career goals and has portrayed a number of models for the consideration of women who are currently entering the professional ranks or who are contemplating doing so.

Interventions

Although the professions are generally viewed as the occupational elite, the examination of the respondents' careers indicated that the gross professional classification conceals substantial differences in career orientation and progression. Career choice was the prime determinant of career outcomes, but the essential determinants of career choice usually originate long before the moment of decision.

Sex discrimination does not begin in the marketplace; it begins at home. It later receives endorsement in school and, indeed, in all social institutions. Differential treatment of the sexes from early childhood instills attitudes and expectations that have the effect not only of routing women toward a limited number of directions but of influencing the treatment that men accord them both in and out of the labor market.

While the respondents' pursuit of further education after college represented willingness to break with tradition, and the rising interest of women in professional careers reflects alterations in female conceptions of their future role, most women who study beyond the bachelor's degree continue to select female dominated professions that have inferior prospects for career success.

The fact that the rise in the proportion of women who are entering training in nontraditional professions is not commensurate with the increase in the total pool of female graduate students suggests that interventions are still needed to dilute male dominance. Since the family derives its values from the larger society, it is in the latter that solutions must be sought. Teachers and counselors below the college level have the obligation to encourage able female students to seek the same educational goals as those they recommend to male pupils. To this end, counselor training institutions and boards of education must be alert to the need for providing student advisors with up-to-date information about women's career prospects. In addition, the public sources of occupational information which form the basis for most advisory opinions must pay more attention to changing career opportunities for women. These include not only specially designed informational resources, but the media in general, and television in particular. Certainly one of the most significant differences between the environment in which the respondents were raised and that of today is the omnipresence of television. No one doubts its influence upon the pursuits and plans of young people, and it is therefore a powerful vehicle for the presentation of female role models who depart from the traditional mold.

Faculty, counselors, and placement personnel at colleges and universities must become more aware of their responsibilities to female students who seek their assistance in choosing career options. The rapid acceleration of coeducation may become a mixed blessing if it results in a shortage of models for female students; a more limited opportunity to shine in the extracurricular arena; or greater concentration on male career decisions. Female models, campus leadership opportunities, and assistance in vocational choice are essential for the many young women who seek a long-term career involvement.

Although women have been entering non-traditional professions in great numbers in recent years their proportions are still low relative to male professionals. More women should be encouraged to pursue careers in these fields, particularly in certain areas where their representation remains minimal. For instance, when this study was originally undertaken in the early 1960's, the absence of participants who had studied dentistry or engineering resulted from a dearth of females in these fields. Although more women have opted to enter these professions recently, their proportions remain low: 11 percent of first-year students in dentistry and six percent in engineering in 1974.[6] By steering women into these and other professional fields, college advisors turn them towards areas that hold promise of superior career opportunities.

The attention of women students should also be directed to employment opportunities in business organizations. Rising female enrollment in graduate business schools testifies to the influence of changed personnel practices in many profit-making concerns upon the goals of women and upon the responses of educators. There is a distinct advantage for women in the new emphasis upon hiring females for management training and upon integrating them into managerial staffs. Other graduate programs in such fields as library science, journalism, and the liberal arts also have a responsibility to publicize job opportunities in corporate settings as an attractive alternative to more traditional employment settings.

The introduction of a significant female component to enrollments in professional training has resulted in demands for greater flexibility in training schedules to enable women to deal simultaneously with study and home needs. While not a significant problem in professions in which training is limited to three or four years, flexibility is desirable in a field like medicine which requires prolonged post-graduate training. The fact that the duty schedules of all members of hospital house staffs have been shortened considerably in recent years is evidence of the adaptability of residency training. Both mothers and fathers can benefit from part-time residencies.

In addition, as more and more females enter non-traditional professions, they may be able to induce a restructuring of time requirements after training as well. There is nothing inherent in the nature of these professions that must confine achievement only to those who conform to the male norm. Indeed, instructive exceptions among physicians, lawyers and other respondents indicated that periods of interrupted or part-time labor force participation were not always a bar to the highest rungs of the professional ladder.

The existence of such exceptions among these women commands a reexamination of employment and training practices that insist upon full-time involvement as a condition for admission and advancement. Since qualitative measurements of productivity in most professions are difficult to devise at best, judgments of performance based on working time may seem an easy substitute but they have no necessary relationship to professional effectiveness. The introduction of more women into male strongholds behooves employers to give consideration to greater flexibility of time requirements, within prescribed limits, in the assurance that females who initially opt for such fields generally have a strong career orientation.

Many respondents maintained their allegiance to their professions by engaging in part-time employment, in most cases as a temporary expedient during periods of heavy home responsibilities and, in some cases, as a continuing means of labor force participation. In neither of these instances could customary inferences about the peripherality of part-time work be supported. Hardly any women took part-time employment because of the lack of full-time opportunities and part-time earnings were not always lower than income earned from similar full-time employment.

Considering the professional dedication that was demonstrated by many of the women who opted for part-time professional commitments rather than withdrawal from the labor force, it is questionable whether it is in an employer's interest to penalize such women by limiting their access to normal channels of job mobility. There was sufficient evidence of a high level of accomplishment among women who had devoted some amount of their worklives to part-time work to suggest that employers who recognized the depth of their commitment benefited from their services. If more employers of professional women recognized the savings to be realized from permitting women employees to bridge periods of full-time work with part-time employment versus the costs incurred by hiring new and often untried replacements, it is possible that they would conclude that it is in their own interests to provide such opportunities. Moreover, public and private action to include the same fringe benefits for part-time as for full-time jobs should be initiated.

If part-time work were a viable option at all career levels, some professional husbands and wives might consider job sharing, at least during the years when child care responsibilities were at their height. While their individual earnings might drop, their combined income would still be equivalent to what the male alone might otherwise have made. If such an arrangement maintained advancement potential, it might be a partial answer to the problem of equity posed by Rivlin:

> People with high earning capacity tend to marry each other, and this tendency might well be increased if job status became a more central part of the average woman's life. In a world in which professionals and managers

married each other, while unskilled workers did the same, and in which male and female patterns of working and earnings were similar, the concentration of money income among husband-wife families at the high end of the scale would be even greater than it is now, and the income share of those at the bottom would be lower.[7]

It is too early to discover whether any substantial number of professional or managerial females and males would be willing to participate in dual careers that involve time sharing and earnings loss. But consideration should be given to providing flexible scheduling in many different types of occupations. Professions, in particular, lend themselves to new forms of time allotment because of the great degree of autonomy they often permit. If high skills are to be utilized fully in the future, restructuring of work and of work time may be an imperative.

Educational institutions have a special responsibility to provide equal opportunities to qualified women who pursue academic careers. Colleges and universities have an obligation to the women upon whom they confer doctorates. This degree is an endorsement of merit but the practice of sex discrimination transforms it into a delusion that makes a mockery of its significance. Considering the lengthy work histories of most of the academics among the respondents and changes in the life patterns of the younger generation of women, there is no reason why the goals of women academics should not be supported in the same way as those of men.

The lack of success of attempts to encourage women to bypass feminine fields because of their inferior opportunities and rewards may not always be due to prior conditioning. These occupations fill important community needs and some women, after consideration of other options, will continue to prefer them. Exhortations to select non-traditional occupations when these have been weighed and found wanting serve no social or altruistic purpose.

As long as large numbers of women continue to select female dominated professions an alternative approach would be to seek upgrading of their job opportunities. All workers in these fields should be stimulated and assisted to achieve greater parity with workers in male dominated fields. Instead of the passivity that has been a hallmark of women in female fields, they should be urged to press for treatment both equal to their male coworkers and to women in non-traditional professions.

Unionization in such fields as teaching and social work has already acted to raise female earnings, although often without a concomitant rise in female job status. A significant indicator of women's inertia is the prevalence of male leadership of unions in female-dominated fields.

When workers are complacent, employers have no incentive to make improvements. A certain number of women deliberately choose occupations in which females predominate because of a preference for flexibility of work participation over high achievement since they do not anticipate being primary earners, and such women who have comprised a substantial portion of employment in these fields tend to be grateful for relatively small favors. However, among the young women who will choose to enter traditional professions in the foreseeable future is likely to be a large component who plan to make careers a more central concern throughout their lives than did most of their predecessors. They will be less likely to settle for second best because they have reached maturity or will do so in a period when second best is no longer considered acceptable, particularly by women with superior educational attainment.

A change in stress by those urging rearrangement of sex ratios of employment to rectification of the inequities that characterize sex-stereotyped occupations, both with respect to internal sex differentials and to external occupational differentials, should be considered. In view of the increasing numbers of women who are entering advanced education, the likelihood of the absorption of all of them into male dominated professions is remote. Nor is there any reason to expect a large-scale movement of men into predominantly female fields. There is nothing invidious in female occupational predominance, per se, but only in its customary consequences. If these consequences were to be reversed, occupational segregation would be descriptive rather than pejorative.

Evidence that a professional woman's career commitment was of secondary importance to her sex as a qualification for advancement indicated that personnel policies are often founded upon misconceptions about women's future decisions. Despite the career implications of graduate and professional training, many employers seem to maintain traditional expectations of women employees and to treat them as if they are only temporary staff members. Women who behaved like men by maintaining a continuous labor force attachment frequently declared that they had been subject to discrimination presumably because by the time an employer realized that they were serious about lifelong careers, it was too late to make up for earlier losses.

It is essential that enforcement of anti-discrimination regulations strike at employers who place the onus upon women to prove that they will not act the way employers expect them to act. Females should be no more subject to interrogations about their personal lives and responsibilities than males. Nor should they be quizzed about future intentions in this respect. Women whose career motivation is evident by virtue of the time and effort devoted to the acquisition of proficiency should not be discouraged in their quest to utilize their skills in the same manner as their male peers.

Since many respondents utilized a good deal of time spent out of the labor force in the performance of volunteer activities that enabled them to maintain and to improve their skills, and that also frequently contributed to the development of new competencies and career interests, the value of non-market work of this type in later job search and job performance deserves wider recognition. If employers had clearer perceptions of the responsibilities assumed by many volunteers, they might be willing to treat volunteer experience as an integral part of a job applicant's work history rather than as an irrelevant addendum.

Affirmative action regulations and equal opportunity legislation were instituted in a period of economic growth when such efforts were greeted by employers with passivity, if not enthusiasm. The true face of the opposition is shown in periods of job shrinkage when women's claims to top jobs must compete with those of males who are conventionally assumed by their fellows to be more deserving of consideration because they are presumed to have heavier financial responsibilities.

However, aside from the fact that many women with high credentials are themselves wholly or partially responsible for their own or their family's support, attempts to justify discriminatory treatment on non-work-related grounds are difficult to support. Personnel decisions that are not associated with job performance hardly constitute rational employer behavior. Professional women who have been tested in the same crucible as their male peers deserve identical consideration.

Furthermore, as the study indicates, the progress of professional women was more commonly undermined by deficient promotional opportunities than by unequal hiring practices. While it is possible that increased numbers of female professionals may act to exacerbate entry inequities, if equality is to be achieved, monitoring of hiring practices should not preclude attention to advancement opportunities. Employers do not discharge their responsibility to comply with regulations ordaining non-discriminatory treatment of the sexes solely by raising the number of female hires. Assignment on a par with that of male entrants is no less important as a measure of an employer's intent, and equitable promotion with commensurate rewards is the fundamental proof of good faith.

Hand in hand with efforts to introduce women throughout the business hierarchy should be policies that assure that the accent is not only on youth. A widened area of search for qualified women employees must pay equal attention to older women, many of whom, as we have seen, are well qualified for responsible positions. The weight of all evidence is that employers who engage women of middle age can anticipate a prolonged employment relationship characterized by reliability and stability. Caution is warranted in all sectors of the economy to assure that attempts to eradicate sex discrimination are not vitiated by biased treatment of older job aspirants of both sexes.

Respondents' reports of discrimination in workplaces covered by affirmative action regulations underscored the need for more effective enforcement. Apparent reluctance to apply the available weapons of public contract cancellation or denial possibly has served to convince employers that they are exempt from drastic action and, as a result, many may have continued to take their chances. Moreover, while individual and concerted action by women has sometimes resulted in successful resolution of complaints of sex discrimination, the high cost of challenges to employer practices could be substantially reduced by more effective government monitoring and by the imposition of available penalties.

Government policies that serve to unify enforcement of anti-discrimination measures can be of great value. For example, the placement of affirmative action supervision under the umbrella of one agency would improve the amount of attention given to this phase of public contract compliance which heretofore has been but one facet of the total compliance procedure and, in many agencies, a minor concern at best. If the Equal Employment Opportunities Commission proceeds to examine employment patterns and practices in large firms in order to determine whether they conform to non-discriminatory requirements, this procedure can have a salutary influence, not only upon female employment in the organizations concerned, but upon women workers in a broad range of establishments which use industry leaders as models for their own personnel policies.

State and local government and non-profit agencies also warrant intensified monitoring of employment practices by the EEOC. Substantial proportions of women in the traditional professions work in these sectors and they have an important stake in any actions designed to improve equal accessibility to supervisory and managerial positions.

Increasing support for women's career goals has not resulted in any significant concrete assistance to help mothers realize their aspirations in the same manner as fathers. The United States is uncommon among industrialized nations in the limited participation of government in providing child-care assistance to families above the poverty level and there is only minimal public involvement in institutional arrangements even for children of the poor. Yet as Darling points out, "Many today view the problem of child care as the most important social issue related to changing attitudes of women toward work and of society toward women working."[8] The American position reflects an anachronistic view of women's current roles which hearkens back to the days when wives give their primary attention to homemaking and child care. It gives no recognition to the fact that increasing numbers of mothers are demonstrating the need or desire to retain a continuing attachment to work.

In families like those of the respondents, women's financial need to work is usually secondary to their wish to fulfill professional responsibilities. Yet the absence of adequate child-care facilities often means that high skills must lie fallow while mothers perform child-care services. It is paradoxical that government is willing to participate in the financing of professional education and to insist that it is available to all regardless of sex, while it simultaneously refrains from assisting women to fully utilize their skills. Nor does it make sense for government to act to widen women's job opportunities (or to allow tax deductions for a portion of child care expenses) when the ability to take advantage of new options is restricted by the unavailability of day care. The assumption that middle class parents can obtain and affort acceptable child care without outside intervention is open to question. There was no evidence in the study that respondents were either readily able to obtain adequate mother substitutes from a declining pool of domestic workers or to find satisfactory alternative private services. This accords with Ruderman's observation:

> Day care . . . is a complex and costly service. It is, by and large, beyond the ability of individuals or individual families to set up, finance and supervise— just as it is, by and large, beyond the ability of individuals or individual families to create and supervise hospitals, schools, and many other institutions. . . . Complex services require societal (organizational) involvement, regardless of the income or social level of the users.[9]

Employers of women with valuable skills also have a stake in child-care arrangements since these can prevent turnover among women whom they have trained and whose careers they have nurtured. Employers also should give greater attention to the provision of paid maternity leave for female employees and to policies permitting paid or unpaid absences for mothers (and fathers) for a period following childbirth. Such policies enhance women's opportunities for continued professional involvement while at the same time assuring their employers of a more stable and experienced professional work force.

The interest shown by the respondents in working after reaching the age of 65 suggests that many of these women welcome the recent extension of the statutory retirement age to 70 years, especially those who who have reentered the work force and wish to compensate for lost time. The prevailing sentiment was in favor of part-time employment during these years, but present social security and tax policies penalize elderly temporary and part-time employees as well as older full-time workers. As the younger labor force contracts in the years ahead while the population at the other end of the age spectrum expands, legislative reform that encourages labor market activity among the latter group, particularly those with the desire and capacity to make productive social contributions would not only enhance the later years of many highly skilled workers but also could produce a more equitable tax burden.

Any change in retirement, social security, or general taxation policies in order to increase work opportunities for older women and men must be considered in conjunction with macroeconomic policies aimed at providing full employment of all population groups.

The Future

The changes that have taken place in society's view of women and in women's view of themselves since the middle of the 1960's are likely to be irreversible. The strength of tradition in the setting of female goals is likely to continue to be dissipated as parental influence upon their children is itself influenced by changing perceptions of woman's role.

As more women move into domains that were formerly almost exclusively occupied by men, and as increasing numbers of women opt to give precedence to their careers, old models of appropriate female behavior will be supplanted by a new look that should lead to female role expectations parallel to those of males.

This prediction must be hedged, however, since so much of what will happen to professional women in the future depends upon forces beyond their control. No matter how effective the women's movement is in changing female expectations, and no matter how forceful government is in removing discriminatory barriers to female occupational achievement, the fact remains that much of what happens to female professionals in the future depends upon the condition of the economy. Only with an expansion of economic activity can women with high credentials be assured of obtaining jobs commensurate with their qualifications. Otherwise, there will be accelerated competition with males for entrance into preferred professional positions. The entire female work force, including professional women, must rely on a buoyant economy to assure effective utilization of their skills.

Yet, even in the best of times, an increased number of professional aspirants may eventually fulfill their career goals in restructured jobs. They may be employed during shorter workweeks and under other innovative conditions that will have to be initiated to accommodate all men and women job seekers, unless unforeseen opportunities eventually develop. Additionally, in some families, time may be spent in the pursuit of non-market careers by both husbands and wives, in turn.

The supply of professionals will rise as more women with strong career motivation enter their ranks, and women's worklives will lengthen because of continued low fertility. The task of satisfying the aspirations of an enlarged corps of professional workers will be difficult at best; and there probably will be a certain amount of skill under-utilization in certain fields where redundancy will result as the demand for labor slackens in response to demographic and other social changes.

In sum, the best that a clouded crystal ball can predict at present is that 20 years hence there will be more women with superior qualifications who have every intention of maintaining an enduring career commitment, and that contrary to precedent, more of the conflicts that arise in achieving their goals will be generated from without than from within.

Notes

1. K. Patricia Cross, "The Woman Student," in *Women in Higher Education*, W. Todd Furniss and Patricia A. Graham, eds. (Washington, D.C.: American Council on Education, 1974), p. 38.

2. An example of such pressure is the work incentive (WIN) provisions of the Social Security Amendments of 1967, reinforced by the Talmadge Amendment of 1972, which were designed expressly to stimulate the employment of adult welfare recipients, almost all of whom are mothers of young children.

3. Bernice Sandler, "Backlash in Academe: A Critique of the Lester Report," *Teachers College Record*, LXXVI, 3 (February 1975), p. 403.

4. Alice S. Rossi, "Summary and Prospects," Chapter 21 in *Academic Women on the Move*, Rossi and Calderwood, eds. (New York: Russell Sage Foundation, 1973), p. 527.

5. Marnie W. Mueller, "Economic Determinants of Volunteer Work by Women," *Signs*, I, 2 (Winter 1975).

6. John B. Parrish, "Women in Professional Training—an Update," *Monthly Labor Review*, XCVIII, 11 (November 1975), p. 49.

7. Alice M. Rivlin, "Income Distribution—Can Economists Help?" *The American Economic Review*, LXV, 2 (May 1975), p. 2.

8. Martha Darling, *The Role of Women in the Economy* (Paris: Organisation for Economic Co-operation and Development, 1975), p. 75.

9. Florence A. Ruderman, *Child Care and Working Mothers* (New York: Child Welfare League of America, 1968), pp. 347–48.

APPENDIX

Follow-up Survey—Life Styles of Educated Women

Letter used for the study

June 1975

Dear

Your cooperation in a research study that we conducted at Columbia University in the early 1960's was very much appreciated. The results of that survey were published in two volumes: LIFE STYLES OF EDUCATED WOMEN and EDUCATED AMERICAN WOMEN: SELF PORTRAITS, Columbia University Press, 1966. These publications were very well received and have been used extensively in teaching, counseling, and further research.

The scarcity of longitudinal information about all groups in our society, well educated women in particular, has been a serious barrier to understanding and to policy formulation. The rapid growth of the women's movement and related developments during the past decade have made such data especially desirable. To meet this need, we are undertaking a follow-up study, under a grant from the U.S. Department of Labor, in order to examine changes over time among the participants in our earlier inquiry.

We have designed the accompanying questionnaire with an eye to conserving your time, although provision has been made for you to comment at length if you wish. Please note that all questions are not applicable to everyone.

In accordance with our past practice, your answers will be treated as confidential and will be reported only in the form of statistical summaries and unattributed quotations.

We hope that you will find the questionnaire interesting and that you will complete and return it to us as soon as possible. We believe that the information we gather can be of significant value to policy makers, educators, counselors, employers, and the public.

A return postage-paid envelope is enclosed for your convenience. If you have any questions about the study, please feel free to communicate with me at the above address.

Thank you for your past assistance and for your participation in this current endeavor.

Sincerely,

Alice M. Yohalem
Research Associate

Follow-up Survey—Life Styles of Educated Women

Conservation of Human Resources, Columbia University

Name _____
                (first)   (maiden)   (married)

Address _____

_____

Date _____

All information in this questionnaire will be held in strict CONFIDENCE.

---

1. *a.* On the average, approximately how many hours a week do you regularly devote to each of the following activities?

Average number of hours weekly

Salaried employment. _____

Self-employment. _____

Other paid work (consulting, free-lance, etc.). _____

Homemaking (including child care). _____

Volunteer work. _____

Education (including study time). _____

Other activities. (Specify.) _____ _____

b. Are there any changes you would like to make in this schedule?   Yes. ☐   No. ☐

c. If so, list the activities to which you would prefer to devote different amounts of time than at present.

Preferred weekly hours

_____ _____

_____ _____

_____ _____

_____ _____

d. If you have indicated a preference for some alterations in your weekly schedule, which among the following circumstances might enable you to make the change(s) you desire? *Please check all that apply.*

Your retirement. ☐   Less need for your earnings. ☐
Your husband's retirement. ☐   Relocation to a smaller home. ☐
Availability of the right kind of work. ☐   Completion of studies. ☐
Fewer family responsibilities. ☐   No foreseeable circumstances. ☐

Other. (Specify.)

210

Questions 2 through 9 concern your employment between 1963 and the present. If you were not gainfully employed at any time during this period, skip to Question 10.

2. *Employment experience 1963 to present:* Starting with your *most recent* employment and working back to 1963, list all full-time and part-time positions, including self-employment and free-lance work. Simultaneous paid work can be listed for a single time period.

From 19____ to 19____	Employer: Location: Job title and major functions: Hours weekly (average):	Reason for leaving: Reason for taking this job: How you learned of this job:
From 19____ to 19____	Employer: Location: Job title and major functions: Hours weekly (average):	Reason for leaving: Reason for taking this job: How you learned of this job:
From 19____ to 19____	Employer: Location: Job title and major functions: Hours weekly (average):	Reason for leaving: Reason for taking this job: How you learned of this job:
From 19____ to 19____	Employer: Location: Job title and major functions: Hours weekly (average):	Reason for leaving: Reason for taking this job: How you learned of this job:

If more space is required, continue at the end of the questionnaire.

3. For your most recent full year of employment since 1963:

   a. What were your *own* total annual earnings from employment and related activities (consulting fees, royalties, honoraria, etc.)? Do not include fringe benefits paid by your employer nor income from other sources.

Under $2,500 ☐	$10,000-$11,499 ☐
$2,500-$4,999 ☐	$12,500-$14,999 ☐
$5,000-$7,499 ☐	$15,000-$19,999 ☐
$7,500-$9,999 ☐	$20,000-$29,999 ☐

   $30,000 and over ☐

   b. In what year did you receive this amount? _____

   c. Were you in a higher earnings bracket in any previous year?   Yes. ☐   No. ☐

   d. If so, please give reason(s) for decrease in earnings.

4. If you shifted your emphasis within the same general area of work or changed your line of work *after 1963*, which among the following considerations prompted your action? *Check all that apply.*

   No good job opportunities in your former area or field. ☐
   No good job opportunities *for women* in your former area or field. ☐
   No relevant jobs in your vicinity. ☐
   Change of interests. ☐
   Avoidance of anti-nepotism regulations. ☐
   No part-time jobs in your former area or field. ☐
   A good job opportunity was offered in another area or field. ☐
   Other. (Specify.)

5. If you are employed at present, under which of the following circumstances would you *probably* change your present employer (or change your self-employed status)? *Check all that apply.*

   Mandatory transfer to a new job location. ☐
   The offer of a more responsible position. ☐
   The chance to make better use of your skills. ☐
   A job opportunity nearer your home. ☐
   A higher salary offer. ☐
   Your husband's job relocation. ☐
   Your husband's retirement. ☐
   Dissatisfaction with future conditions of employment. ☐
   No foreseeable circumstances. ☐
   Other. (Specify.)

6. Financial considerations aside, if you are employed at present and under the age of 65, and if the following options are available when you reach that age, which *one option* would you choose?

   Retirement. ☐
   Continuation in same job or field on a full-time basis. ☐
   Continuation in same job or field on a reduced schedule. ☐
   A new career. (Specify.) _____
   Independent writing and/or research. ☐
   Other. (Specify.)

7. If you are currently employed on a part-time weekly schedule, indicate the reason(s). *Check all that apply.*

      No acceptable full-time job available. ☐
      Family responsibilities. ☐
      Housekeeping requirements. ☐
      Part-time study. ☐
      Desire for more free time. ☐
      Husband's preference. ☐
      Other. (Specify.)

8. With respect to your most recent employment, do you think that governmental and/or social pressures against sex discrimination in employment (Affirmative Action, EEOC, Women's Liberation, etc.) have had any effect on:

   a.   your own job and rewards?   Yes. ☐   No. ☐   If yes, explain.

   b.   the policies of your employer?   Yes. ☐   No. ☐   If yes, explain.

   c.   the attitudes of your male supervisors and colleagues?   Yes. ☐   No. ☐   If yes, explain.

   d.   your relations with clients, students, customers, patients, etc.? Yes. ☐ No. ☐ If yes, explain.

9. Do you think that your treatment as a worker has been at least equal to that accorded males with similar qualifications and experience?   Yes. ☐   No. ☐   If not, in which of the following aspects of employment do you believe you have not received equal treatment? *Check all that apply.*

      Hiring. ☐
      Promotion. ☐
      Salary. ☐
      Tenure. ☐
      Responsibility. ☐
      Assignment of duties. ☐
      Grants. ☐
      Other. (Specify.)

10. If you *ever* dropped out of the labor force for a year or more in order to fulfill family obligations, or if you delayed entering paid employment for the same reason:

  a. Did you engage in volunteer work during that period?   Yes. ☐   No. ☐

  b. If so, did your volunteer experiences make a contribution to your subsequent employment in any of the following ways? *Check all that apply.*

     Maintained and/or improved your career skills. ☐
     Developed new skills later used on the job. ☐
     Inspired new career interests. ☐
     Provided contacts useful in your job search. ☐
     Advanced your personal growth and self-confidence. ☐
     Other effects. (Specify.) _____
     Had no effect. ☐

11. If you *ever* entered or reentered employment after three or more years out of school or out of the labor force, in which *one* of the following ways did you obtain your first job after this period? (If you had more than one period of temporary retirement, answer for the most recent.)

     Personal contact. ☐   Private or nonprofit employment agency. ☐
     Former employer or colleague. ☐   Response to your want ad. ☐
     Acquaintance in your field. ☐   Response to employer's ad. ☐
     Former teacher. ☐   University placement office. ☐
     Public employment agency. ☐   Other. (Specify.)

The next question concerns only respondents who were not in the labor force at any time after 1963. If you were employed at all during that period, skip to Question 13.

12. If you were not gainfully employed between 1963 and the present, indicate the reason(s). *Check all that apply.*

     Retirement. ☐
     Husband's preference that you not work for pay. ☐
     No suitable job available in your vicinity. ☐
     Child-care responsibilities. ☐
     Demands of elderly family members. ☐
     Anti-nepotism policies of husband's employer. ☐
     Poor health. ☐
     Preference for other activity(ies). (Specify.) _____
     Other. (Specify.)

13. Note any prizes, honors, or government appointments; election to political office; books, articles, etc.; or other achievements of a similar nature.

Questions 14 and 15 concern additional studies *after 1963*. If you did not pursue any course of study during this period, skip to Question 16.

14. Did you receive one or more academic degrees after 1963, or are you at present a candidate for a degree?
       Yes. ☐   No. ☐

   a. If yes, what degree(s)? _____

   b. When received or expected. _____

   c. Field(s) of study. _____

   d. What was the length of time between your entrance into required course work and the acquisition of

       your most recent degree? _____

15. Which of the following reasons explain(s) why you undertook studies *after 1963? Check all that apply.*

       Completion of course of study begun earlier. ☐
       Updating of knowledge in original field of study. ☐
       Improvement of chances for job promotion. ☐
       In compliance with employer's suggestion or requirements. ☐
       Change of interests. ☐
       Wish to enter field with better job opportunities. ☐
       For personal fulfillment rather than vocational aims. ☐
       Other. (Specify.)

16. If there were any changes in your marital status *after 1963*, give the year(s) of *each* change.

       Married for first time   _____

       Divorced   _____

       Separated   _____

       Widowed   _____

       Remarried   _____

If you are currently married and living with your husband, answer Question 17. If not, skip to Question 18.

17. Provide the following information about your husband.

       Age: _____ years.

   a. Occupation _____

   b. Type of employing institution _____

   c. Highest school grade completed or highest degree _____

18. *a.* What was your approximate total income in 1974 (family, if married and living with your husband) from *all* sources?

Under $10,000	☐	$20,000-$29,999	☐	$50,000-$74,999	☐
$10,000-$14,999	☐	$30,000-$39,999	☐	$75,000 and over	☐
$15,000-$19,999	☐	$40,000 $49,999	☐		

b. About what proportion of your total family income in 1974 came from *your* earnings from employment? _____ percent.

Questions 19 through 22 concern children of respondents. If you have no children, skip to Question 23.

19. Give the ages of all of your children who are living at home. _____

20. *a.* Provide the following information about the educational status of *each* of your children.

Age	Sex	Present grade (if student)	Highest grade completed or highest degree (if not attending school)
____	____	_____	_____
____	____	_____	_____
____	____	_____	_____
____	____	_____	_____
____	____	_____	_____

b. Approximately what proportion of your *total family income* is used to meet your children's educational expenses (tuition, fees, room, board, transportation, etc.)? _____ percent.

Question 21 concerns your children's employment. If you have no employed adult children, skip to Question 22.

21. Provide the following information for *each* adult child who is now employed either full or part time.

Age	Sex	Occupation*	Full or Part time	Marital status	If parent, number of children
____	____	_____	____	_____	_____
____	____	_____	____	_____	_____
____	____	_____	____	_____	_____
____	____	_____	____	_____	_____
____	____	_____	____	_____	_____

*including graduate assistant

22. In retrospect, if you consider the amounts of time that you allocated to family and to career pursuits (including study), do you: (Select *one* of the following statements.)

feel satisfied with the way you apportioned your time? ☐
wish you had spent more time on family concerns? ☐
wish you had spent more time developing your career? ☐
have any other response? (Specify.)

23. If an able woman undergraduate consulted you about the following options for the future, what advice would you give her?

a. Combining family and career.

b. Attending graduate or professional school.

c. Entering the same field of study as yours.

24. Apart from employment-related concerns already noted, in what ways have recent efforts to improve the status of women had any effect upon your own attitudes, relationships, self-image, activities, etc.?

25. Additional comments. Please elaborate on or clarify any of your answers if you feel that this would be helpful to us. Also comment on any other points that you consider important with respect to yourself and educated women in general. If the remaining blank pages are insufficient for your comments, please attach as many additional sheets as you require.

INDEX

ABOUT THE AUTHOR

Alice M. Yohalem is Research Associate, Conservation of Human Resources, Columbia University. She is the author of *Educated American Women: Self-Portraits* and *Desegregation and Career Goals* and co-author of *Life Styles of Educated Women, Talent and Performance,* and *The Middle-Class Negro in the White Man's World.*